Praise for

THE GILDED CHALET

'Rooney's thoroughly absorbing book bundles up all of Switzerland's "gilded ambiguities" into a dazzling package that is part road trip, part reading list, part memoir, and part historical exposé. [It] makes one want to pick up old favourites and seek out new literary discoveries. It is a book for those who love to travel, whether in the mind or on the road. It [is] easy to tear through the volume in a few voracious sittings.'
Times Literary Supplement

'With a sharp eye for detail and a historian's capacious knowledge, Padraig Rooney has written a superbly amusing guide to all the writers who've been drawn to or emerged from Switzerland.'
Edmund White, author of *Our Young Man* and *The Flâneur*

'Constantly engaging… and highly entertaining. Rooney is almost casually brilliant on Joyce, Nabokov and Mann, but revelatory on such as Durrenmatt and Frisch. He shows a deftness of touch but can, too, be powerful. A love letter to reading that does not shy away from the sins of reality.'
Herald

'An enjoyable wander around literary Switzerland. *The Gilded Chalet* tracks the snow prints, shattered booze-glasses and missed spy drops of the likes of Rousseau, Byron, Hemingway and le Carré, sniffing the air of inspiration they found in the hills, huts and bars.'
Wanderlust

'A gossipy feel [with a] touch of Clive James in its humour. What has Switzerland ever done for us? Quite a bit.'
Irish Mail on Sunday

THE GILDED CHALET

For Y

THE GILDED CHALET

Travels through Literary Switzerland

PADRAIG ROONEY

NICHOLAS BREALEY
PUBLISHING

London · Boston

First published in 2017 by Nicholas Brealey Publishing
An imprint of John Murray Press

An Hachette company

1

Previous edition published 2015 in UK, 2016 in US
Copyright © Padraig Rooney 2015, 2016

The right of Padraig Rooney to be identified as the Author of the Work
has been asserted by him in accordance with the Copyright, Designs
and Patents Act 1988.

British Library Cataloguing-in-Publication Data
A catalogue record for this book is available from the British Library.

ISBN 978-1-85788-652-8
eBook ISBN (UK) 978-1-85788-987-1
eBook ISBN (US) 978-1-47364-502-8

Printed and bound by Clays Ltd, St Ives plc

John Murray Press policy is to use papers that are natural, renewable
and recyclable products and made from wood grown in sustainable forests.
The logging and manufacturing processes are expected to conform to the
environmental regulations of the country of origin.

Nicholas Brealey Publishing
John Murray Press
Carmelite House
50 Victoria Embankment
London, EC4Y 0DZ, UK
Tel: 020 3122 6000

Nicholas Brealey Publishing
Hachette Book Group
Market Place Center, 53 State Street
Boston, MA 02109, USA
Tel: (617) 523 3801

www.nicholasbrealey.com
www.padraigrooney.com

CONTENTS

INTRODUCTION

The gilded chalet opens rooms with a view to Julius Caesar,
the Irish Earls, Lord Byron and me

LA SUISSE A TRAVERS LES AGES

Puisque nos ancêtres
ont fait l'Helvétie,

les États confédérés,
enfin la Suisse ;

nous voulons aussi faire quelque chose : c'est
pourquoi nous instituerons la Kadence et le drill.

Switzerland through the ages: Charles Addy cartoon dating from the First World War

It is perhaps only in little states that one can find the model for a perfect political administration.
Jean Rond d'Alembert

One blue June evening in 1973 I was hitchhiking across the Susten Pass in my army-surplus jacket, clogs and a wealth of hair. There was snow on the ground. A car stopped, heading north to Basel. George Harrison's *Here Comes the Sun* played on the radio. My summer in Switzerland had begun. I got a job, a room, picked up some Swiss German and read Hermann Hesse and Vladimir Nabokov. As an Irishman, I learned what it means to be continental, to be a little bit Swissy, to cross my sevens and cut the butter straight. By summer's end I had acquired an education and a beard. My first glass of champagne was above Basel's Café Spitz. My first espresso was across the Rhine in Bachmann's Konditorei. There were other firsts, best passed over. It was a gap summer.

The Cold War was still going strong. Earlier I'd got a lift from an American GI Joe living on a military base called Patrick Henry Village, on the edge of the Black Forest. He dropped me off outside a collection of Quonset huts, jerrybuilt bungalows and a pizzeria – a gated community, exotic to me as pizza in 1973. My next lift was from a hippy living in a commune. Nobody over forty mentioned the war. Old men clicked their heels.

Like my longhaired arty self in 1973, foreign writers fetched up in Switzerland by hook or by crook, by the seat of their pants. The poet Shelley, sixteen-year-old girlfriend Mary in tow, ran out of money on his gap summer in 1814. He got her pregnant. Two years later Lord Byron tumbled across the border in a bling Napoleonic coach, but was on the run from creditors and paparazzi. Our romantic notion of Swiss mountain landscape derives from these poets, from Byron's 'thousand years of snow'. Switzerland was a walk on the wild side, a view that no longer obtains.

That wet summer of 1816 has gone down in literary history. Byron, the Shelleys, Claire Clairmont, Polidori and maybe even baby William sat around the crackling fireside in the Villa Diodati. Horror literature was misbegotten. Mary Shelley's *Frankenstein* (1818) and the first sketch of *The Vampyre* (1819), penned by Byron's doctor Polidori, are the storm's forbidding fruit. The party came under the spell of ghoulish German folk tales. Indeed the Alp (kin to the word 'elf') is a mountain vampire or incubus that attacks by sitting on the sleeper and inducing nightmares – *Alpträumen*.

Mountains the world over have inspired a folklore of otherworldly beasts: the Yeti, the abominable snowman and malevolent devils guarding the passes. The Alp drinks blood from the nipples of men and children, and sucks milk from the breasts of women. This theme of man tormented by monster is resurrected in Hermann Hesse's *Steppenwolf* (1927), a novel begun in Basel and exploring the wolfish character of Harry Haller. The gothic-horror literary tradition is the progenitor of so much in our contemporary culture, from the New Romantics to *Gay Bride of Frankenstein* (2008) to *Twilight* (2005).

The original Romantics drew inspiration from Switzerland's William Tell foundational myth, but it was Schiller's nineteenth-century play about the crossbow-wielding Tell that caught the popular imagination. (Hitler banned performances of *Wilhelm Tell* and had it removed from the German school curriculum.) Freedom was in short supply in Russia too. Switzerland became a refuge, a beacon for nineteenth- and twentieth-century anarchists, revolutionaries and refusniks of all stripes. Fleeing the Tsarist regime, the workers of the world began uniting in the watchmaking Jura towns. It was from Zürich that Lenin's sealed train made its way to the Finland Station and the 1917 October Revolution.

Swiss writers, on the other hand, seem to head for the borders and keep on running. In the mid-eighteenth century, Geneva-born Rousseau fell foul of that town's tight-pursed Calvinism. They burned his books and he fled to Paris. He is Switzerland's first world-class writer. Twentieth-century Swiss writers – Dürrenmatt and Frisch – owe their irreverence to Rousseau's tell-it-like-it-is example, picking at the dry rot behind the Protestant ethic and the spirit of capitalism. Likewise the travellers, the itinerants – Eberhardt, Maillart, Schwarzenbach and Bouvier – are descendants of Rousseau's wanderlust. Writers from small countries seek elbow room and Swiss writers fight their corner in four languages. How do you negotiate a literary space different from your neighbours?

Deep in Victorian England, Switzerland was a breath of fresh air. Charles Dickens, like the Romantics before him, saw the country as an invitation to escape:

> *Gradually down, by zigzag roads, lying between an upward and a downward precipice, into warmer air, calmer air, and softer scenery, until there lay before us, glittering like gold or silver in the thaw and sunshine, the metal-covered, red, green, yellow, domes and church spires of a Swiss town.*[1]

And so Switzerland emerged from the cloud of history like a chalet, an Alpine refuge, an earthly paradise. A chalet was originally a small mountain cheese hut rather than the wealth and status symbol it has since become. Mark Twain in *A Tramp Abroad* (1880) gives us a wonderfully matter-of-fact description:

> *The ordinary chalet turns a broad, honest gable end to the road, and its ample roof hovers over the home in a protecting, caressing way, projecting its sheltering eaves far outward. The quaint windows are filled with little panes, and garnished with white muslin curtains, and brightened with boxes of blooming flowers. Across the front of the house, and up the spreading eaves and along the fanciful railings of the shallow porch, are elaborate carvings – wreaths, fruits, arabesques, verses from Scripture, names, dates, etc. The building is wholly of wood, reddish brown in tint, a very pleasing color. It generally has vines climbing over it. Set such a house against the fresh green of the hillside, and it looks ever so cozy and inviting and picturesque, and is a decidedly graceful addition to the landscape.*[2]

Swiss writer Daniel de Roulet, conversely, has a historical awareness of the role of the chalet in the national psyche. His definition touches on many of the themes that run through my book: Alpine tradition stretching back to the Romans and beyond, psycho-geography, the interpenetration of foreign and local views, moneyed exclusivity and the common weal, the home of literature and myth, a refuge, maybe even a redoubt for travellers:

> *For us Swiss, the chalet, the* Swiss *chalet, as English-speakers say, is the matrix of all dwellings. From the Latin* cara, *which means 'the place where one is sheltered', I retain the earliest meaning. The poor have their thatched cottages, the rich their palaces, but the chalet is a shelter for travellers, a piece of common property; for anybody to claim it as his or her own would be unseemly. A wooden structure with a pitched roof whose ridgeline is perpendicular to the contours, this model was popularised by Jean-Jacques Rousseau in* The New Heloise, *reproduced ad infinitum in suburbs, plains, on the shores of lakes. Flaubert found chalets ugly, Proust made fun of them (the comfort chalet), but we Swiss learn how to draw them in childhood. It is the home of Heidi and William Tell, the immediately intelligible symbol of an Alpine tradition.*[3]

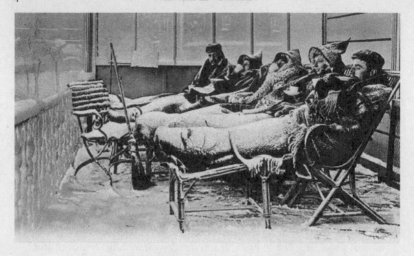

Treatment at the Schatzalp sanatorium in Davos, setting for
Thomas Mann's *The Magic Mountain*

Switzerland was a land of milk, honey and fresh air for generations of well-to-do tubercular patients. Davos had plenty for sale; you could breathe easy. Symonds, Stevenson and Conan Doyle, those late Victorian gentlemen, saw Switzerland as a health farm, a happy valley. Pastoral imagery – cows, chocolate, cheese – as well as pristine air became desirable commodities for the crumbling industrial age. Conan Doyle may have killed off Sherlock Holmes in the Swiss mountains, but the figure of the pursuing and pursued spy-detective is alive and well and living under an alias with a numbered account.

Thomas Mann spent a thousand pages up his particular *Magic Mountain* (1924), in an enclave of elusive health and exclusive wealth, a brand still maximising its shareholder value. This gave rise to a literature of illness with Switzerland as panacea. As the bacillus retreated, Swiss sanatoria morphed into psychiatric clinics and finishing schools – a home away from home for wealthy sprogs and the broken in mind and body of two world wars. Hemingway and Fitzgerald both escaped into the magic mountains – from war, from the Roaring Twenties, in a search for sanity. In our time fresh air is once again on the wellness menu, with aromatherapy and lashings of liquid soap.

Besides mainstream health, back-to-nature fads at the close of the nineteenth century led wayward writers off the track to nude sunbathing and communal living at Monte Verità. They escaped the strictures of little

Male bathing area, with hip baths, at Monte Verità, 1903

England and a militarised Germany for little Switzerland. H.G. Wells imagined Switzerland as Shangri La, a utopian escape from the machine age. D.H. Lawrence, confined with his German wife to wartime England, recalled walking through Switzerland in *Twilight in Italy* (1916). Hermann Hesse, like Thomas Mann, withdrew for decades to Switzerland and became a sage on the literary and hippy trails. Their books were in my rucksack when I first came to Basel.

My compatriot James Joyce eloped from Ireland in borrowed boots in 1904. He fled both world wars to the safety of Zürich. War too caught the fifteen-year-old Borges in Geneva, where his dad arranged for the boy to get laid. Ian Fleming was recovering from a dose of the clap. The seventeen-year-old John le Carré turned spy in Bern and polished his German. It would prove useful. For all of them Switzerland was a hideout, a refuge, the quiet good place.

Switzerland's neutrality nurtured espionage in Geneva and Bern through both world wars. Joseph Conrad's *Under Western Eyes* (1911) explores *la petite Russie* in Geneva during the first decade of the twentieth century. Somerset Maugham's *Ashenden* (1928) plays the Great Game during the First World War, prefiguring the spy and criminal worlds of John le Carré and Ian Fleming, both Swiss educated. Le Carré's agents, double agents and prisoners of conscience continue to see Switzerland as haven, but also as manager of the world's slush funds. Friedrich Glauser is the daddy of the detective genre – the *Krimis* – in the German-speaking world. Following his example, Friedrich Dürrenmatt's plays and detectives, and other Swiss *noir* practitioners, pick away at the gilt. All that glitters is not gold for espionage and detective writing in Switzerland, but often enough it hits the jackpot.

Switzerland prospered during and after the Second World War. Writing in 1952, Patricia Highsmith noticed the abundance of food and American cars in contrast to post-war deprivations across the border. Like Madame de S— in Conrad's *Under Western Eyes*, we might be inclined to shout: 'You have no idea what thieves those people are! Downright thieves!'[4] An anonymous letter sent in 1758 to Rousseau cites the want of empathy in Geneva for the outside world's travails: 'it often sees everything in flames around it without ever feeling them; the events which agitate Europe are for it only a spectacle which it enjoys without taking part'.[5] There is something of this attitude in Switzerland as a whole. What began in utopia in the first decade of the twentieth century seems to have ended in funny money by century's end.

This view of Switzerland as a beneficiary of one if not two world wars gains currency, literally and literarily, throughout the twentieth century. Swiss and foreign writers alike take up residence in the gilded chalet. The popular view of little Switzerland on the world stage is that it did well – shiny on the outside, although ill gotten underneath. This obscures the virtues of industry, innovation and imagination that Switzerland undoubtedly possesses. But it also occludes the holier-than-thou nations, conniving banks and military-industrial complexes that have prospered from wars. Skulduggery across the field is doing rather nicely as I write. Neutral Switzerland plays it well, but the bellicose nations play hard to catch too. It is convenient to target Switzerland. Transparency has never been its strong point, except in the air.

Switzerland is partly a creation of our own guilt and desires: freedom, fresh air, money, corruption, chocolate, a winter holiday, heaven on earth. It's the playground of Europe, far from prying eyes, where royalty go skiing, former royalty hide out, and collapsed dictators count their filthy lucre. For Swiss writers it is home, and a local home at that. The individual cantons, the narrow valley or city street, one's *Heimat* – these often figure more strongly than the federation as a whole. It is surprising how cantonal – *cantonné* – the Swiss sense of self can be. Their literature exists on the edge of the great literatures of the age by an accident of geography and history. They might be rather tired of people dropping in, but they are also used to being on the periphery – it has its uses for the imagination.

I must belong to the last generation to have studied Caesar's *Gallic War* (circa 46 BCE) at school – the hearts and minds operation of the day. Early on, Caesar dispatches the expansionist Helvetii, tribal ancestors to the Swiss. He commandeers them as porters and begins a long tradition of Swiss mercenaries that ends with the Pontifical guards at the Vatican, in their natty Renaissance motley.

Caesar's firm grasp of Helvetian geopolitics still holds true today:

> *The Helvetii are confined on every side by the nature of their situation; on one side by the Rhine, a very broad and deep river, which separates the Helvetian territory from the Germans; on a second side by the Jura, a very high mountain, which is between the Sequani and the Helvetii; on a third by the Lake of Geneva, and by the river Rhone, which separates our Province from the Helvetii. From these circumstances it resulted, that they could range less widely, and could less easily make war upon their neighbors.[6]*

Orgetorix is the Helvetian man of the hour, but in the short term Caesar prevails. He secures the Alpine passes. Roman roads across the Alps are still there under the scrub, alongside the newer highways. Once off the beaten track, as a later emperor, Napoleon Bonaparte, discovered, you never know which way a valley will swing. The Helvetii are entrenched and wary of strangers. The Romans came and went (and did a little shopping), but Caesar is the first writer to leave his mark on Helvetia.

Coins showing Helvetian leader Orgetorix at the time of Julius Caesar's Gallic Wars (58–50 BCE)

Basel's Paper Mill dates from the late Middle Ages

In March 2008 I was drinking coffee in the Paper Museum down by the Rhine. The museum sits alongside a fast-running little canal called the St Alban Teich, in a district of Basel that owes its name to an eleventh-century monastery. I was back living in the city of firsts, after a gap of thirty-five years.

The Paper Museum houses the oldest printing works in Switzerland. Putting words on paper with moveable type – the right words in the right order – has been going on here since Gutenberg set up his bible. Paper has been made in the St Alban valley since the late Middle Ages. It requires a special sort of chutzpah to take time out here to write. What else is there to say? Who needs more words?

But the Paper Museum is where I got the idea for this book: a book about books, about writers and travellers.

Basel has always been Switzerland's point of entry from the north. You follow the river and water your horses before the assault of the mountains. It's where French and German trains stop. Travellers with a few shillings stayed at the Hotel des Trois Rois, overlooking the Rhine – writers as diverse as Thomas Mann, Patricia Highsmith and Lord Byron. Mann was in retreat from the Nazis in 1933 when he heard marching music and singing from his hotel window.[7] Hitchcock had just filmed Highsmith's *Strangers on a Train* (1950). We have no record of Byron's stay, but he might have bedded one of the room maids or a willing stable boy.

There wasn't just Byron frightening the horses. Many of the writers in this book came to Switzerland with romantic ideas. However, the writer on my mind that March evening in the Paper Museum was a scribe like myself: Irish, an Ulsterman, a bit of a travel writer.

He passed through Basel en route to Rome 400 years before, in March 1608. His name was Tadhg Ó Cianáin, scribe in the party of Hugh O'Neill, Earl of Tyrone. *Tadhg* means 'poet' or 'storyteller' in Irish. He was one of a hundred-strong band accompanying the Earls of Ulster from Ireland, following the Nine Years' War (1594–1603). This is known as the Flight of the Earls – but, as is the way in Ulster, it depends whose side you're on. It depends on the way you tell it. Were they fleeing or leaving? Was it a 'tactical retreat', as Irish historians tend to see it, or were they traversing Switzerland with their tails between their legs?

It was with some trepidation that these Irish chieftains crossed the border into Protestant Reformed Basel. Tadhg's is the earliest account of Switzerland we have in Irish. A thousand years before, Irish monks founding monasteries in Helvetia – St Columbanus, St Gallen – must have scratched their thoughts in an idle moment, but such marginalia are now lost to us.

Tadhg's is also the first travel diary in Irish. As an old travel journalist myself, I want to salute him across the centuries in *Gaelige*, with the somewhat clichéd greeting we both learned in school: *Go n-éirí an bóthar leat*, may the road rise with you, may you succeed.

The road does rise steeply from Basel, across the Jura and into the Alps, but our Earls did not succeed:

> *They moved on to Basel, a fine, strong, ancient, remarkable city which is built on that river [the Rhine]. There is a very good bridge in the very centre of the city over the river, and numerous boats afford a means of leaving it and getting to it from Flanders and the country around the river. Those who occupy and inhabit it are heretics. There is a very large church in the very centre of the city in which there are statues and pictures of Luther and Calvin and many other bad, devilish authors.*[8]

Tadhg is an observant scribe. Holbein's portrait of Luther the heretic now hangs in Basel Kunstmuseum. At the city gates a toll had been exacted for the number of horses. Drivers entering Switzerland still fork out forty francs at the toll bridge for the privilege of using the country's excellent motorways, tunnels and mountain passes.

As Tadhg was leaving Switzerland he summarised its politics:

*In themselves they are a distinct, remarkable, peculiar state. They make
their selection of a system for the government of the country each year.
They have fourteen famous great cities. Half of them are Catholics and
the other half are heretics, and by agreements and great oaths they are
bound to one another for their own defence and protection against any
neighbour in the world who should endeavour to injure them or oppose
them in upholding the public good with moderation and appropriateness.*[9]

Switzerland provided the Earls safe passage. At Hospental – known to
the Romans as Hospitaculum – near the Gotthard Pass an inscription in
the church makes no bones about where we are. 'The ways part here, my
friend, so where do you want to go? Down to eternal Rome? Down to holy
Cologne, the German Rhine or westward and way into Franconia?' Many
of the writers in our story paused here to get their bearings. Tadhg took
stock of the Swiss character:

*It is said of the people of this country that they are the truest, most honest
and untreacherous in the world, and the least given to breaking their
word. They allow no robbery or homicide to be done in their country without punishing it at once. Because of the perfection of their truth they
alone are guards to the Catholic kings and princes of Christendom.*[10]

This seems to me a just measure. Writers since Tadhg have commented on
Swiss probity. At times it is the epitome of dullness, smug righteousness; at
other times highly prized. I once left my bag at the motorway stop south of
the Gotthard tunnel. Phone, credit cards, cash, camera, passport, residence
permit and notebook – all gone in a moment. Back in Basel I opened up
Find My iPhone, saw its GPS blinking south of the mountains, and con-
tacted the service station. We have your bag, the attendant said, we'll post
it in the morning. And so she did. And refused any reward.

The late, lamented historian Tony Judt tackles the gilded ambiguities
of Switzerland head on:

*Switzerland did remarkably well out of World War II – trading with Berlin
and laundering looted assets. It was the Swiss who urged Hitler to mark
Jewish passports with a 'J' ... Then there are the tax evaders, although it
has never been clear to me why what Swiss banks do in servicing a hand-
ful of wealthy foreign criminals is significantly worse than what Goldman
Sachs has done with the proceeds of millions of honest US tax dollars.*[11]

He ends by giving the country a thumbs up, and so do I. There is gold surely in these mountains, and there is gilt – and there is guilt. When the sun strikes the roof of the chalet it glitters with borrowed or stolen light. The tracks in the snow criss-cross off-piste, by curious paths and old logging trails, and you add to them. Inside, the heating is on, and gives a piny, medicinal fragrance to the communal area, its carved woodwork, its tatty boxes of games, a shelf of well-thumbed books in many languages.

Upstairs, the room is spotless and faces a picture window. A chair. A desk. That incomparable view.

RUN OUT OF TOWN

Rousseau's walk on the wild side

JEAN-JACQUES ROUSSEAU QUITTE GENÉVE EN 1728

Nineteenth-century illustration of the young Rousseau leaving Geneva in 1728

Gilt covers the whole surface.
Jean-Jacques Rousseau

The volume gets turned down on a winter Sunday in Switzerland. You'll find one shop open at the train station. In the small towns you might hear the slither of onionskin Bible pages and a clutch of dark teenagers around a kebab outlet. On the approach to Geneva, speed cameras are out to get you and the high rises suggest little room. On the lake, the fog, nature's very own anaesthetic, muffles the ducks. They know today is Sunday and are on their best behaviour. You could quietly top yourself and nobody would pay much attention.

Nature in Geneva seems to flow southwest into France: the Rhône, the Jura, the Savoy Alps, the long drooping crescent of the lake, all head in that direction. They tumble over themselves to escape, like weekenders at the border. The wind off the water – the Bise – blows them westward. Geneva's writers look to Paris. When Calvin's city got too much for them there was always the City of Light. The playgrounds there were in full swing.

It's a conference town chock-a-block with laptops and leadership. The august buildings flaunt their acronyms – UNHCR, UNBRO, UNESCO – a kind of concrete poetry, with an army of functionaries watching the clock. Now and then the bigwigs come to town, engaged in talks, ironing out the world's trouble spots, followed by heavies whispering into their wrists. Bono does Geneva. Geldof does Geneva. It has always been a town of worthies.

Rousseau is Geneva's very own bigwig. He was born here into a world of clocks and gets ticked off when you ask people to name a Swiss writer. More often than not they say *Heidi* or *The Swiss Family Robinson* and can't name the authors, but the well-read mention Rousseau. He was a polymath: when he turned his pen towards a subject – justice, romance, education, autobiography, nature – he changed it. His buzzing ideas got up Calvinist Geneva's nose and so he was often on the road, in a huff, mostly across the border in France. He handed down this role – the writer challenging orthodoxy – to his Swiss successors. *Man was born free, and everywhere he is in chains*: that's Rousseau.

We all need to rattle our chains.

He had a bestseller: *Julie, ou la nouvelle Héloïse* (1761). Tutor falls in love with student, daddy marries her to money, tutor wanders off, comes back and still they're in love. Social conventions get in the way of high-flown hanky-panky: a story that remains with us. All set against a backdrop of vineyards, lake, mountains. *Julie* did for Switzerland what the Waverley

Rebel without a cause: The teenage Rousseau

Novels did for Scotland and *Huckleberry Finn* for America: it put a land-scape on the map. Half a century after publication the Romantics had it in their backpacks.

Rousseau's father, Isaac, had been clockmaker in the seraglio of Constantinople in the first decade of the eighteenth century. A seraglio is where the Ottoman big turbans kept their women. I can see why they might want the clocks on time. Newly married Isaac was busy, winding and tightening the springs, polishing the works, assembling ever more ornate timepieces for his new masters in the east. Geneva's population of 17,000 was tiny compared to Istanbul's 700,000. The Ottomans were the command economy of the day and the Swiss were the immigrant labour. Swiss artisans, clockmakers and pedagogues were in demand. Ticino architects laid out swathes of St Petersburg. The tutor to the future Tsar Alexander I of Russia was Swiss. Geneva's craftsmen, its jobbing teachers and writers tended to follow the river and achieve fame elsewhere.

There was nothing unusual in this. In his autobiographical *Confessions* (1782), Rousseau acknowledges 'a charm in seeing different countries which a Genevese can scarcely ever resist'. Many of his relatives in the clock business were on the road. A brother of Isaac's went to Amsterdam;

another to London; and a brother-in-law went to Charlestown in the new colony of Carolina. A cousin travelled with Louis XIV to Persia, settled in Isfahan and brought up a Farsi-speaking family. His son, Jean François, speaking Farsi, Turkish, Arabic and Armenian, became the French consul at Basra. Geneva may have been small but its emigrants saw the world.

Jean-Jacques Rousseau, born into this artisan milieu, was set ticking like a fat gold watch in 1712. His mother died ten days later. Motherless children have a hard time. Jean-Jacques spent his first six years right in the heart of the old town, in hearing of the bells and in sight of the town hall. Hours reading in his father's workshop in St-Gervais, in the poorer area across the Rhône, gave him a restless mind:

> Good or bad, all were alike to me; I had no choice, and read everything with equal avidity. I read at the work table, I read on my errands, I read in the wardrobe, and forgot myself for hours together; my head became giddy with reading; I could do nothing else.[1]

At the beginning of the eighteenth century, Geneva was a university and clockmaking town in the Calvinist tradition. The tectonic plates of Enlightenment France and a deep-seated Puritanism rubbed against each other, just as, millennia before, the Alps had reared up against the Jura. On the doors of the town hall a Latin inscription called the Pope 'the Antichrist'. An influx of French Huguenot refugees had only emboldened the reformist character of the town. Stoutly walled, independent, Geneva was wary of the Dukes of Savoy on its doorstep and the king of Sardinia to the south. Its characteristic openness to refugees and prickliness with strangers were established early.

Solidly Protestant, not too much garlic. I've never heard of Jean Calvin having a sense of humour. Picardy French, he initially fled to Basel in 1536 from oppression across the border and then found a foothold in Geneva, gradually hijacking the town as his own fiefdom against local opposition. Calvinism preached an individualised and egalitarian reading of the Bible and Geneva became its spiritual home. Following the St Bartholomew's Day massacre, when a French mob turned on and slaughtered thousands of Huguenots, those who could escape across the border to the safety of Geneva were the human rights refugees of the day. The English poet John Milton commemorated an earlier slaughter bordering Switzerland in his sonnet 'On the Late Massacre in Piedmont':

Geneva's reformer: Jean Calvin (1509–64)

Avenge, O Lord, thy slaughtered saints, whose bones
Lie scattered on the Alpine mountains cold

Geneva thereby gained a reputation as a refuge from religious persecution. Initially they were Reformers fleeing Catholic orthodoxy, but later refugees fled Russian serfdom and the Tsar's police, conflicts and persecution of all stripes. The UN High Commission for Refugees based in Geneva has been long in the making.

Rousseau was brought up with a firm view of Catholics as the dreaded other:

I had an aversion to Catholicism peculiar to our village, which repre-
sented it as a frightful idolatry, and painted its priests in the blackest
colours. This feeling was so strong in me, that at first I never looked into
the inside of a church, never met a priest in a surplice, never heard the
processional bell, without a shudder of terror and alarm, which soon
left me in the towns, but has often come upon me again in country
parishes.[2]

Calvin left his stamp on the city-state. Sumptuary laws forbade goldsmiths from making jewellery and so stimulated watchmaking, a neat motif for the plain, utilitarian, industrious virtues that he espoused. A history of time-pieces is a history of enslavement to the nine to five, to twenty-four–seven, to clocking in and signing out. Taskmasters like their clocks: they are a measure of control. Geneva's early watchmakers were of French origin and their skills spread to the Jura towns of Vallée de Joux and La Chaux-de-Fonds, where there was a ready supply of labour.

The Grand Council – the leadership team of the day – kept the popu-lace in check with the help of Calvinist pastors. They had their PowerPoints, their bullet points, their protocols and their hymn sheets, from which every-body was singing in unison. A strategic plan was in place. All knew the staff handbook by heart, policies and procedures for everything. They were moving forward, striving for excellence, researching and developing their souls, busting a gut for heaven, reflecting on that mansion on the hill – and gaining on the competition: the papists, who clearly were not with the pro-gramme. The aristocratic families in Geneva's Old Town and the more rad-ical forces across the Rhône in St-Gervais were often in dispute. Rousseau was never one to side with management and was clearly thinking outside the box. His writings fell foul of the quasi-theocratic power of the Grand Council. For all the talk of predestination, what was wanted was obedience.

Apprenticed to an engraver, carousing with his mates outside the city one Sunday in 1728, the teenage Rousseau got locked out. It was the third time. Curfew was at dusk and he was tardy. The Porte de Rive banged shut. Geneva had a lockdown procedure in place that would be the envy of any high school. The sixteen-year-old Rousseau had had enough. In his *Confessions* he makes much of this call to freedom:

> During our walks outside the city I always went further than any of them without thinking of my return, unless others thought of it for me. Twice I was caught: the gates were shut before I was back. ... I was returning with two companions. About half a league from the city I heard the retreat sounded: I doubled my pace; I heard the tattoo beat, and ran with all my might. I arrived out of breath and bathed in perspiration; my heart beat; from a distance I saw the soldiers at their posts; I rushed up and cried out with a voice half-choked. It was too late![3]

Rousseau's brush with authority set the template for the later rebellion of the Romantics. Percy Shelley read Rousseau's novel *Julie* to Byron, neither philandering poet averse to a tumble in the hay should the occasion arise. Mary Shelley locks her Victor Frankenstein – 'by birth a Genevese' – out of his hometown in the manner of the teenage Rousseau:

> It was completely dark when I arrived in the environs of Geneva; the gates of the town were already shut, and I was obliged to pass the night at Sécheron, a village at the distance of half a league from the city.[4]

For Rousseau, freedom meant Savoy, the Piedmont, women in furbelows and Mother Church. Having run away from home and the hated apprenticeship, he converted to Catholicism at sixteen and put himself beyond the pale of Geneva citizenship. The catalyst that sent him over to 'the scarlet woman of Rome', as Ian Paisley used to put it, was called Madame Françoise-Louise de Warens.

She was twenty-nine when the sixteen-year-old Rousseau clapped eyes on her in 1728. 'I was approaching an age when a woman of her own years could not with propriety express a desire to keep a young man with her.'[5] Originally from Vevey, she had been married at fourteen to de Warens, a marriage she annulled. Rousseau was smitten. She welcomed him as a *pensionnaire* into her home in Annecy, seat of the Catholic bishop of Geneva. Her specialty was conversions to the Catholic faith, for which she received a Church stipend. She was a covert recruitment agency in frocks, to counteract the bastion of reformism that was Geneva. Rousseau quickly got himself baptised into the Catholic Church in Turin. The motherless boy had met the woman of his life:

> From the first day, the most complete intimacy was established between us, which has continued during the rest of her life. 'Little one' was my name; 'Mamma' was hers; and we always remained 'Little one' and 'Mamma', even when advancing years had obliterated the difference between us.[6]

Sweet, we might think, but Mamma was no nun and had several lovers. *Le petit* wanted to keep her on a pedestal as a surrogate mother. They had the decency to wait until the autumn of 1733 before bedding down and establishing 'relations of a different character'. They performed the deed in a *guinguette* – a sort of suburban dancing garden – in Chambéry. Maman became Madame. She was already the mistress of her manservant, Claude Anet. The three conducted a *ménage à trois* for a year in Chambéry, until

Rousseau's 'Mamma', Mme de Warens, and her welcoming bedroom in
Les Charmettes, Chambéry

Anet's death. Rousseau loved her, but like all his loves, there was a certain
amount of sex in the head to contend with:

> Her image, ever present to my heart, left room for no other; she was for me
> the only woman in the world; and the extreme sweetness of the feelings
> with which she inspired me did not allow my senses time to awake for oth-
> ers, and protected me against her and all her sex. In a word, I was chaste,
> because I loved her.[7]

Rousseau then began a long wandering apprenticeship as a teacher,
dancing master, fiddler and *valet de chambre*, but always coming back to
Mamma's apron strings. He did a bit of tutoring here, hung around the
great houses there, tried his hand at music, lusted after young women and
a few older ones, and sang for his supper. The philosopher Edmund Burke,
taking issue during the French Revolution with what he saw as Rousseau's
bad moral example, lamented his 'men of wit and pleasure, of gay, young,
military sparks, and danglers at toilets'. Burke lays the moral degeneracy of
the French Revolution firmly at the feet of poor old long-dead Rousseau.
These new tutors 'infuse into their youth an unfashioned, indelicate, sour,
gloomy, ferocious medley of pedantry and lewdness'.[8] Burke seems to be
losing the plot here, although 'danglers at toilets' is worth it. But certainly
the unschooled Rousseau had a jumped-up quality – and from Burke's

point of view he was continental to boot. Lackey to the rich and titled in Piedmont and Savoy, Rousseau seems to me like an early international schoolteacher, eavesdropping at the coffee klatches of the mothers, at times bored by their pushy wittering, at times amused by their advances.

Obliged to give Geneva a wide berth by virtue of his conversion, Rousseau settled along the lakeshore in Vevey, the 'small town at the foot of the Alps' where the youthful scenes of his bestseller *Julie* take place. Madame de Warens infamously hailed from those parts, so he had to be circumspect:

> her birthplace was only twelve miles from Lausanne, I spent three or four days in walking there, during which a feeling of most tender emotion never left me. The view of the Lake of Geneva and its delightful shores always possessed a special charm in my eyes which I cannot explain, and which consists not only in the beauty of the view, but in something still more attractive, which moves and touches me ... it is always the Canton of Vaud, near the lake, in the midst of enchanting scenery, to which it draws me. I feel that I must have an orchard on the shore of this lake and no other, that I must have a loyal friend, a loving wife, a cow, and a little boat.[9]

Rousseau had more than forty different addresses in his life and the wife, cow and boat never materialised for long. They were his equivalent of a little cabin in the woods. In Vevey he lodged at La Clef just behind the market hall, where a plaque commemorates his stay. The old rooming house is now a restaurant serving fillets of perch from the lake, just as *le petit* liked them, done in butter.

This is the landscape that Rousseau made synonymous with romance, Switzerland's equivalent to the Lake District or Brontë Country. He invented the idea of a natural landscape as possessing beauty (and the idea of the 'noble savage'), even though the shoreline here has been cultivated for over two thousand years, its vineyards stretching back to Roman times. The Savoy Alps rear across the lake, vines come down to the water's edge, the lacustrine villages are crowned with pretty castles and a tradition of peace.

Sometimes you just have to rattle the chains.

Throughout the nineteenth century, writers and travellers came in pilgrimage to Rousseau's fictional places. The Romantics only added to the way stations with an admixture of sulfurous sex and poetry. They were like rock stars who die young – members of the twenty-seven club – quickly canonised and thought of as bad boys in heaven, strumming their air guitars: Shelley on vocals, Byron playing lead guitar, Coleridge overdosing in the dressing room and refusing to come out. I think I'd put Wordsworth on a Moog synthesiser. Hazlitt, Dickens, Dean Howells, Twain and Henry James were the groupies. These writers of the nineteenth century broadened the audience to include a transatlantic readership and contributed to the development of Switzerland as a mass tourism destination.

Rousseau sets a famous trysting scene, Julie's kiss, in a grove of trees above Clarens, along the shore from Vevey. The feminist Mary Wollstonecraft urged the social reformer William Godwin to read *Julie* – it first appeared in English translation in 1761 – as a test of the tenor of his heart when they were courting. Their daughter Mary Godwin in turn pressed the novel on Percy Shelley. It became a kind of literary litmus test. Shelley read it to Byron as they were boating around the lake in the summer of 1816. The two of them hoofed it up the hill, Byron limping, in search of that hand-me-down grove of trees. Byron's *Childe Harold* did the rest:

> 'Twas not for fiction chose Rousseau this spot,
> Peopling it with affections; but he found
> It was the scene which passion must allot
> To the mind's purified beings; 'twas the ground
> Where early Love his Psyche's zone unbound,
> And hallow'd it with loveliness...

'Where early Love his Psyche's zone unbound' is a killer line. Byron's early love was for a boy at Harrow, Lord Clare. Rousseau's early love was, of course, Madame de Warens. She had had her own dalliance with a tutor when she was a girl and there is a sense in which Rousseau is living vicariously through her relationships. Here's the effect of aristocratic Julie's kiss on the humble tutor Saint-Preux: 'Julie's lips ... placed on, pressed against mine, and my body clasped in your arms! No, lightning is no more fiery nor quick than the fire that instantly inflamed me.'[10] Hot stuff.

When Rousseau published *Julie* in 1761 he was forty-nine. In 1762 *Émile*, his book on education, was burned in Paris. In that same year Rousseau brought out *The Social Contract*, which together with *Émile* made him persona non grata in Geneva.

The Social Contract is a political analysis of what binds people together 'each to all and all to each'. Might does not make right, says Rousseau: the

Vevey town councillors in a 1905 wine festival poster

individual forfeits some of his freedoms for the good of all; the delicate balance of rights and duties is what constitutes civil society. Geneva as a citystate, with its Grand Council and freedom from princely rule, is clearly a template for this view of society. By seeing the relation between sovereign and subject as a social contract rather than power exercised by divine right, Rousseau ushered in the demos – the crowd. Along the way, he comments on slavery, the death penalty, the lawmakers (among whom he lauds Calvin) and the rise of nations – among which he counts Switzerland.

The philosophical works were for the few. But *Julie* was wildfire in the popular mind and *Émile* proposed unorthodox religious and educational views; the reintroduction of breastfeeding, for example. Marie Antoinette was the first queen in centuries to breastfeed her children, courtesy of Rousseau. His writings made him the pariah of moral guardians (both Paris and Geneva issued warrants for his arrest) but the darling of the literate, especially the women.

The gatekeepers were wary of novels. Calvinism conceived of God as the Great Author, so puny rivals were suspect. Edicts and censorship followed. If novels were to be admitted, then they should be moral and didactic. The spread of printing two centuries earlier had given way to the triumph of reading. Lost in reading, women neglected their wifely and household duties. In Switzerland still, the racks of pink-covered chic lit tempt the housewife at every post office.

Rousseau had been living at the Hermitage in Montmorency outside Paris since 1757. The jobbing music teacher and gadfly gallant of the Savoy years had given way to the august man of letters, still squatting in other people's houses. He feared a fatwa following the publication of *Émile* and was obliged to find refuge. He didn't much like cities but was a great one for the cabin in the woods, the gazebo in the garden, the potting shed. He was on the lookout for a safe house across the border. In 1762 a friend offered him half a house in the hamlet of Môtiers in the Val-de-Travers, a remote valley in the Jura above Neuchâtel. Rousseau called it 'Scotland in Switzerland'.

The Val-de-Travers is infamous as the birthplace of absinthe, but we are getting ahead of ourselves. Had absinthe been distilled in Môtiers at the time, the world might have lost Rousseau's *Confessions* (1781). The disreputable drink, after a century of proscription, was legalised again in Switzerland in 2005. A museum to the green fairy – the Absinthe House – sits not far from Rousseau's house on the Grand Rue in Môtiers.

I have a very beautiful fountain beneath my window and the sound of it is one of the things I love. These tall fountains in the shape of columns or obelisks, with water running through iron pipes into big pools, are a typical feature of Switzerland. I can't express how agreeable it is to see all this beautiful water flowing in the midst of rock and wood during the hot weather. You feel refreshed just by looking at them, and tempted to drink from them when you're not even thirsty.[11]

Rousseau's humble house was closed the Sunday I visited and after pacing the tiny gallery as the Master used to on rainy days – three paces, no more – I headed to the Absinthe House for a tour and a drink. In Rousseau's time there can't have been much to do in Môtiers except hike to the waterfall and back.

I settled into reading at the bar while working my way through the museum's 'tasting menu'. It consisted of three types of absinthe: the first at 52% proof, the second at 63% and the third – the veritable green fairy, named Esmeralda, whose name means emerald – at 72%. On the label was a fairy in a skimpy nightie, holding a lantern. She had gossamer wings, blonde hair and a crown of bay leaves. She looked as though a Japanese manga team had designed her. The three respectable drams went down remarkably well with Jean-Jacques' letters, which I called up on wi-fi, deep in the *Complete Works* of over twenty volumes.

At Môtiers he wrote to dukes and barons, to titled ladies, to the literary pussycats of the day. Boswell came to call. Celebs, we might call them. I gave Esmeralda a complicit wink. I remembered, à propos of nothing, that the boat at the beginning of Visconti's *Death in Venice*, conveying Aschenbach to his fate, is called *Esmerelda*. On second look the winged creature was more like a porno star than a manga fairy – one of those new floozies, all peroxide, piercings and tattoos. It took a while to scroll down to Rousseau's letters addressed to the Maréchal de Luxembourg in January and February 1763.

'Imagine a valley,' writes Jean-Jacques – I'd laboured through him at college, had stalked his movements for weeks and felt this familiarity was earned – 'a good half a league wide and two leagues long, through which runs a little river called l'Areuse, running north-west to south-east. This valley, lying between two mountain chains branching off from the Jura, narrows at either end.'

He was a Genevan on the run, back in Switzerland after a lifetime in foreign parts. I felt sympathy for his predicament. He'd blotted his copy-book. This eighteenth-century Salman Rushdie went to ground under the protection of the King of Prussia (Neuchâtel was a principality in his kingdom) and Lord Maréchal Keith, a Jacobite exile from Britain who was governor of Neuchâtel. These were his minders.

I thought I would rediscover here what delighted me in youth; all is changed: a different landscape, a different air, a different sky, different people; and, no longer seeing my mountains with the eyes of a twenty-year-old, I find them aged. I miss the good old days, indeed. We attribute to the world changes that have taken place in us, and when pleasure goes we think it gone from the world. ... To know Môtiers, you need to have some conception of the canton of Neuchâtel, and to know Neuchâtel you need to keep the whole of Switzerland in mind.[12]

Jean-Jacques provides the Maréchal de Luxembourg with a potted history of Switzerland, attributing the corruption of a pastoral way of life to the mercenaries who loaned their services to neighbouring armies. French dress, food and court manners become pretentious and airy-fairy once brought back to the cantons of the home country. 'Gilt covers the whole surface' is Jean-Jacques' memorable phrase for the Swiss aping the *beau monde* of Paris. It's the perennial story of old money and new money, the centre and the fringe. Here and there, glimmers of modern Switzerland flash forward to us from the age of Enlightenment: 'So many bandits hide out in the country that those who govern can't distinguish between wanted criminals and innocent refugees, or can't be bothered to find out.' Now *that* sounds familiar.

The second absinthe bottle sported an even more curious label. It was called La Fine Clandestine. I had grown up with *poitín* in Ireland so Christophe Racine's under-the-counter spirit from Môtiers would present no problem. The label showed a dance of death, a *Totentanz*, with a skeleton linked to a cadaverous doctor – a tall Doctor Death sporting a white T-shirt with a blue cross on it. He was dancing with a green-skinned, black-haired fairy in that nightie again; she had the addition of a garter strap and what looked like Jimmy Choo heels. This dance took place on the shore of Lake Neuchâtel under a full moon.

Jean-Jacques liked to sneak out the back door for a walk without being spotted. He explored a branch of the river called La Côte aux Fées, the Fairy Shore, where the little people are said to have their abode. We can confidently say that he was away with the fairies. He compares the Areuse river to the Fontaine de Vaucluse, in that both surface fully formed as rivers. The Fontaine de Vaucluse is where Petrarch retreated with his lover Beatrice in 1338, so maybe Jean-Jacques is beginning to have delusions of grandeur.

In *The Confessions* he turns bitter and critical of his hosts: 'The inhabitants of Neuchâtel, who are fond of nothing but trifles and tinsel, who are no judge of genuine goods, and think that talent consists in long phrases.'[13] He has it in for his hometown as well:

> determined to renounce my ungrateful country, in which I had never lived, from which I had received no kindness or assistance ... Clergymen, relatives, bigots, persons of all sorts came from Geneva and Switzerland, not for the purpose of admiring or making fun of me, like those who came from France, but to scold and catechise me.[14]

The winter of 1762–63 was one of the coldest of the century. The Thames and the Seine froze over and Môtiers was snowed in.[15] Jean-Jacques wore his Armenian robes and hat, in which Scottish portraitist Allan Ramsay had captured him (a painting now in the National Gallery of Scotland). Thérèse, Jean-Jacques' live-in servant and mother of his four abandoned children, joined him. She was Catholic, Neuchâtel was a Reformist canton, and their irregular household didn't help relations with the neighbours.

Allan Ramsey's portrait of Rousseau in Armenian costume, painted in London, 1766

Jean-Jacques' dalliance with the Scarlet Woman of Rome may have been over, but Thérèse was off to Mass most Sundays while he sat at home upstairs writing his *Confessions*.

On 6 September 1763 matters came to a head. Villagers threw stones at the house. Jean-Jacques and Thérèse had to cower in the kitchen. It was like living in a mixed marriage up on the Falls Road circa 1969 with both the B-Specials and the Royal Ulster Constabulary knocking at the door. The writer and his common-law wife did a runner a couple of days later. Market day in Môtiers, with drinking and carousing, might turn ugly. He was on the road again.

But Môtiers this evening looked the picture of peace after my three shots of absinthe. I also remembered that the current heir to the collapsed Principality of Neuchâtel is Patrick Guinness, of the stout family. Main Street had begun to darken and shadows lengthen.

Then I spotted him skulking along by the wall opposite, decked out in his long Armenian robes that had something of the maxi-coat about them,

the fur hat covering his bald spot. Rousseau's get-up had a kind of oriental wackiness – Jean Paul Gaultier crossed with the Ayatollah. He moved
fast for a man approaching sixty, determined to make it to the Fairy Coast
before night.

He must have had a good day at the writing.

I never made it to the Ile Saint-Pierre on Lake Biel where Rousseau escaped
after Môtiers. He lasted two months on the tiny island before he was chased
out of there too. In *Meditations of a Solitary Walker* (1782), an old man's
book, we hear the sound of settling after fitful upheavals.

> *Of all the places where I have stayed (and there have been some lovely
> ones), none has left me as truly happy as St. Peter's Island. I was only able
> to spend a couple of months on the island, but I would have spent two
> years, two centuries or even an eternity there without ever being bored. I
> look upon those two months as the happiest time of my life. It was such
> a happy time that it would have satisfied me throughout my life and I
> would never once have yearned to be in another place.*[16]

Each period of history reinvents Rousseau. The Enlightenment philoso-
phers blamed his influence for the French Revolution. Byron in *Childe
Harold* saw him as

> *wild Rousseau,*
> *The apostle of affliction, he who threw*
> *Enchantment over passion, and from woe*
> *Wrung overwhelming eloquence*[17]

Mary Shelley makes Victor Frankenstein and his monster outcasts from
Geneva. Later writers echo Rousseau's picture of his hometown as closed
to intellectual enquiry but open for business. In the mid-nineteenth century, Nathaniel Hawthorne summarised this Swiss mix of plain living and
business acumen:

> *This being a Protestant country, the doors are all shut – an inhospitality
> that made me half a Catholic ... The Swiss people are frugal and inex-
> pensive in their own habits, I believe, plain and simple, and careless of*

ornament; but they seem to reckon on other people's spending a great deal of money for gewgaws.[18]

Even Henry James doesn't mince words about 'the Presbyterian mother-city':

> *the Helvetic capital is a highly artificial compound. ... the want of humour in the local atmosphere, and the absence, as well, of that aesthetic character which is begotten of a generous view of life. There is no Genevese architecture, nor museum, nor theatre, nor music, not even a worthy promenade – all prime requisites of a well-appointed foreign capital; and yet somehow Geneva manages to assert herself powerfully without them.*[19]

Rousseau pointed out the truism that the wellbeing of the rich is rooted in the exploitation of the poor – 'Thus it is that the substance of the poor always goes to enrich the wealthy'[20] – an observation that gave grist to nineteenth-century socialism and twentieth-century Communism. You could make a good case for it being true also of the twenty-first-century banking crisis and the 99% in our own day. At the end of Joseph Conrad's spy novel *Under Western Eyes,* about Russian revolutionaries in Geneva, Razumov the double agent pointedly visits Jean-Jacques Rousseau's island in the Rhône, the city's homage to its wayward son:

> *a hexagonal islet with a soil of gravel and its shores faced with dressed stone, a perfection of puerile neatness. A couple of tall poplars and a few other trees stood grouped on the clean, dark gravel, and under them a few garden benches and a bronze effigy of Jean-Jacques Rousseau seated on its pedestal. ... This was the place for the beginning of that writing which had to be done.*[21]

A century after Rousseau's birth in Geneva, a group of free-love practitioners descended on the town and met up with lead guitarist Lord Byron. He was trying to shed a few pounds, finish his triple concept album and keep out of the way of the groupies. The summer of rain and love had begun.

2

HERE COME THE MONSTERS

Boating with Byron and frolicking with Frankenstein on Lac Léman

1820 print of Lord Byron at the Villa Diodati near Geneva, 1816

I saw their thousand years of snow
On high – their wide long lake below,
And the blue Rhone in fullest flow
Lord Byron

It begins with a volcano. In April 1815 Mount Tambora erupted on the Indonesian island of Sumbawa, the largest volcanic eruption in recorded history. Ash rained across the northern hemisphere and brought cold weather and torrential downpours to Europe the following summer. In June 1816 snow fell in Albany, New York. Volcanic winter caused freaky summer weather in Switzerland, where a group of English free-love advocates were in and out of each other's beds on the southern shore of Lake Geneva. They passed the inclement evenings inventing tales of vampires and monsters. Mary Shelley took up her pen and began *Frankenstein*, looking out at the downpour on the lake. It was good writing weather.

'I passed the summer of 1816 in the environs of Geneva', she wrote in the introduction to her gothic horror story:

> *The season was cold and rainy, and in the evenings we crowded around a blazing wood fire, and occasionally amused ourselves with some German stories of ghosts which happened to fall into our hands. These tales excited us in a playful desire of imitation. Two other friends (a tale from the pen of one of whom would be far more acceptable to the public than anything I can hope to produce) and myself agreed to write each a story founded on some supernatural occurrence.*[1]

The two friends were Lord Byron and Mary's lover Percy Bysshe Shelley.

Mary Godwin and Shelley had eloped from England two years earlier, in the summer of 1814, when she was not yet seventeen. Shelley was already married and turning twenty-two, the father of a child, with a second on the way. Here he is in June 1814, waxing lyrical to his old university friend Hogg:

> *The originality and loveliness of Mary's character was apparent to me from her very motions and tones of voice. The irresistible wildness and sublimity of her feelings showed itself in her gestures and her looks – Her smile, how persuasive it was, and how pathetic! She is gentle, to be convinced and tender.*[2]

They were soon meeting at her mother's grave in St Pancras Churchyard. Her mother, Mary Wollstonecraft, had written A *Vindication of the Rights of Woman* (1792), studied and translated French and German and had read Tom Paine's *Rights of Man*. The French Revolution cast its light and shadow over the late eighteenth century the way the fall of Communism – or perhaps the Twin Towers – does over ours. Nonconformist William Godwin took up with Wollstonecraft when he was forty and she the unmarried mother of Fanny, born of a stormy affair with a young American in Paris. When Wollstonecraft became pregnant with Mary, Godwin made an honest woman of her. She died in childbirth. Her daughter, canoodling at her grave with the young poet, seems to have inherited the tangled apron strings of feminist revolt and its consequences.

Muriel Spark makes no bones about what attracted Shelley:

> *Mary offered fresh, 16-year-old sexuality combined in the most extraordinary way with the precocious intellectual flair of her Godwinian upbringing. She was both naïve and knowing, both flesh and spirit, burning with a youth and intelligence which blazed out all the more hypnotically against the gloomy, hopeless, complicated collapse of Shelley's married relationship with Harriet.[3]*

Shelley was a bit of a dish, but you mightn't want your daughter meeting him on the sly among the tombstones. His family were squires of Horsham in Sussex. He had been expelled from Oxford for distributing an atheistic pamphlet and was wrangling with his father about inheritance and money. A pretty boy, pugnacious, he had behind him three years of utopianism, communal living and a spell of revolutionary rabble-rousing in Ireland. Mary was sixteen and impressionable.

It was a hot day in London and they had a stormy crossing from Dover on the night of 28 July 1814. Sheet lightning lit the channel. They stayed at an inn in Calais and three days later in Paris Shelley bought a notebook, now at the Bodleian, in which both of them recorded their travels. Shelley wrote a letter at Troyes to his pregnant wife with a curious proposal for a threesome about which biographers can only speculate:

> *I write to urge you to come to Switzerland, where you will at least find one firm & constant friend, to whom your interests will be always dear, by whom your feelings will never wilfully be injured ... you shall know our adventures more detailed, if I do not hear at Neuchâtel, that I am soon*

to have the pleasure of communicating to you in person, & of welcoming
you to some sweet retreat I will procure for you among the mountains.[4]

Harriet – the spurned wife left holding the baby – did not rise to the bait:
'Every age has its cares. God knows, I have mine. Dear Ianthe is quite well.
She is fourteen months old, and has six teeth.'

Why Switzerland? Napoleon's war had despoiled France and Shelley
had read his Rousseau. Switzerland was safe, romantic. The elopement of
these young lovers was harum-scarum. The presence of Claire Clairmont,
Mary's stepsister, underlines the devil-may-care recklessness. She thought
she was half-Swiss, although later evidence would prove this unfounded.
Shelley and Mary's co-authored journal, published in 1817 as *History of a*
Six Weeks' Tour, has a backpacker quality. This early Lonely Planet Guide
describes their first view of Switzerland:

> *On passing the French barrier, a surprising difference may be observed*
> *between the opposite nations that inhabit either side. The Swiss cot-*
> *tages are much cleaner and neater, and the inhabitants exhibit the same*
> *contrast.*[5]

Eastern France 'had been entirely desolated by the Cossacks' in the
Napoleonic wars. Flush with some money Shelley managed to procure
from the bank, they arrived at Lucerne, and from there boarded the boat
down the lake to Brunnen. Always interested in revolutionaries, Shelley
focused on William Tell:

> *The high mountains encompassed us, darkening the waters; at a distance*
> *on the shores of Uri we could perceive the chapel of Tell, and this was*
> *the village where he matured the conspiracy which was to overthrow the*
> *tyrant of his country; and indeed this lovely lake, these sublime moun-*
> *tains, and wild forests, seemed a fit cradle for a mind aspiring to high*
> *adventure and heroic deeds. Yet we saw no glimpse of his spirit in his*
> *present countrymen. The Swiss appeared to us then, and experience has*
> *confirmed our opinion, a people slow of comprehension and of action; but*
> *habit has made them unfit for slavery, and they would, I have little doubt,*
> *make a brave defence against any invader of their freedom.*[6]

The lovers spent three weeks on the run, with the vague intention of
founding a commune. Renting a house for six months, they moved in full

of excitement, but the next day did a flit. There were bedbugs and they had £28 in the kitty. With the lack of foresight that characterised all their movements, they left Lucerne on 28 August, taking the boat-diligence to Laufenberg on the Rhine. River travel was the cheapest way to get around Switzerland at the time. From Laufenberg they hitched a flat boat to Mumph, where they managed to board a cabriolet to Rheinfelden. The cab broke down and some Swiss soldiers gave them a lift:

> we were directed to proceed a league further to a village, where boats were commonly hired. Here, although not without some difficulty, we procured a boat for Basle, and proceeded down a swift river, while evening came on, and the air was bleak and comfortless. Our voyage was, however, short, and we arrived at the place of our destination by six in the evening.[7]

Shelley's biographer Richard Holmes remarks on the young people's whingeing about other passengers: 'their democratic spirit was often strained by the coarseness and proximity of their fellow-travellers, and a peculiarly English kind of fastidiousness emerged'.[8] Like schoolkids on an excursion, plugged into their Tacitus, they looked down their noses at the local oiks: 'Our companions in this voyage were of the meanest class, smoked prodigiously, and were exceedingly disgusting.' After punching one of the boat passengers, 'Mad Shelley', who had been bullied at Eton, managed to procure the seats he wanted.

Mary was soon pregnant. The child, born prematurely in February 1815, died in March. A second child, William Shelley, was five months old when the two teenagers and the married man attempted continental escape again in May 1816. Stepsister Claire had already slept with Lord Byron in April and was out to snag him in Geneva. Both poets that spring were waiting on financial and marital settlements: Byron, like Shelley, was shaking off the dust of a bad marriage and the bailiffs.

This time they entered Switzerland in blizzard conditions (that volcano) across the snow-covered Jura, travelling in a large carriage Shelley had ordered constructed in London three years previously. The cash flow for our young free-lovers had improved somewhat. They booked into Monsieur Dejean's Hotel d'Angleterre in Sécheron, at the time outside Geneva's city walls. Today the original building and its stables still face a park and the lake – it was a well-appointed hotel with all the amenities for English expats on the Grand Tour. Mary describes their first glimpse of Lake Geneva:

Hotel d'Angleterre at Sécheron, where Byron and the Shelleys stayed in 1816

blue as the heavens which it reflects, and sparkling with golden beams.
The opposite shore is sloping, and covered with vines, which however do
now so early in the season add to the beauty of the prospect. Gentlemen's
seats are scattered over these banks, behind which rise the various ridges
of black mountains, and towering far above, in the midst of its snowy
Alps, the majestic Mont Blanc, highest and queen of all. Such is the
view reflected by the lake; it is a bright summer scene without any of that
sacred solitude and deep seclusion that delighted us at Lucerne.[9]

Claire Clairmont shared the first six years of the Shelley couple's life
together. Richard Holmes describes her: 'With thick, black unruly ring-
lets of hair parted round an oval face, a compact and generously moulded
figure verging on chubbiness, and large dark bright eyes, she was volatile,
childish and outgoing.'[10] Claire spoke the best French of the three of them.
That spring Byron had got her pregnant and was trying to shake her off.
There was a touch of the groupie about her. Byron described her in a letter
as 'the 18 year-old plump girl ... who had scrambled 800 miles to unphilos-
ophise me'. In 1820, with the benefit of hindsight, he said: 'I think Madame
Claire is a damned bitch'.

His Lordship was a bit on the plump side himself. He spent the summer
of 1816 trying to lose weight on a diet of spritzers, toast, tea and vegetables,
with the help of his live-in doctor, Polidori. At twenty-eight, the oldest of
the group, Byron was beginning to feel his age.

Polidori – Byron called him 'Dr. Pollydolly' – had travelled in the poet's coach from London. Young, good-looking and voluble, he was Edinburgh trained. Like his employer, he had a decade of exposure to Aberdeen Calvinism behind him. In Geneva, Polidori's street fights drew the attention of the local gendarmes. Byron's drug of choice was magnesia, a purgative administered as part of his diet. Polidori's job was to procure it – personal trainer and dealer rolled into one. This led him to a scrape with a Geneva apothecary over quality. The brawl went before the magistrates. There was also laudanum going around. Byron cashiered Polidori at the end of the summer after one fight too many and the doctor returned to London, where he wrote and published under Byron's name *The Vampyre*, a story of blood-sucking and depravity that the poet disowned. That rainy summer in Geneva is responsible for the creation of not one but two monsters in the shock-horror tradition.

Polidori records for posterity the first meeting between Byron and Shelley on the shore of the lake that would forever be associated with their names. The hotel buzzed with English tourists of the better sort and the presence of Lord Byron only led to more gossip. He had made his ostentatious way down the Rhine valley in a grandiose copy of Napoleon's travelling coach.

> Dined. P[ercy] S[helley], the author of Queen Mab, came; bashful, shy, consumptive; twenty-six; separated from his wife; keeps the two daughters of Godwin, who practise his theories; one L[ord] B[yron]'s.[11]

'Consumptive' refers to Shelley's slight, pale appearance, while 'practise his theories' suggests he might be sleeping with both women. The last phrase refers to the hanky-panky between Byron and Claire and tells us that Polidori was observant. Byron's publisher, John Murray, was paying Pollydolly to keep a kiss-and-tell journal.

The Shelley party moved into Maison Chapuis on the lakeshore opposite the hotel. It was a smallish two-storey house uphill from the stormy water. A surviving nineteenth-century photo shows a foursquare structure that would easily fetch a couple of million Swiss francs today on location alone. From the upper windows there was a perfect view of the lake and the Jura mountains. Rising behind the house were the vineyards; across the slippery slope there was a good deal of to-ing and fro-ing that downpouring summer. The Villa Diodati commanded the rise, as befitted the lordly Byron. He ensconced himself there with Pollydolly, Byron's faithful valet

Nineteenth-century photograph of the Maison Chapuis (above right)
where Mary Shelley wrote *Frankenstein*

William Fletcher and a young footman, Robert Rushton. The two servants
had been in Byron's entourage since their teens and knew what was what
and on which side their bread was buttered.

Byron was the literary lion of the age. Infamous for his entanglements
with high-society women and chambermaids alike, he was happy to have
them cloak an underlying interest in adolescent boys. Indulging this pre-
dilection at Harrow and Cambridge, he fully explored it during his year in
Greece. An early poem puts his closeted dilemma succinctly:

> To one, who thus for kindred hearts must roam,
> And seek abroad the love denied at home.[12]

He was an early sex tourist. Writing to his Cambridge friend Hobhouse
about his Athenian year of living dangerously, Byron was graphic: 'none
female nor under ten nor Turk'.[13] For Byron they were willing to drop their
drawers for a drachma. Middle-aged women, dumpy women, temple boys,
pageboys, a boy on the beach at Brighton, his half-sister – all were grist to
his philandering mill.

Chalk drawing of Lord Byron by George Henry Harlow, 1815

Shelley, on the other hand, was unknown as a poet outside a small circle. Like Byron, he had a reputation as a skirt-chaser and a squire who didn't pay his bills. Byron admired the younger poet's work, although he found Shelley himself a bit too ethereal. Shelley was a couple of rungs down the social ladder from Lord Byron, and occasionally got tired looking up. They shared an interest in sailing.

For the men it was one of the most productive periods in poetry the world has known. For the women there was a good deal of running across the vineyards. At one point, Byron's servants found a slipper on the path below the house. Baby William was in nappies. It's a wonder *Frankenstein* came to light at all. From the hotel opposite, English guests trained lorgnettes and telescopes on the goings-on of the two poets and their women.

On 23 June the weather cleared and Byron and Shelley set off with Maurice, their Swiss boatman, to circumnavigate the lake. Shelley was an early riser while Byron, with aristocratic indolence, was a lie-abed. The younger poet was heading on a literary pilgrimage to the places mentioned in Rousseau's *Julie*, a bestseller subtitled *Letters between two lovers living in a small town at the foot of the Alps*. It was on the Catholic index of banned books. For Shelley it was a Romantic bible and he was so much a fan that he read passages to Byron on the boat.

On that first afternoon they rowed and sailed to Hermance and spent the night at Nernier on the Savoy coast. Shelley noted the thyroid deficiencies of the children playing ninepins on the shore. Due to an iodine deficiency in drinking water, these goitres were prevalent at the time in Alpine regions. Shelley remarked on the contrasting beauty of one boy in particular:

> Most of them were crooked, and with enlarged throats; but one little boy had such exquisite grace in his mien and motions, as I never before saw equalled in a child. His countenance was beautiful for the expression with which it overflowed. There was a mixture of pride and gentleness in his eyes and lips, the indications of sensibility, which his education will probably subvert to misery or seduce to crime; but there was more of gentleness than of pride, and it seemed that the pride was tamed from its original wildness by the habitual exercise of milder feelings. My companion gave him a piece of money, which he took without speaking, with a sweet smile of easy thankfulness, and then with an unembarrassed air turned to his play.[14]

Shelley was gestating his 'Hymn to Intellectual Beauty' and this boy's charm seems to have been one of the sparks. The poets spent the following night at Evian.

English poetry nearly lost two of its chief practitioners off the rocks between Meillerie and the village of St Gingoux, today called St Gingolph, on the border between Savoy and Switzerland at the eastern end of the lake. At Meillerie they dined on honey, in the manner of Rousseau's Julie and her lover. A storm came up and Byron, an excellent swimmer (veteran of the Tagus and the Hellespont), proposed to rescue Shelley, who could not swim. Shelley huffed on a locker in the bows. 'But I knew that my companion would have attempted to save me,' he wrote in a letter, 'and I was overcome with humiliation when I thought that his life might have been risked to preserve mine.'[15] Byron was more sanguine: 'I ran no risk, being so nearby the rocks and a good swimmer,' he wrote to his publisher. 'The wind was strong enough to blow down some trees as we found at landing.'

Two soaked poets and their crew came ashore at the fishing village of St Gingolph. They must have caused a flurry of excitement. Shelley was sufficiently shaken by his near drowning to draft his will that night in the inn, naming Byron one of his executors. Had he gone further and asked Byron to teach him to swim, he might have avoided his fate off the coast at Positano ten years later.

Today St Gingolph sits half in Switzerland and half in France, sep- arated by a mountain stream, the Morges, rushing through the tightly packed houses down to the lake. Official notices on the two footbridges warn about exporting currency, but you can happily cross from France into Switzerland and back again without being challenged. A tiny baroque chapel and a castle survive on the Swiss side, but much of the village on the Savoy side was destroyed by fire in the 1920s. The valley of the Morges was a crossing point for Jewish refugees attempting to flee Occupied France during the Second World War. Many were caught and sent back to their deaths. 'The infamous Sergeant Arrettaz of Saint-Gingolph always handed over refugees with sadistic pleasure', reported a local eyewitness. 'His col- league the customs officer, on the other hand, always walked off and made himself scarce so as not to have to see the terrible expressions on the faces of the people who were handed straight over to the militiamen at the fron- tier.'[16] At Evian, up the road on the French side of the lake, the World Refugee Conference in July 1938 tried to solve the crisis brought about by Nazi policy and Hitler's annexation of Austria. The Swiss government of the day withstood American pressure to hold the conference in Geneva and imposed an entry ban on Austrian Jews in September, following the *Anschluss* earlier that year.

Down by the lake a small group of summer campers were learning life- saving. Their unwieldy rowboat held an inflated dummy on a stretcher. Once on shore, they took turns at artificial respiration. On the plump side, the boys had difficulty keeping their shorts up. Pinching the dummy's nostrils, they counted breaths in French. I thought of Byron proposing to abandon ship and assist wan Shelley ashore. I thought of those fleeing Jews. Maybe Byron relished the prospect of rescuing white-knuckled Shelley. Any one of Europe's women would have leapt at the prospect of being rescued by Byron. A touch of his nether lip and a spot of mouth-to-mouth resuscitation would have set their fans aflutter.

Further along the promenade a picnicking Thai family had their trot- lines out, catching small grayling and grilling them on a charcoal burner. I remembered that King Bhumipol, the world's longest-reigning monarch and the only king born on American soil (Elvis excepted), had been edu- cated across the water at Lausanne University. This stretch of Lake Geneva is rich in associations and history.

1890 silver-gelatin print of the Château de Chillon

Byron and Shelley dried off at the inn and went on an evening ride to see the nearby mouth of the Rhône, flowing into the lake from the Valais. The next morning they visited Clarens, where Rousseau had set the trysts between his young lovers, and stopped at the eleventh-century Château de Chillon. Shelley was particularly affected by its gloom and monumental tyranny, but it was Byron who wrote the poem that forever links the castle to his name. It memorialises François Bonivard, imprisoned there in 1530 by the Duke of Savoy, and led to a nineteenth-century Byronic cult. The poet's early death defending little Greece contributed to the myth of the swashbuckling hero. Shelley walked in Rousseau's footsteps, but the tourists followed Byron around the lake.

Such was Byron's fame that twenty-five years later, in 1839, the first of the grand hotels named after him, the Hotel Byron, opened its doors at Villeneuve, a mile up the hill from the lake. It was at the time the largest hotel on the Swiss Riviera. Listed in the first edition of Baedeker, the hotel commanded a stunning view west, the Jura lazily rising from one shore and the more dramatic Savoy Alps from the other. Before the advent of the railway, 'Going over the Simplon' often involved a pit stop at Le Byron. Its guest list was an artistic *Who's Who*: Franz Liszt, Richard Wagner, Victor Hugo, Stefan Zweig and Rabindranath Tagore are among the scribbling luminaries who got a night's kip in its rooms.

Henry James in his 'Swiss Notes' gives it five stars on his Trip Advisor scale:

> *There is a charming Hôtel Byron at Villeneuve, the eastern end of the lake, of which I have retained a kindlier memory than of any of my Swiss resting-places. It has about it a kind of mellow gentility which is equally rare and delightful ... It has none of that look of heated prosperity which has come of late years to intermingle so sordid an element with the pure grandeur of Swiss scenery.*[17]

In 1929, the Hotel Byron, always financially precarious, fell on hard times. The ambiguously named Chillon College, a private boarding school catering to the sons of British colonialism, precursor to the many international schools around the lake today, occupied the building. The *Lausanne Gazette* described the students as 'a battalion of little Anglo-Saxons animating the corridors of the hotel'. *The Straits Times* went so far as to describe it as the 'Eton of Switzerland'. On the night of 23 January 1933, at fifteen minutes past midnight, the Hotel Byron burned down, fortunately with no casualties among the boarders. Today there is an old people's home on the site, still called Le Byron. Its chameleon career – from hotel to private school to retirement home – epitomises the Swiss ability to adapt to changing circumstances.

Our two Romantics, filled with fervour after Chillon, paused in Lausanne to view the house and garden (now Lausanne Post Office) where Gibbon penned his *Rise and Fall of the Roman Empire*. Byron wrote his 'best bad poem' – *The Prisoner of Chillon* – in Room 18 of Auberge de l'Ancre in Ouchy, Lausanne's port.

Now the Hotel d'Angleterre, it has a Byron Room in the pavilion and offers a Late Riser Package – his Lordship would have been in his element. The hotel wears its exclusivity lightly. I wander unchallenged up to the Salon Byron on the second floor, filled with large-format glossy magazines advertising the watch and fashion industries. Not a smell of literature about the place. Nothing even vaguely resembling a book, never mind a poem. It exudes that slick designer culture I was to encounter all through Switzerland. The hills are alive with the sound of business class. Bling with bells on. The Zen bling of mountain spas. Bling-aling. Down on the lakeshore, coveys of Chinese tourists, their spectacles catching the morning sun, follow guides to the nearby Olympic Museum. The Salon Byron is entirely empty in the middle of August, beautifully upholstered in the grand austere manner. I could have read the whole of *The Prisoner of Chillon* undisturbed.

Swiss painter Alexandre Calame's view of the Villa Diodati
where Byron stayed in 1816

My hair is grey, but not with years,
    Nor grew it white
    In a single night

In a letter to his publisher, Byron enclosed sprigs of acacia from Gibbon's
garden:

> *I have traversed all Rousseau's ground – with the Heloise before me – and*
> *am struck to a degree with the force and accuracy of his descriptions –*
> *and the beauty of their reality: – Meillerie – Clarens – and Vevey – and*
> *the Chateau de Chillon – are places of which I had no, I shall say little,*
> *because all I could say must fall short of the impressions they stamp. ... I*
> *have finished a third Canto of Childe Harold (consisting of one hundred*
> *and seventeen stanzas).*[18]

On their return to the Villa Diodati, Byron was careful to absent himself
from an excursion with the women to view the glaciers above Chamonix.
He was no doubt aware of Claire's pregnancy by this time and his response
in a letter is seigniorial: 'Is the brat mine?' The relative lowliness of the cottage by the lake in contrast to the grand villa up the hill is emblematic of

the relationship between the two households. Byron pacified the ladies by calling occasionally at Shelley's cottage. Shelley had been brought up the eldest in a house of girls, and had a soft spot for a female entourage. Byron disliked bluestockings and preferred all-male company.

Byron was lionised by Geneva's *bon ton* and at the literary salon of Madame de Stäel at Coppet. He warned opinionated Pollydolly to be on his best behaviour: 'Above all, speak as little as possible, and only when she addresses you. She has met everybody, and after Goethe, Schiller and Napoleon we are all inferior.' On 30 July, he attended a gala gathering of English at the villa of Charles Hentsch, his financial adviser in Switzerland, where historian Jacques Augustin Galiffe described him: 'His features are handsome, but his eyes now and then horrid. He has composed a poem of Chillon on our lake, the heroes of which are two brothers who suffer death for the faith of their fathers.'[19]

An excursion along the banks of the river Arve and up to the Montenvers glacier was a standard piece of sightseeing for the well-to-do English tourist, growing in popularity as the nineteenth century advanced. Robert Macfarlane, in his hymn to elevation, *Mountains of the Mind*, describes Victorian ladies edging towards crevasses in the ice, in the arms of their local guides. They were thrill-seekers. Even in the earliest illustrations of glaciers, dating from the mid-1700s, tiny sightseers in the foreground give a sense of the awe-inspiring Alps. Part of the attraction of glacier watching was a growing awareness that nature at home in Britain had been spoiled by the industrial revolution. The word glacier itself only entered the English language towards the end of the eighteenth century, from the French for ice.

> But then [1863] the glaciers were superb enigmas in an age which, beset by mechanization and materialism, was hungry for mysteries. Their history and their motion were imperfectly understood. No one really knew how they moved their bulks over the land, or even whether glacial ice was a liquid, a solid or some category-defying hybrid substance which both flowed (like a liquid) and fissured (like a solid). It had also since the 1840s become apparent that at some point in the spans of geological time glaciers had been far more extensive than they presently were.[20]

Nineteenth-century Bible readers were familiar with the verses in the Apocrypha, portending the ice next time: 'He poureth the hoar-frost upon the earth. It abideth upon every gathering together of water with a breastplate. It devoureth the mountain, and burneth the wilderness, and consumeth the grass as fire.' Such dire prognostications put ice in the soul.

Mary Shelley's excursion into the mountains forms the template for the encounter between creator and monster in *Frankenstein*. It inspired Percy Shelley to write his poem 'Mont Blanc' at the Hotel de Londres in Chamonix.

They climbed to see the so-called Sea of Ice. Mary describes the climb in *Frankenstein*:

> *In a thousand spots the traces of the winter avalanche may be perceived, where trees lie broken and strewed on the ground, some entirely destroyed, others bent, leaning upon the jutting rocks of the mountain or transversely upon other trees ... I suddenly beheld the figure of a man, at some distance, advancing towards me with superhuman speed. He bounded over the crevices in the ice, among which I had walked with caution; his stature, also, as he approached, seemed to exceed that of a man.*[21]

That summer of 1816 the rivers were in full spate with volcano-induced rains. As they abated, eighteen-year-old Mary advanced her first draft. Dr Victor Frankenstein echoes Rousseau's *Confessions*: 'I am by birth a Genevese, and my family is one of the most distinguished of that republic'. Mary gives him Percy Shelley's interest in galvanism, a theory that the dead could be reanimated – galvanised – by electricity:

> *When I was about fifteen years old we had retired to our house near Belrive, when we witnessed a most violent and terrible thunderstorm. It advanced from behind the mountains of Jura, and the thunder burst at once with frightful loudness from various quarters of the heavens. I remained, while the storm lasted, watching its progress with curiosity and delight. As I stood at the door, on a sudden I beheld a stream of fire issue from an old and beautiful oak which stood about twenty yards from our house.*[22]

The Plainpalais behind the old town of Geneva is the setting for the child murder of Victor Frankenstein's brother. Today the Plainpalais hosts a skate park and a weekend antiques market. Returning from Ingolstadt, where he has been studying, Dr Frankenstein follows Mary Shelley's footsteps, but also Rousseau's – who as a youth had missed the last bus and been locked out of town:

the gates of the town were already shut, and I was obliged to pass the
night at Sécheron, a village at the distance of half a league from the city.
The sky was serene, and I was unable to rest, I resolved to visit the spot
where my poor William had been murdered. As I could not pass through
the town, I was obliged to cross the lake in a boat to arrive at Plainpalais.
During this short voyage I saw lightnings playing on the summit of Mont
Blanc in the most beautiful figures.[23]

The Maison Chapuis where Mary wrote was separated from the water
by an overgrown garden of trees. Visiting two years later in 1818, Thomas
Medwin, Percy Shelley's cousin and old prep school chum, described the
spot as 'one of the most sequestered on the lake, and almost hidden by
a grove of umbrageous forest trees, as is a bird's nest by leaves'. A photograph of the house where Mary Shelley wrote *Frankenstein* shows the
trees still there, the lakeshore embanked and the house oddly suburban
and tamed.

Doctor and monster criss-cross the lake in a game of hunter and hunted,
under the electrically charged weather of that summer. The Jura range
on the northern bank is pitted against Mont Blanc on the southern. At
one point Mary Shelley's scientist quits Ireland, hailing 'the darkness that
shut Ireland from my sight, and my pulse beat with a feverish joy when I
reflected that I should soon see Geneva'. She knew that Percy had undertaken a scamper to Ireland with his estranged wife some years earlier. It
is entirely possible that Mary Shelley, a communard herself, knew of the
failed settlement of New Geneva in County Waterford in 1782. This early
utopian project envisioned a thousand Genevois watchmakers relocating
to Ireland, escaping the heavy-handed repression of Geneva's city fathers.

Lake Geneva forms a backdrop to the vengeful murder of Dr
Frankenstein's bride on their wedding night. Bride and groom depart from
Belrive. The imagery of opposing tectonic plates feminises Mont Blanc
and sees the older Jura as a champion of freedom.

it was agreed that Elizabeth and I should commence our journey by
water, sleeping that night at Evian, and continuing our voyage on the fol-
lowing day. The day was fair, the wind favourable ... where we saw Mont
Salève, the pleasant banks of Montalègre, and at a distance, surmount-
ing all, the beautiful Mont Blanc and the assembly of snowy mountains
that in vain endeavour to emulate her; sometimes coasting the opposite
banks, we saw the mighty Jura opposing its dark side to the ambition that

*would quit its native country, and an almost insurmountable barrier to
the invader who should wish to enslave it.*[24]

Mary Shelley knew her readers were armchair travellers and she accordingly makes her landscape both sublime and threatening. Perhaps she was thinking of her own return to the weather and petty scandals of England:

*The sun sank lower in the heavens; we passed the river Drance, and
observed its path through the chasms of the higher and the glens of the
lower hills. The Alps here came closer to the lake, and we approached the
amphitheatre of mountains which forms its eastern boundary. The spire of
Evian shone under the woods that surround it and the range of mountain
above mountain by which it was overhung.*

   *...as I touched the shore I felt those cares and fears revive which soon
were to clasp me and cling to me forever.*[25]

The strangling of Victor Frankenstein's bride takes place on a stormy night at Evian. The author borrows gothic trappings from Monk Gibbon. Frankenstein expects the monster, and the denouement is swift: 'The murderous mark of the fiend's grasp was on her neck, and the breath had ceased to issue from her lips.' The monster disappears into the lake, pursued by Dr Frankenstein across the Black Sea, 'the wilds of Tartary and Russia' and the polar ice.

   Mary Shelley's masterpiece is a product of that stormy summer of love and forked lightning. The inhospitable town, the glaciers, the sea of ice are properties of a Hammer movie set that she observed all around her. Who would have thought that Geneva, righteous and dull, could give birth to such a monster?

   A second monster creation of that summer was John Polidori's *Vampyre*, a tale of blood sucking and the living dead that the doctor passed off as the work of Byron. Polidori had seen a fragment of a novel that Byron was writing on 17 June 1816. It concerns the narrator and a dying nobleman called Darvell:

*I was yet young in life, which I had begun early; but my intimacy with
him was of a recent date: we had been educated at the same schools and
university; but his progress through these had preceded mine, and he had
been deeply initiated into what is called the world, while I was yet in my
novitiate.*[26]

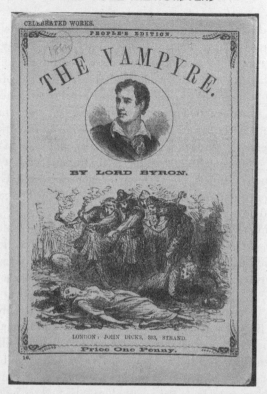

CELEBRATED WORKS.

PEOPLE'S EDITION.

THE VAMPYRE.

BY LORD BYRON.

LONDON: JOHN DICKS, 313, STRAND.

Price One Penny.

16.

1884 penny dreadful edition of Polidori's *The Vampyre*, misattributed to
Byron, first published in 1819

Polidori expanded the situation and had *The Vampyre* published under
Byron's name in 1819, in *New Monthly Magazine*. He named his vampire
Lord Rutheven and attributed to him his former master's lordly hauteur
and scandalous behaviour. Polidori's tale was successful and much copied.
When it was adapted for the stage, Paris theatres picked it up and made it a
hit. Nikolai Gogol and Alexandre Dumas wrote their own vampire tales. The
pulp fiction aspect was there from the start. By the time the Irish manager
Bram Stoker pitched up at London's Lyceum Theatre, Polidori's vampire
had recrossed the channel. Stoker tried out such names as Wampyr, Ordog
and Pokol for his nobleman protagonist, none of them fetching. Finally he
hit on Vlad 'the Impaler' Dracula. *Dracula* (1887) had risen from the dead.
    Once the Shelley party was safely on its way to England and Polidori
given his marching orders for his indiscretions, Byron accompanied his old

Cambridge chums, Hobhouse and Scrope Davies, on a trip to Chamonix. Davies forms a lucrative pendant to the events of that stormy summer of 1816. An inveterate gambler, he spent some £17,000 in the following year and in 1820 fled to Paris to escape his creditors. Before leaving he deposited a suitcase of papers in a Pall Mall bank vault. He died a wastrel in Paris in 1852. The suitcase remained undiscovered until 1976. Among its papers was a manuscript copy of Byron's *Childe Harold* Canto III (the triple concept album), letters from Byron (a superb letter writer), as well as manuscripts of Shelley's 'Hymn to Intellectual Beauty', 'Mont Blanc' and two previously unknown Shelley sonnets. The poems had been entrusted to Davies on the diligence from Geneva to London. The find was valued at half a million pounds. Had he lived he would have been solvent.

Three children were on board the boat to Portsmouth that September: eight-month-old William, Claire's unborn child by Byron and the manuscript of Byron's *Childe Harold*. William Shelley died at the age of four in Rome, and is buried there in the Protestant Cemetery, under the cypress shade by the Pyramid of Cestius. Allegra, Byron's illegitimate daughter by Claire, was born in Bath, a safe distance from the chattering classes of the capital. Byron removed the four-year-old Allegra from her mother to a convent near Ravenna, where the child died of typhus the following year.

In September 1816, Fanny Godwin, Mary's stepsister and the original love child of Mary Wollstonecraft and her American paramour, committed suicide in Swansea by overdosing on opium. She had recently discovered her illegitimacy. Nobody claimed the body, the suicide was hushed up, and she was buried anonymously in a pauper's grave. Shelley's first wife Harriet was found drowned in the Serpentine on 10 December 1816. She was 'far advanced in pregnancy'. Her death allowed Shelley to marry Mary Godwin and to make an honest woman of her too. Polidori, the progenitor of a thousand vampire stories, movies, television series, Halloween masks and T-shirts, committed suicide in 1821 by swallowing prussic acid.

In October the Byron circus crossed the Alps into Italy. Byron himself had dropped a few pounds and wrote about the wonder of that Swiss summer:

> It is the hush of night, and all between
> Thy margin and the mountains, dusk, yet clear,
> Mellowed and mingling, yet distinctly seen.
> Save darkened Jura, whose capped heights appear
> Precipitously steep; and drawing near,

There breathes a living fragrance from the shore,
  Of flowers yet fresh with childhood; on the ear
Drops the light drip of the suspended oar,
Or chirps the grasshopper one good-night carol more.[27]

It was illness rather than poetry that brought the next band of Englishmen to Switzerland, as tuberculosis moved through the smog of nineteenth-century industrial cities. Those who could afford it could breathe the rarefied air of the Swiss Alps. The tiny mountain village of Davos was about to undergo an invasion that would transform it forever into a synonym for wealth, health and the good life.

3

THE BLUE HENRYS

Symonds, Stevenson, Conan Doyle and Mann
on the magic mountain

The Waldsanatorium in Davos, inspiration for Thomas Mann's
The Magic Mountain

death by gradual dry-rot, each in his indifferent inn...
Robert Louis Stevenson

Davos owes its origin as a spa town to the district physician Dr Spengler. He noticed that returning emigrants with pulmonary complaints quickly recovered in the mountain air. In the *Deutsche Klinik* for 1862 he published his findings. Soon patients came from all over Europe, as tuberculosis racked and coughed its way through nineteenth-century lungs. Treatments included cold morning showers, fresh milk, long spells of lying on deckchairs, breathing clean mountain air and spitting into their Blue Henrys, or Blauer Heinrich, a cobalt blue glass sputum bottle.[1]

English writer and traveller John Addington Symonds arrived in 1867 and spent his winters in Davos until his death in Rome in 1893. Symonds was an art historian and man of letters with a classical bent. He built a splendid chalet, Am Hof, on a meadow of the same name in Davos Platz, which became the locus for visiting English intellectuals and artists. Writers Robert Louis Stevenson and Arthur Conan Doyle followed him to this quiet valley in search of fresh air and a measure of health. Thomas Mann, visiting his wife Katia at the Waldsanatorium in the spring of 1912, was inspired to set his quintessential novel of spa life here, *The Magic Mountain* (1924).[2]

Symonds' early life followed a predictable enough curve: home tutoring, Harrow, Oxford, continental wanderlust in search of art and health. Calculatedly married, he produced four daughters and many now unread books on art and literature. Behind the façade of family man, however, he conducted mostly platonic relationships with Davos village lads and with gondoliers on his forays to Venice – Sodom-on-Sea for Victorian homosexuals, as it had been for an earlier generation of Regency bucks.[3]

Symonds was never short of a Greek epigram. If you were male, young and attractive around him you had to watch your bum. The Hellenic flummery that cloaks his writing reminds me of Alan Bennett's line in *The Habit of Art* about Benjamin Britten and W.H. Auden's final meeting: 'and all that counterfeit classical luggage – we know it's boys'.[4]

Symonds knew it was boys early on. His earliest childhood fantasies featured sailors: 'I used to fancy myself crouched upon the floor amid the company of naked adult men; sailors, such as I had seen about the streets of Bristol.'[5] A classical education spruced up this rough trade a bit:

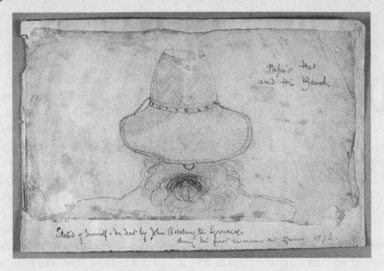

Papa's Hat
and his Beard

Sketch of himself & his Dad by John Addenton Symonds
during his first summer at Harrow 1876.

J.A. Symonds' self-portrait in a hat, Davos, 1876

*What I really wanted at this period was some honest youth or comrade,
a sailor or a groom or a labourer, who would have introduced me into
the masculine existence for which I craved in a dim, shrinking way. My
equals repelled me.*[6]

He kept up an enormous, knowing correspondence with the great
bearded men of his time, always ready with a Latin or Greek tag where
plain English would suffice. Slipped between the sheets of Davos
notepaper were his dirty snaps from Rome and Sicily.[7] This dualism
began early. While his dorm mates seemed to 'spoon' all before them,
he remained aloof from the bed-hopping of Harrow life. He describes
one classmate as 'a good-natured longimanous ape, gibbering on his
perch and playing ostentatiously with a prodigiously developed phal-
lus'. Another 'suddenly dared to throw his arms round me, kissed me,
and thrust his hand into my trousers. At that moment I nearly gave way
to sensuality.'[8]

Sex in the head always seemed to win out over the hand in the trousers. Many years later, writing from Davos, this fundamental dilemma
remained unresolved: 'Eros Pandemos is everywhere. Plato lends the light,
the gleam, that never was on sea or shore.'[9] It would take a later English
sexual rebel, D.H. Lawrence, to give the boot to Plato and put a bit of flesh
on Eros Pandemos.

J.A. Symonds tobogganing in Davos

Part of Switzerland's attraction for Symonds was its democratic ethos, so different from class-bound England: 'Had Willie [a Bristol chorister] been a boy of my own rank, our friendship need not have been broken; or had English institutions favoured equality like those I admire in Switzerland, he might have been admitted to my father's home.'[10] His coming to terms with homosexuality involved consigning the class baggage of England to the hold. Symonds' relationships with the lower orders strike us now as a kind of sex tourism: 'When I came to live among peasants and republicans in Switzerland, I am certain that I took up passionate relations with men in a more natural and intelligible manner.'[11]

Poor health brought him to Switzerland for the first time in the summer of 1863. The 23-year-old fellow of Magdalen College, Oxford stayed at the Silberhorn in Mürren. Here the young virgin spied his future wife, Catherine North, at a time when he was attempting to wean himself off a taste for choristers and onto a 'coaxed-up emotion' for women. 'Alpine inns are favourable places for hatching acquaintance and gaining insight into character,' Symonds notes.[12] It is clear from his *Memoirs* that he had no genuine interest in women and that Catherine's own tetchiness of temper stems from their passionless marriage. Mother and daughters in time grew tolerant of father's 'special friendships' in a way that seems remarkably enlightened.

A year later he followed Catherine to Switzerland, calculatedly a-wooing:

> Paris, Basel, Zürich, Chur: I do not well remember how I did the journey.
> I only remember crossing the Lenzer Heide and the Julier in the ban-
> quette of the diligence, and feeling the aridity of Graubünden in painful
> contrast to what I had so fresh in memory of Mürren ... There is a bridge
> above the stream at Pontresina; and this became our meeting place; and
> here, one afternoon, I think, when snow was falling in thin flakes, I asked
> her to be my wife.[13]

The bridge and the stream at Pontresina are still there, and the five-star
Grand Hotel Kronenhof is still in the business of welcoming the betrothed.
Symonds had few illusions about what he was doing: 'I could not so conquer
the original bent of my instincts as to feel for her in the brutal unmistakable
appetite of physical desire.' Faute de mieux is how sexologist Havelock Ellis
describes this state of affairs.[14]

A serious haemorrhage of the lungs brought Symonds and his family to
Davos on 7 August 1877. His initial impression was unfavourable:

> As the valley opened before me from the height of Wolfgang, veiled in
> melancholy cloud, towards the close of a weary day, I thought that I had
> rarely seen a less attractive place to live in. Everything looked so bleak
> and bare; and though I loved the Alps, I discerned little of their charm
> in Davos. What should I have thought, had I then been told that twelve
> years afterwards, on the anniversary of that day, I should be penning
> these lines in a house built for my habitation here?[15]

Soon Symonds was eyeing up the Tyrolese peasantry as it took a quick pee
in a meadow.

> He had probably taken too much wine, and there was licence in his gait.
> Desire for the Bursch [youth] shot through me with a sudden stab. I fol-
> lowed him with my eyes until he passed behind a haystall; and I thought
> – if only I could follow him, and catch him there, and pass the afternoon
> with him upon the sweet new hay! Then I turned to my Campanella's
> sonnets, and told myself that these things were forever over.[16]

Symonds initially stayed at the Belvedere Hotel, where he soon befriended
nineteen-year-old Christian Buol, youngest in a family of sixteen. Along
with Christian Palmy, 'my friends and fellow-travellers', they are the ded-
icatees of Symonds' collection of articles Italian Byways (1883), which

includes three essays about Davos and Graubünden. The apparently chaste friendship with Christian Buol lasted for the dozen years Symonds lived at Davos. They became travelling companions to the cities of the plain – Milan, Venice, Genoa.

> We often slept in the same bed; and he was not shy of allowing me to view, as men may view the idols of their gods, the naked splendour of his perfect body. But neither in act nor deed, far less in words, did the least shadow of lust cloud the serenity of that masculine communion.[17]

Italian Byways includes a fair bit of high-flown art appreciation and circumspect comment on gondoliers. A fine essay on wine, 'Bacchus in Graubunden', and a piece on 'Winter Nights at Davos' bear up well as journalism goes. The rest has the tedium of 'chronicling small beer', as Symonds himself suspects from time to time.

Symonds gave generously to local causes and helped many young men starting out in business. The Buol boys and Symonds were instrumental in the establishment of an English church in Davos, which opened its doors in January 1882. He funded most of the cost of the Davos Gymnasium, founded the Davos Gymnastic Club, and hosted wine parties for its members; we can see where all this is going. In *Our Life in the Swiss Highlands* (1892) he's off again, waxing lyrical about Swiss gymnasts:

> Bruisers like Milo of Croton, brawny, thick-set men, of bone and muscle, able to fell oxen with a fist-blow on the forehead. Most people think the Swiss an ugly, ill-developed race. They have not travelled with 600 of these men on a summer day, as lightly, tightly clad as decency and comfort allow. It is true that one rarely sees a perfectly handsome face, and that the Swiss complexion is apt to be muddy. But the men are never deficient in character; and when denuded of the ill-made clothes they usually wear, they offer singular varieties of strength, agility, and grace.[18]

At the same time as Symonds was ogling Swiss musclemen, Tchaikovsky was visiting his former student and lover, Iosef Kotek, in Davos in November 1884. Soso Kotik ('Joe the Tomcat') was Tchaikovsky's nickname for him. They had met when Tchaikovsky was teaching composition at the Moscow Conservatory. The composer described his pupil in these terms:

The Swiss bobsleigh team takes off, Davos, ca. 1910

*When he caresses me with his hand, when he lies with his head inclined
on my breast, and I run my hand through his hair and secretly kiss it ...
passion rages within me with such unimaginable strength ... Yet I am far
from the desire for a physical bond. I feel that if this happened, I would
cool towards him. It would be unpleasant for me if this marvellous youth
debased himself to copulation with an ageing and fat-bellied man.*[19]

Seven years later, in November 1884, the composer described his arrival at
Davos to visit his erstwhile lover, who died there in January 1885 aged only
twenty-nine:

*Driving up to Davos I imagined it to be a wilderness and feared that I
would not be able to get either cigarettes or cigars. But I found that at this
great height there is a row of first class hotels, and shops where you can
get whatever you like. They have their own newspaper, theatre. ... At last
Kotek appeared. I was afraid that I would see only a shadow of his former
self and imagine my joy when I saw him looking much fatter, with a clear
complexion, and seeming perfectly well. But this is only on the surface.
When he started talking I understood how bad his lungs are. Instead of a
voice he has a hoarse croak and an incessant heavy cough.*[20]

Though Tchaikovsky and Symonds never met, it would be interesting to
commission Alan Bennett to script their meeting in one of those fevered

Robert Louis Stevenson thought Davos was 'death by gradual dry-rot'

hotel drawing rooms or on a deep white balcony. Both men married in attempts to cover their homosexual tracks or to bring about a cure. Both carried on liaisons behind the scenes, and expressed their true selves through music and writing.

Robert Louis Stevenson was a writer of an altogether different calibre and stamp to Symonds. Consumptive Stevenson spent two successive winters on the mountain, 1881 and 1882, from November until April, with his wife Fanny and stepson Samuel Lloyd Osbourne, age twelve. He completed *Treasure Island* at Davos, in a winter of feverish work.

Like Symonds, the sun-loving Stevenson was at first disillusioned by the atmosphere of 'death by gradual dry-rot, each in his indifferent inn'.[21] The two writers got on and shared a passion for tobogganing, although we get the impression from letters and stray comments that Stevenson had scant regard for the older man's books: 'He is a far better and more interesting thing than any of his books.' Other letters betray a more ambiguous, qualified response to Symonds' sagacity.[22]

Lloyd Osbourne brought with him a small portable printing press, now on display at the Writers' Museum in Edinburgh. The press, a gift from Stevenson, had travelled from San Francisco to Silverado, to Edinburgh and Davos. It was used in Davos to print the programme for the weekly concerts at the Hotel Belvedere. Stevenson was much more adventurous and less hidebound than Symonds. He regarded his surroundings in Davos with a sharp eye:

> *For about the health resort the walks are besieged by single people*
> *walking rapidly with plaids about their shoulders, by sudden troops of*
> *German boys trying to learn to jödel, and by German couples silently*
> *and, as you venture to fancy, not quite happily, pursuing love's young*
> *dream. You may perhaps be an invalid who likes to make bad verses as*
> *he walks about.*[23]

His second winter in the mountains was particularly productive. In the
spring he collected together the stories that would make up *New Arabian
Nights* (1882). In addition, he wrote four short pieces for the *Pall Mall
Gazette* on the benefits of mountain air. Together with his lively letters,
these give a quick view of invalid experience and the mountain environment. He was particularly taken by tobogganing:

> *You push off: the toboggan fetches away; she begins to feel the hill, to*
> *glide, to swim, to gallop. In a breath you are out from under the pine tree,*
> *and a whole heavenful of stars reels and flashes overhead ... in an atmos-*
> *phere tingling with forty degrees of frost ... and adds a new excitement to*
> *the life of man upon his planet.*[24]

Stevenson's eye for local detail, his rapid sketch of a scene, remind us that
he was an early exponent of travel journalism in *Travels with a Donkey
in the Cevennes* (1879). In 'Health and Mountains' he brings the feverish
world of the spa town alive.

> *a few noble peaks seen even from the valley; a village of hotels; a world*
> *of black and white – black pine-woods, clinging to the sides of the valley,*
> *and white snow flouring it, and papering it between the pine-woods, and*
> *covering all the mountains with a dazzling curd; add a few score invalids*
> *marching to and fro upon the snowy road, or skating on the ice-rinks, pos-*
> *sibly to music, or sitting under sunshades by the door of the hotel – and*
> *you have the larger features of a mountain sanatorium.*[25]

Productivity apart, Stevenson's two winters in Davos were marked by crisis
and death. Fanny fell ill with kidney stones in December 1881 and was treated
in Bern. They returned to Davos on Christmas Day by open-air sleigh:

> *seven hours on end through whole forests of Christmas trees. The cold was*
> *beyond belief. I have often suffered less at a dentist's. It was a clear, sunny*

day, but the sun even at noon falls, at this season, only here and there into the Pratigau.[26]

Fanny wrote of the proximity of death in Davos, shadowing the beauty of the valley:

> *Louis is much cut up because a young man whom he liked and had been tobogganing with has been found dead in his bed. Bertie still hovers between life and death. Poor little Mrs. Doney is gone; my heart is sad for those two lovely little girls. In a place like this there are many depressing things, but it is encouraging to know that many are going away cured.*

By the time the crocuses had pushed through the snow of their second spring, the Stevensons had had enough. Inveterate travellers and sun worshippers, they settled for good in Samoa.

Another well-travelled Edinburgh writer, the thirty-four-year-old Arthur Conan Doyle, came to Switzerland in August 1893 to give a series of talks in Lucerne. Perhaps it was his final school year spent with the Jesuits at Feldkirch in Austria that gave him a taste for the Alps.

Conan Doyle was a sporty doctor. He had seen skiing in Norway and imported one of the first pair of Norwegian skis to Davos. Along with the Branger brothers (who possessed the other two pairs), he scaled the saddle of the Jacobshorn in the Albula range, now served by cable car and renowned for snowboarding. They then tackled the 2,253-metre pass between Davos and Arosa, rising at 4 am, heading to Frauenkirch, crossing the Maienfelder Furka pass and sliding down to Arosa. Since 2008 this area has been added to the list of UNESCO World Heritage sites, traversed by the wonderful Rhaetian railway and by 'lads leaping about on planks tied to their feet'.[27] Doyle wrote up his travels for *The Strand*, the magazine that had been serialising his Holmes stories:

> *But now we had a pleasure which boots can never give. For a third of a mile we shot along over gently dipping curves, skimming down into the valley without a motion of our feet. In that great untrodden waste, with snow-fields bounding our vision on every side and no marks of life save the tracks of chamois and of foxes, it was glorious to whizz along in this easy fashion.*[28]

He predicted that 'the time will come when hundreds of Englishmen will come to Switzerland for a skiing season'. Time has proved him right.

Besides skiing, Conan Doyle left his mark on Switzerland by setting one crucial Sherlock Holmes story here. Holmes is the first of many detectives and spies to stick their noses into Swiss literary history. Somerset Maugham, Friedrich Glauser, Ian Fleming, Friedrich Dürrenmatt and John le Carré have all peopled the genre in the course of the twentieth century. 'I think of slaying Holmes ... and winding him up for good and all. He takes my mind from better things,' Conan Doyle wrote to his mother in November 1891.[29] He attempted to kill off Holmes in the story 'The Final Problem', published in the December 1893 issue of *The Strand*, while the author was safely wintering at Davos.

Switzerland hosts two Conan Doyle museums. Holmes, like Ian Fleming's Bond, has become a literary brand, diversifying into television, film and costume. The Hotel Parc du Sauvage in Meiringen is where it is thought the writer stayed with his wife. Here he conceived the idea of killing off Holmes in a struggle with Moriarty, 'the Napoleon of crime', at the nearby Reichenbach Falls. He renamed the hotel 'The Englischer Hof'. Holmes is the only fictional character to have been made an honorary citizen of Meiringen, with full voting rights. Renamed Conan Doyle Place in 1988, the village square proudly sports a statue of Sherlock Holmes. The little faux-gothic English Church hosts a tiny museum featuring one of two Swiss replicas of 221b Baker Street. A plaque up on the Falls commemorates the detective's apparent demise.

Meiringen in winter is a lonely place to die. Dirty snow littered Place Sherlock Holmes when I visited in late January. The bakeries were selling *Haslikuchen*, made from hazelnuts, with a prancing caster-sugar cock on the crust. The main street was almost deserted and the Hotel Parc du Sauvage wasn't serving lunch. In the Portakabin adjoining the ice rink, staff kept warm and sheepskins were spread on the benches of the café. I mooched around town, noticing everything. A hotel up the hill was called The Sherlock Holmes. A man in the bakery was speaking loud Russian into his phone.

In the story Holmes escapes from Victoria station disguised as an Italian priest. Watson is along for the ride in the first-class carriage. Baker Street is in flames and Moriarty is in hot pursuit. They make their way 'into Switzerland, via Luxembourg and Basle', across the Gemmi Pass and along the Daubensee. It's a curious, roundabout route:

Sidney Paget's 1893 illustration of Sherlock Holmes' demise at the Reichenbach Falls

It was on the 3rd of May that we reached the little village of Meiringen, where we put up at the Englischer Hof, then kept by Peter Steiler the elder. Our landlord was an intelligent man, and spoke excellent English, having served for three years as waiter at the Grosvenor Hotel in London. At his advice, on the afternoon of the 4th we set off together, with the intention of crossing the hills and spending the night at the hamlet of Rosenlaui. We had strict injunctions, however, on no account to pass the falls of Reichenbach, which are about half-way up the hill, without making a small detour to see them.[30]

Conan Doyle dovetails his real circumstances with those of Watson and Holmes:

an English lady had arrived who was in the last stage of consumption. She had wintered at Davos Platz, and was journeying now to join her friends at Lucerne, when a sudden hemorrhage had overtaken her. It was thought that she could hardly live a few hours, but it would be a great consolation to her to see an English doctor, and, if I would only return, etc. The good Steiler assured me in a postscript that he would himself look upon my compliance as a very great favor, since the lady absolutely refused to see a Swiss physician, and he could not but feel that he was incurring a great responsibility.[31]

Doctor Watson falls for the ruse and returns to the Englischer Hof. Moriarity
tackles Holmes at the Falls. Watson realises his mistake and returns to find

> Holmes's Alpine-stock still leaning against the rock by which I had left
> him. But there was no sign of him, and it was in vain that I shouted. My
> only answer was my own voice reverberating in a rolling echo from the
> cliffs around me.[32]

Clear and melodramatic, Holmes' end allows the possibility he might rise
again from the 'dreadful caldron of swirling water and seething foam'.
Thousands of readers cancelled their subscriptions to The Strand magazine
in December 1893 in protest. Conan Doyle was obliged to resurrect his
detective in a later story, 'The Adventure of the Empty House'.

A second Conan Doyle museum is in Lucens, between Lausanne and
Lake Neuchâtel. The writer's son, Adrian Conan Doyle, established it with
lordly aplomb in the resplendent château overperching the town. He built
a replica of the sitting room in 221b Baker Street for the 1951 Festival of
Britain. The room is authentic down to the last sourced detail. Since 2001,
when the château was sold, the museum has moved to the Maison Rouge
in the village.

It was the German novelist Thomas Mann who made the most sus-
tained use of Davos in his long novel The Magic Mountain. In 1911 he had
been writing Death in Venice in Bad Tölz in Bavaria, where the Manns had
a summer home. In 1912 he journeyed to Davos for three weeks to visit his
wife, flush with the knowledge that he had just written a small masterpiece
and feverish with his own demons.

Mann, like Symonds, was another of those old-style married homosexuals, with their Hellenic baggage, a clatter of children and a patient
wife. Katia Mann bore her husband six children: proof perhaps of the
ascendancy of hydraulics over chemistry. Three of their children were
homosexual – two sons and a daughter. Katia was fully aware of her husband's infatuations behind the carapace of the family man. In 1912 she
was recovering from two recent miscarriages and the birth of their fourth
child, Monika. She had contracted tuberculosis and booked into the
Waldsanatorium above Davos.

Thomas Mann's visit from mid-May to mid-June gave him the germ
of the thousand pages of The Magic Mountain, a story he would drop and
pick up again over the following war-torn decade. It is a swansong to the
Belle Époque and to the class that propped it up. A curious fact about

Katia Mann's six-month stay emerges from her X-rays, which have been preserved. They do not present any evidence of tuberculosis, according to present-day experts.[33] Perhaps it really was all in the head. Perhaps *Death in Venice*, 'the paradigmatic master-text of homosexual eroticism',[34] had brought their marriage into sharp focus and she needed a rest cure.

The Magic Mountain's twenty-four-year-old protagonist, Hans Castorp, travels by train to Davos to visit Joachim, a sick cousin, at the International Sanatorium Berghof (today the Hotel Schatzalp). Musing in the mountains, he describes what appears to be the Solis Viaduct, built in 1902, as it curves across the Albula River on the Rhaetian Railway.

> He looked out – the train was winding through a narrow pass; you could see the forward cars and the laboring engine, emitting great straggling tatters of brown, green and black smoke. Water roared in the deep ravine on his right; dark pines on his left struggled up between boulders towards a stony gray sky. There were pitch-black tunnels, and when daylight returned, vast chasms were revealed, with a few villages far below.[35]

What traps the thoroughly bourgeois Castorp is the cloying atmosphere of illness. His initial visit of three weeks extends to seven years. Balconies and terraces give the sanatorium the appearance of a sponge, but also the baroque spectacle of a theatre. Time becomes a sponge too, and not just for Castorp. The reader of this novel gets drawn into its cavities. Mann elaborates illness as a metaphor for artistic sensibility, for the sexual drive and for the malaise of Europe on the eve of the First World War. He always liked to think big. In *Death in Venice* there is a similar linkage of illness (cholera-ravaged Venice) and artistic creativity. Mann's first novel *Buddenbrooks* was the *Downton Abbey* of the early twentieth century. The boy aesthete Hanno dies of typhus at the end. Hanno, Aschenbach and Castorp attempt to kick over the traces of bourgeois existence and become prey to decadence and desire. Their ramrod-straight author never did.

Mann was conversant with the health crazes, fitness regimes and rest cures of his day, many of which anticipate the expensive therapeutic culture of present-day Switzerland. *The Magic Mountain* could be read as a bible of the spa class, where healing, money, splurge and purge meet. Spa people are not great readers, however. The rich like to render their illnesses as exclusive, and Davos found ways of catering to them over the years – first the tubercular Russians, then the Germans, now the Russians again.

No sooner well-met at Davos than cousin Joachim shows Hans Castorp his Blue Henry:

> now he pulled something halfway out of the nearer side pocket of his ulster, showed it to his cousin, and put it away again at once – a curved, flattened bottle of bluish glass with a metal cap. 'Most of us up here have one,' he said. 'We even have a name for it, a kind of nickname, a joke really.'[36]

Castorp breathes his first lungful of Davos air: 'it lacked odor, content, moisture, it went easily into the lungs and said nothing to the soul'. Installed in a room where an American has died two days before, he marvels at the humour of corpses ferried down by bobsleigh from a sanatorium higher up the mountain.

Among the last corpses bobsleighed to the cemetery was that of Grand Duke Dmitri Pavlovich, one of three assassins of Rasputin. Carried out of Room 309, exited by the back door of the sanatorium, he was ferried by sled down to his final resting place in the forest cemetery in March 1942. The assassin was first cousin to Prince Philip. The Grand Duke's son, Prince Romanovsky-Ilyinsky, became mayor of Palm Beach, Florida. Russian royalists have made overtures and offered him the position of Tsar, but he's staying put in the Sunshine State.[37]

A florid and voluble Italian called Settembrini joins the cousins on their walks through the Davos woods. He is one of Mann's caricatured exotics, a Faustian littérateur, a turn-of-the-century gadfly. Castorp says of his pedagogic conversation: 'listening to him always reminds me of fresh hot buns'.[38] The schedule of the International Sanatorium Berghof reminds me of a New Age retreat centre crossed with a Catholic seminary, where a young priest with sideburns might ask you if you like Simon and Garfunkel. At any moment a conversation about cigars might veer off into the higher truths of why we're here. To be ill is to be of the elect, pontificating above the treeline. When Mann wants to suggest wayward sexuality or bohemian culture, as he does with Settembrini, he gives his characters yellow trousers. He adds, 'his greeting was precise and melodious. And now he stopped, striking a graceful pose in front of them by propping himself on his cane and crossing his ankles.'[39] Camp, the reader thinks, as Christmas.

Mann gives us a snapshot of Davos transformed by the coming of the spas, typical of the change in Swiss mountain villages of the time:

*One could not really call Dorf a village; at least, nothing except the name
itself was left now. It had been devoured by the resort spreading relent-
lessly towards the entrance to the valley, and that part of the settlement
called Davos-Dorf merged imperceptibly, without transition, into what
was called Davos-Platz. Hotels and boarding houses, all of them amply
equipped with covered verandas, balconies, and rest-cure arcades, lay on
both sides, as well as private homes with rooms for rent. Here and there
new buildings were under construction, but sometimes the line of houses
was broken by an open space that allowed a view of the valley's green
meadows.*[40]

Mann's pinched face with close-set eyes and bristly moustache stares out at
us from his photos, not unhandsome but not forthcoming either. He's very
much the author. He has a Prince Charles way of handling a pocket, always
anxious to look the picture of probity.

In the early twenty-first century Davos is a byword for skiing and economics rather than tuberculosis. Castorp's observations of sanatorium life
have an eerie poignancy, reminding us of the reality of medicine before
penicillin:

*Those balloon-shaped containers with short necks, for example, which
were set out beside the doors in the corridor and which had caught his eye
on the evening of his arrival – Joachim explained about them when he
asked. They held pure oxygen, for six francs the demijohn, and the stimulating gas was provided to dying patients in order to help preserve their
energies and rouse them one last time – it was sipped through a rubber
hose. And behind the doors where these potbellied containers stood lay
the dying or the moribundi.*[41]

On page 301 we finally get down into the village for a glimpse of the bob-
sled races. Our cousins observe, characteristically, but don't take part:

*A little hut had been built at the finish line, and inside was a telephone
that rang whenever a sled began its run. Steered by men and women in
white wool and with sashes in various national colors across their chests,
the low, flat frames came shooting down, one by one, at long intervals, taking the curves of the course that glistened like metal between icy mounds
of snow. You could see red, tense faces with snow blowing in their eyes.
There were accidents, too – sleds crashed and upended, dumping their*

*teams in the snow, while onlookers took lots of pictures. There was music
playing here, as well. The spectators sat in a little grandstand or thronged
the narrow pathway shovelled free next to the course itself. Farther up,
wooden bridges spanned the course, and they, too, were crowded with
people, who could watch the competing sleds hurtle by under them from
time to time. The bodies from the sanatorium on the far slope whizzed
down the same course, taking its curves, heading down to the valley.*[42]

Hans Castorp, his cousin Joachim and a young girl soon to die pay a mor-
bid visit to Davos village cemetery in mid-winter:

*The gravestones and crosses were unpretentious affairs placed there at no
great expense. As for the inscriptions, the names came from every corner
of the earth, were written in English, Russian or other Slavic languages,
in German, Portuguese, and many more tongues. The dates, however, had
their own delicate individuality – on the whole these life spans had been
strikingly short, the difference in years between birth and demise averag-
ing little more than twenty. The field was populated exclusively by youth
rather than virtue, by unsettled folk who had found their way here from
all over the world and had returned now for good and all to the horizontal
form of existence.*[43]

Shortly after reading that graveyard scene from *The Magic Mountain* I
gave up. It was a mylar-covered school library edition, so I refrained from
throwing it across the room. The 'Date Due' card on the inside back cover
was virginal. At the end the words FINIS OPERIS seemed fatuous. Life
got too short to dutifully struggle through a novel I wasn't much enjoying.
Lugubrious, ponderous, stuffy, garrulous – all the old epithets thrown at
Mann, like so many playground snowballs, were true. The famed rolling
periods left me cold. His stuffed shirts I found preposterous. His straight
relationships didn't work and his gay ones were all talking heads. Where
Anthony Heilbut saw grandeur I saw obfuscation. Re-reading *The Magic
Mountain* had been one of those challenges of late reading – would the
monumental writer of one's youth meet the older reader's eyes?

And what of the magic mountain itself? During the Second World
War a little coven of Nazi sympathisers controlled at least one of the
sanatoria, as Danielle Jaeggi has outlined in her documentary *À l'Ombre
de la Montagne*. Behind the clean façade, Switzerland's chic spa turned
nasty.

The Thomas-Mann Way follows in Castorp's footsteps from the Waldhotel Davos, pausing at benches, winding through the trees – a literary stations of the cross that takes up a good deal less time than reading the novel. The Schatzalp Hotel in Davos hosts an annual four-day conference in August, focusing on *The Magic Mountain*. Speakers from German, British and Italian academies toss the ball about, in much the same way as their fictional counterpart in the novel, Dr Krokowski, lectures the inmates on love and illness. Sessions end with wine tasting and an aperitif.

Alexander Fleming's discovery of penicillin in 1928 emptied the sanatoria after the Second World War. The remaining institutions, like their inmates, are dying out. Re-marketed as spas and wellness hotels, they offer a full range of treatment, catering to what Ian Fleming calls 'the modern managerial diseases'. Since health insurers have cut back on paying for a stay in the Swiss Alps, only two bona fide sanatoria remain, catering to mostly asthma patients. Davos began to look for new ways to market fresh air and snow. Skiing at Klosters, taken up initially by Conan Doyle, became the sport of royalty in the last decades of the twentieth century. That old magic, money, was back in town. The wealth managers themselves were not far behind, talking filthy lucre as their forefathers had talked ideas.

While the tuberculars were spitting into their Blue Henrys, at the other extremity of Switzerland anarchists, nihilists and fellow travellers plotted to bring down capitalism's house of cards. A dark room off Geneva's windy quays held portly men called Boris and Ivan and Vladimir – a secret army of sleepers, bomb merchants, propagandists and spies. Their revolution would mark the twentieth century like no other: reds were under the bed and living it up in Hotel Helvetia, replete with room service and plenty of vodka.

4

GOING TO POT

Anarchy, cross-dressing and kif: Eberhardt and Conrad

Le Grand Hôtel de Russie in Geneva, where anarchists and royalty
rubbed shoulders

*the respectable and passionless abode of democratic liberty, the serious-
minded town of dreary hotels, tendering the same indifferent hospitality
to tourists of all nations and to international conspirators of every shade.*
Joseph Conrad

R ussian royalty and nobility had always wintered on Lake Geneva,
but in the second half of the nineteenth century they were joined by
anarchists and revolutionaries fleeing Tsarist oppression. These two
politically opposed camps rubbed shoulders along the Avenue de la Paix.
Switzerland embodied the ideal of natural man in a majestic landscape. Its
love of liberty and democracy was also a source of inspiration for Russian
revolutionaries, and the writings of Tolstoy and Dostoyevsky had nurtured
these views among educated Russians. Geneva's exile *petite Russie* spawned
two wildly different literary responses.

Tsar Alexander II had emancipated the serfs in 1861 but turned increasingly autocratic, countering further concessions with a crackdown on dissent. Members of the People's Will movement in 1881 eventually assassinated
him. The Crimean War of the mid-nineteenth century had been a struggle
between great powers in the vacuum left by the Ottoman Empire, a battle
still flaring in the twenty-first century along the shores of the Black Sea. The
Tsar reigned over a rag-tag army of exiled nihilists, anarchists and revolutionaries, whose calls for change would eventually bear bitter fruit fifty years later
in the century of Communism. Many of them plotted from Switzerland.

They congregated around Lake Geneva and in the Italian-speaking
Ticino. After escaping from the Peter and Paul Fortress in St Petersburg,
the anarchist Mikhail Bakunin formed the International Brotherhood in
Vevey in 1864, a forerunner of the Communist Party. Conferences of the
League of Peace and Freedom, advocating international socialism, were
held in Geneva and Bern at the same time. At Saint-Imier in the Bernese
Jura, the first International Workingmen's Association was founded in 1872.
Bakunin lived out his last years shuttling between Locarno, Lugano and
Bern, where the old revolutionary died in 1876.

*The workers gathered in Berne on the occasion of the death of Michael
Bakunin belong to five different nations. Some are partisans of a Worker's
State, while others advocate the free federation of groups of producers.*[1]

A backward glance at the nineteenth-century workers' struggle can be
instructive from the vantage point of market capitalism. Switzerland was

not then the banking paradise it has become. The watchmaking Jura towns were split between workers and fat-cat owners. All boats were not lifted. Emigration was high. Seasonal labour and factory work in textiles were poorly paid and badly regulated – or regulated to serve the corporate owners. The twenty-first century of robber barons, bailed-out bankers, short-term contracts, inequality and social unrest is enough to make an old Leftie dust off his Karl Marx for another read.

Isabelle Eberhardt was born into *la petite Russie* in Geneva and couldn't wait to get away. Her short, nomadic life in North Africa on the cusp of the nineteenth and twentieth centuries seems curiously modern. This cross-dressing, hashish-smoking Muslim convert appears to be of our time. Were she living today we might dub her a *jihadi* – but wrongly. Joseph Conrad, a Pole born in the Ukraine who took British citizenship, was the first to write about the spy and anarchist world of Geneva during the first decade of the twentieth century. His *Under Western Eyes* anticipates the espionage novels of John le Carré and the world of oligarchs, poisonings and state-sponsored assassinations of modern Russia. Terrorism was in the air at both ends of the twentieth century. Isabelle Eberhardt and Joseph Conrad make strange bedfellows in straight-laced Geneva.

There was not much of the Swiss nanny or Heidi pigtails about Isabelle. She was born out of wedlock in 1877 in Geneva to the widow of a Russian general, adviser to Tsar Alexander II. A forty-three-year age difference separated the old general and his wife. He sired three children in rapid succession and died of apoplexy in 1873 while his estranged wife was in Switzerland for the waters. A fourth child of doubtful parentage saw the light of day in 1871. Isabelle was the fifth in this curious ménage.

The children, a tutor called Alexander Trophimowsky and the diminutive Madame (she was five foot one inch) must have seemed a mixed bag in Geneva of the 1870s. Madame de Moerder had difficulty keeping up appearances and two apartments. She lived on the rue du Mont-Blanc with the children. Fyodor Dostoyevsky had lived on the same street in 1868. Trophimowsky's digs were in the more downmarket rue des Grottes. When Isabelle was born in 1877 she was officially *fille naturelle* of no acknowledged father. This fractured and uncertain identity was to haunt her all her short life. She was destined to be a wandering soul.

Russian presence in Switzerland was of long standing. Diplomatic relations between the Republic of Geneva and Russia had been established since 1687. *La petite Russie* was inclined to oligarchy and rabble-rousing, but Switzerland, then as now, was also a good place to acquire an education, and not just in French and needlework:

> The prospect of a free education at the universities of Zürich and Berne had sparked an influx of Russian students, especially female students, who were nicknamed 'Cossack fillies' by the locals. This expression was not used pejoratively but out of respect for the stamina, alertness and courage of these young women from a faraway country. Sometimes they were bold indeed: no sooner had they completed their courses in physics, chemistry and anatomy, than they returned to their homeland to embark on perilous adventures by becoming terrorists or socialist agitators.[2]

The tutor Trophimowsky was an anarchist who had abandoned his first family near Odessa to take up with his noble-born mistress. His links to Bakunin and the exiled revolutionaries of 1870 in Geneva are hazy. Isabelle later put Nechayev's views on camouflage and subterfuge into practice as a cross-dressing, dope-smoking Muslim in North Africa:

> The revolutionary may and frequently must live within society while pretending to be completely different from what he really is, for he must penetrate everywhere, into the higher and middle classes, into the houses of commerce, the churches and the palaces of the aristocracy, into the world of the bureaucracy, literature and the military, and also into the Third Section and the Winter Palace of the Tsar.[3]

Nechayev was a nihilist who had founded a secret society called 'The People's Retribution'. He was one of the models for Dostoyevsky's The Demons, but also for Joseph Conrad's assassin in Under Western Eyes.

> Nechayev had organised and participated in the murder of an unfortunate student in Moscow named Ivanov. Eventually arrested in Zürich he was extradited to Russia as a common criminal over the protests of Russian students at Swiss universities.[4]

This cloak-and-dagger Switzerland culminated in the assassination of Empress Elisabeth of Austria in Geneva in 1898 by an Italian anarchist. He stabbed her with a homemade four-inch stiletto while she boarded the ferry to Montreux. She was carried to the Hotel Beau Rivage on a makeshift stretcher of a sail and oars. A concierge found the weapon in the doorway of

3 rue des Alpes the following morning.[5] Mark Twain, who happened to be
in Austria at the time, expressed the grief of his host nation:

> One must go back about two thousand years to find an instance to put
> with this one. The oldest family of unchallenged descent in Christendom
> lives in Rome and traces its line back seventeen hundred years, but no
> member of it has been present in the earth when an empress was mur-
> dered, until now.[6]

Twain's democratic sympathies were with the royal victim. He described
the assassin, Luigi Luceni, an Italian army recruit raised in an orphanage,
in these terms:

> He is at the bottom of the human ladder, as the accepted estimates of
> degree and value go: a soiled and patched young loafer, without gifts,
> without talents, without education, without morals, without charac-
> ter, without any born charm or any acquired one that wins or beguiles
> or attracts; without a single grace of mind or heart or hand that any
> tramp or prostitute could envy him; an unfaithful private in the ranks, an
> incompetent stone-cutter, an inefficient lackey; in a word, a mangy, offen-
> sive, empty, unwashed, vulgar, gross, mephitic, timid, sneaking, human
> polecat.[7]

Twain the seasoned journalist is clearly having a hissy fit here. He gives
an astute glimpse of the political forces – imperialist and anarchist – confronting Europe at century's turn. Three imperial powers were hit by assassination in the space of twenty years: Tsar Alexander II in 1881, Empress
Elizabeth in 1898 and US President McKinley in 1901. Governments
milked the public mood, and in some cases planted *agents provocateurs*.
Terrorism was a fashionable whipping boy (as it was at the beginning of the
twenty-first century) and Geneva was viewed as a hotbed of desperadoes
enjoying Swiss hospitality.

When Isabelle was two and a half her family decamped to Meyrin, west
of the city, then a multicultural community of exiles. The impressively
bearded Trophimowsky – 'one of those bearded Russian faces without
shape', as Conrad puts it – had Tolstoyan back-to-nature pretensions and
liked to cultivate orchids. The family was dysfunctional, as we might now
say. Nathalie, Madame's daughter, later claimed that Trophimowsky had
interfered with her. Isabelle was brought up in boy's clothes and spoiled

by her tutor father, whom she called Vava. A gifted linguist, he taught her Arabic and German, besides the Russian spoken at home. As soon as they could, the boys escaped to the French Foreign Legion. Nathalie absconded in her mid-teens to a lover in Geneva. Swiss police became involved in domestic rows. By the time Isabelle was sixteen, she was polyglot, could read the Koran in Arabic, wrote the language elegantly, and had taken to wandering around the city in boy's clothes:

> I was already a nomad as a young girl, when I used to daydream as I gazed at the enticing white road leading off, under a more brilliant sun, it seemed to me, into the delicious unknown.[8]

In diaries and travel notes written in North Africa, Isabelle returns to the view from Meyrin of the snow-crowned Jura, her blue remembered hills. On the road to Touggourt in the southern Atlas, 'at that frontier between town and desert, I was reminded of those autumn and winter sunsets in the land of exile, when the great snow-capped Jura mountains seemed to come closer and turn into an expanse of pale blond and bluish hues'.[9] At El Oued on the edge of the Sahara, riding out to assignations with a lover or exploring the dry riverbed, she closed her eyes and 'was off in a dream. I felt as if I were back in the big woods along the Rhône and in the Parc Sarrazin on a mellow summer evening.'[10]

Surviving photos of Eberhardt show a sullen, pouty boy dressed as a sailor, or as an Arab under a tarboosh – a boy who might have had to watch his backside in North Africa or on board ship. By all accounts, after a few pipes of hashish Isabelle could be game for anything. The photos give an impression of hardness, posed defiance. She had them taken in Geneva when the dream of life as an Arab began to obsess her.

At sixteen she started smoking and meeting men in bars:

> I go around dressed as a sailor, even in town, right under the noses of agents. The other evening I was sitting in the pharmacy and to my great confusion (I remembered my complaints to you about drinking!) I got so drunk on beer (six of them!), happily in the company of Schwarz [her married lover].[11]

There is some evidence ('under the noses of agents') that she became involved with anarchist and nihilist cells in Lausanne and Geneva in the mid-1890s, when she was in her late teens. She got off on disguise,

Eighteen-year-old Isabelle Eberhardt as a sailor in Geneva in 1895
and, right, in Arab get-up

on assembling different selves into a composite identikit. She reminds me
of teenagers morphing from goody-two-shoes to Goth to punk in a year.
It could get tedious. Like her English counterpart, Lawrence of Arabia,
she liked to swan around in Arab robes, describing her mask as 'a certain
tom-boyishness'.

In North Africa she passed herself off as Si Mahmoud Saadi, a young
Tunisian *taleb* (scholar); the word Taliban derives from the same root.
There was chutzpah in these disguises but also a certain naivety. In the
desert a woman did not go undetected for long and her hosts were tactful
and face-saving:

> They knew perfectly well, from all sorts of European indiscretions, that
> Si Mahmoud was a woman. But, with beautiful Arab discretion, they
> argued that it was none of their business, that it would have been inap-
> propriate to allude to it, and they carried on treating me as they had at
> first, as an educated and slightly superior friend.[12]

In the desert near the Moroccan border she wrote: 'I'm entertained at first,
and it's hard not to laugh hearing them say among themselves: "He's good
looking, the little *spahi*; he has fine skin!"'[13]

She might have been attractive as a boy, but as a woman the desert took
its toll. She was drawn to sex, to the port cities of Marseilles, Algiers, Bône,
Tunis, to the seedy lives of stevedores and garrison recruits. Her writing is
full of people down on their luck, fallen women, sex as a currency of trade.
She was an aficionado of the quickie. A smoker, a drinker and a habitual

user of *kif* – hashish – staid, abstemious Geneva produced her, like a rare orchid from her father's greenhouse.

> *She was particularly drawn to ports, with their wayward, bustling, provisional life, their sense of people always on the point of setting off for the unknown, their coarse virility, their smells, their raucous gaiety, their snatched, rough couplings, and above all their suffering. ... lush colours, desert landscapes, brutal, uncommitted love-making. With the sailors in Toulon and St Mandrier, she was probably dressed in her loose workman's clothes of blue linen jacket, trousers and cap. If she made love with the sailors – and she probably did far less than the scandalised bourgeois later implied – it was as a girl, but as a girl who was their physical equal.*[14]

She sounds and looks like a female Rimbaud passing herself off as one of the lads.

She first travelled to North Africa with her mother in 1897. Madame de Moerder was ailing, quickly converted to Islam and died shortly thereafter. She is buried in a pauper's grave in Annaba. They must have made a strange pair, knocking about in the streets of the Kasbah. Isabelle assumed the identity of her alter ego Mahmoud Saadi:

> *She already had a command of classical Arabic and a good knowledge of the Koran, and, as a natural linguist, she now quickly picked up spoken Algerian Arabic ... She used to lose herself in the street life in the 500-year-old Kasbah, a few streets away from the rue Rovigo, and soon made friends among the local Arab students.*[15]

What pushed these Russian exiles to renounce the comforts of Geneva for the uncertainties of the Maghreb and the Muslim faith? They bear a curious resemblance to modern-day *jihadis* spurning the attractions of the west. As Russian émigrées, their attachment to Switzerland was fleeting. Madame de Moerder seems also to have been somewhat detached, if not unhinged. Marked by marriage to a man forty-three years older than her, she might have been looking for escape. Colonial North Africa was filled with such renegades.

Isabelle began publishing stories and travel vignettes in French journals and newspapers, creating a costumed world of sudden passion, death, fallen women and glorious men. Her characters sometimes seem like Cossacks in disguise: 'Nomads dressed in white wool, *spahis* superbly draped in red, local gendarmes in black *bournouses* lined up along the walls, crouched on benches.'[16]

From 1897 to 1903 she negotiated a path through the often mutually suspicious ethnicities of French North Africa: the indigenous Berber tribes of the Atlas Mountains, the *grande* and *petite* Kabylie, the coastal mix of Greek, Phoenician and Roman followed by Arab blow-ins from the seventh century, nomads and their Somali slaves. The company she kept were the *spahis* of the garrison towns, minstrels, wandering holy men and tribal warriors. They seem remnants of an older nomadic way of life: 'Men pass: Europeans, Jews, turbaned Bedouin, detachments of rowdy Zouaves, hunters, seamen, troops in red tunics.'[17]

She would hunker down and smoke hashish with the troops. We might wonder at their motivation. It wasn't all the finer points of Koranic interpretation by any means. Her hosts in the colonial army treated her to the manly pleasures of military towns at the edge of the desert.

> *Whatever their unenlightened way of life, the lowliest of Bedouins are far superior to these idiotic Europeans making a nuisance of themselves. Where can one go to flee them, where can one go to live far from those arrogant, prying, evil beings who think it is their privilege to level everything and fashion it in their own dreadful image.*[18]

Her disguise allowed her to visit a brothel, which she wrote about in a 1903 text called 'Dark Pleasures'. She describes the back room of a hovel, peopled with Sudanese dancers and musicians. It is a remarkably fresh piece of writing:

> *The others sing without stopping or pausing for breath – the gasping chant, the terrible cry that just now brought the damp flesh of the negresses to a climax of such savage passion.*
>
> *Hashish pipes do the rounds.*
>
> *Bit by bit, with the peppermint tea, the incense smoke, the scents of negroes, the music in the stuffy room, a breath of madness seems to come off the shiny foreheads of the blacks.*[19]

It was a long way from Avenue de la Paix.[20]

Isabelle's flouting of political, social and gender propriety in North Africa did not go unnoticed by the French authorities. As in Geneva, the *gendarmes* kept their eye on her. In October 1903 she met Colonel Lyautey, the man charged with extending French colonial 'protection' into the disputed territory of the Sahel. Lyautey was one of those grown-up boy scouts of the Third Republic; in later life he took to the Scouts with a passion. Graduate of Saint-Cyr, Chief of Staff at Tongking, a colonial pacifier, he was another one who liked to dress up in Arab robes and hang around with young men in steam rooms. French Prime Minister Georges Clemenceau described him as 'an admirable, courageous man, who has always had balls between his legs – even when they weren't his own'.[21]

Mystery surrounds the exact terms of the mission that Lyautey proposed. He needed someone who could infiltrate the desert tribes and win them over to at least a passing French allegiance. Isabelle took on the role of an embedded journalist, sent to the Sud-Oranais by her friend Barrucand to report on the insurgency for his paper in Algiers. Her writing became more focused, urgent. The correspondent of the Paris newspaper *Le Matin* described Isabelle at twenty-six as a 'robust lad, *imberbe*':

> *She was ugly, with an ugliness unredeemed by any pleasing feature of her face, with her very prominent forehead, her high cheekbones, very tiny eyes and an appallingly nasal voice. In contrast her walk, the way she held her shoulders, very squarely, belonged to a more hardened cavalryman, a real* spahi; *unless you had known, you would never have taken her for a woman.*[22]

A German Legionnaire stationed at Ain Sefra confirms this view: 'Besides, she had nothing provocative about her and was far from being pretty.'[23] Lyautey, on the other hand, gives an admirable picture of her, not at all fazed by her gender bending as evidenced by his mixed pronouns:

> *We understood each other very well, poor Mahmoud and I, and I shall always cherish exquisite memories of our evening talks. She was what attracts me most in the world: a rebel. To find someone who is really himself, who exists outside all prejudice, all enslavement, all cliché, and who passes through life as liberated as a bird in space, what a treat!*[24]

Roped into the machinations of the French protectorate, Isabelle's role became more ambiguous. Whose side was she on? Her elective affinities were for the desert tribes, but her company was increasingly that of the garrison towns. Like her husband of three years, the *spahi* Slimene Ehnni, she had thrown in her lot with the occupying power. During the last year of her life her marriage had begun to unravel; she can't have been a domestic goddess. In a piece written in Kenadsa, she declared: 'All love of an individual, carnal or fraternal, is slavery, a more or less complete effacement of the personality. One renounces oneself to become a couple.' Such clarity in a twenty-six-year-old is unnerving.

She was headed for powder country: *bled-el-baroud*, a colloquial term for the desert. Kenadsa was a monastery affiliated to a Sufi confraternity that Isabelle had joined some years before. Territorially it was under the rule of the Sultan of Fez, which Lyautey sought to bring under the protectorate of France in a larger game with Morocco. 'Where, really, is the border? Where does Algeria end and Morocco begin? Nobody bothers to find out. But what good is a border which is knowingly unspecified?'[25] Isabelle's brief was to inform Lyautey of the affiliations of the sheikh, Sidi Brahim. This dovetailed with her interest in secret brotherhoods, remote desert outposts and a search for peace of mind.

> *Under a little tattered tent invaded by flies, someone from Kenadsa has installed a Moorish café. A few government-issue saddles and rifles … the dreaming soul of nomads, reckless and sensual, climbs in wonderful savage songs, raucous at times as cats in the night, and sometimes mild as the gentlest lullaby. Their songs are waves of passion and feeling that cast themselves up on the beach of the sky. Their melancholy breaks on my heart, as well.*[26]

She was attended by Sudanese slaves, given a cell-like room in the monastery precinct, and left to her austere surroundings. As an initiate of a Sufi brotherhood she had perfect credentials with the sheik and his seminarians, who came from all over North Africa to seek instruction. Her observations on slavery have a refreshing matter-of-factness:

> *Sons of captives taken by the Souah and the Mossi tribes, the fathers of these slaves came to Kenadsa after years of suffering and complicated wanderings. Captured first by men of their own race during the constant warring between villages and black chieftains, they were sold to Moorish traffickers, then placed in the hands of the Tuareg or the Chaamba who, in their turn, passed them on to the Berbers.*[27]

Isabelle's late writing achieves a kind of grace, different from her adolescent rumblings. Vignettes are clear, sympathetic, the observer unobtrusive:

For the last few days a black boy named Messaoud has been serving me.
He's about 14 years old, tall for his age and too sharp for his own good.
He dresses in white shirts pulled in at the waist by a belt of grey wool. His
brown face is friendly and expressive, with mischievous, large dark eyes
that seem to have no iris. On his shaved head a tuft of crisped hair, sign of
slavery and also of pre-adolescence, is a comic fixture above his right ear.
This bizarre ornament lends a humourous touch to his otherwise mocking
features. In the pierced lobe of his ear Messaoud wears a piece of rolled
blue paper, in lieu of an earring.[28]

Invited by students to a gathering of tea, music and embroidery, she notices
the handsome Hamiani Abd el Djebbar 'lying full length on the carpet
like a big Saluki hound, he stretches his lean horseman's muscles, which
are clearly unused to inactivity'.[29] One wonders who observes whom
here. Some days later, she spies on him outside at night with a 'young,
waxen-faced village girl ... convulsing in love's superb fury, rolled together
upon the shadowy earth'.[30]

In monasteries and boarding schools nothing remains secret for long.
Isabelle's usual disguise was a ruse on both sides. She had her own day-
dreams 'about the lives of these Muslim students: the long tradition of scho-
lastic studies within the bare, simple confines of the ancient mosques; pious
exercises stirring most of these young men, already affiliated with mystical
brotherhoods, to daily ecstasy. ... many hidden vices. An almost cloistered
life promotes this perversion of the senses.'[31] As her most recent biographer
Annette Kobak puts it, 'she was often overtaken by moments of pure lust'.[32]

'Hidden vices', of course, is disingenuous coming from a cross-dressing
former anarchist reporting back to Lyautey. But it was exactly the voyeur-
ism she enjoyed. She liked to watch people watching. The 'ardent rutting'
did not go unnoticed by her, and she may have joined in. Her observation
of student teatime extended to a whole way of life, a cultural analysis borne
out by her own experiences as a disguised woman in a man's world.

For the well-born Muslim at home, particularly in towns, nothing of per-
sonal affairs, family life, pleasures, or loves, must be revealed outside. The
publicizing of pleasures, as European students love to do, is unknown in
the Islamic world.[33]

In short stories giving voice to North African female characters, Eberhardt
shows the same acute awareness of power relations. In 'Toalith' a girl jumps

to her death down a well to escape a second marriage to an old man, a business partner of her stepfather: 'It was said by everyone that she had run away to become a prostitute in some purlieu of the Kasbah.'[34] Women are either obedient wives or whores; there is no third way. In 'Portrait d'Ouled Nail', translated by Paul Bowles as 'Achoura', Isabelle characterises the semi-nomadic dancers of the Ouled Nail:

> Like all the women of her region, Achoura considered the sale of her body the only escape from want that was available to a woman. She had no desire to be cloistered again by marriage, nor was she ashamed to be what she was. To her prostitution seemed legitimate, and did not interfere with her love for her favourite. Indeed, it never occurred to her to associate in her mind the indescribable bliss they knew together with what she called, using the cynical sabir word, coummerce.[35]

Observations such as these and Isabelle's trail-blazing life have made her a darling of identity politics.

Her ascetic interlude didn't last long and soon she was back on the drugs. She had a way of nosing out a *kif* pipe. *The Oblivion Seekers* (2010) is the arresting title of a collection of her stories translated by that old *kif* smoker and Moroccan hand Paul Bowles. Bowles and Eberhardt were made for each other. In his preface, Bowles renders homage to her father for inculcating Isabelle with anarchist independence:

> he allowed his daughter to have no contact with the Swiss among whom they lived. Very early he instilled in her a healthy contempt for the values of bourgeois society. Indifference to public opinion was essential if she was to be able to lead the kind of life she demanded.[36]

Isabelle's sympathies lay with the underdog, the nomad, the feckless – an 'intellectual nomadism' identified by the writer Norman Douglas as long ago as 1911. He makes an interesting link between the Alps discovered by the Romantics and the Sahara 'discovered' by the same kind of people, fleeing the strictures of bourgeois society. Isabelle's shiny black eyes, *kif* enflamed, anticipated the drug culture of the Beats and the *fin-de-siècle* clubbers:

> The seekers of oblivion sing and clap their hands lazily; their dream voices ring out into the night, in the dim light of the mica-patterned lantern. Then little by little the voices fall, grow muffled, the words are slower.

1904 flash flood at Aïn Sefra, western Algeria, in which
Isabelle Eberhardt drowned

Finally the smokers are quiet, and merely stare at the flowers in ecstasy.
They are epicureans, voluptuaries; perhaps they are sages. Even in the
darkest purlieu of Morocco's underworld such men can reach the magic
horizon where they are free to build their dream-palaces of delight.[37]

In the autumn of 1903, sick with malaria and perhaps syphilis, she checked
into the military hospital at Aïn Sefra in the western Atlas. She asked her
husband Slimene to join her. Both knew their destinies lay in different
directions. She rented an old adobe house in the lower town in anticipation of his arrival and her discharge. They had been living separately for
eight months.

In those southern Atlas towns flash floods sweep all in their path with
sudden fury. Barely two hours after Isabelle had checked herself out of
hospital, the water surged down the dry *wadi* and took the town by surprise.
Husband and wife were upstairs, probably smoking *kif*. Slimene managed
to escape. Isabelle was found trapped under the stairwell two days later,
drowned with her hands behind her head as though protecting herself
from falling masonry. She was buried according to Muslim rites in the
cemetery nearby. Slimene didn't turn up for the funeral.

Lyautey ordered a search for her papers and a month later the manuscript of what was to become 'Sud-Oranais' was found inside a large urn.
Her editor Barrucand in Algiers supervised publication of her writings in
the following decades. Two stage plays in the 1920s about her life, a film
and the diaries began to build the legend of the tragic twenty-seven-year-
old desert wanderer of Russian-Genevan heritage who liked to hang with
the sailors.

Three of the Moerder children came to bad ends: Vladimir gassed
himself in 1898; Isabelle drowned in 1904; in 1914 Augustin committed
suicide. Slimene died of tuberculosis three years after escaping from the
flood that killed his wife. The Australian writer Robert Dessaix makes an
apt comment about happiness: 'I'm not at all convinced now that happy
childhoods are a good thing. I think they can lead to a kind of moral para-
lysis, a sort of smug Swissness of the spirit.'[38] No one could accuse Isabelle
Eberhardt of smug Swissness of spirit. In her diary she wrote: 'I will vanish
from this earth, where I have always been a spectator and outsider among
men.'[39] She hasn't vanished yet.

Joseph Conrad was well placed to understand the anarchist threat among
imperial powers. The Tsar's police had imprisoned his Polish parents for
sedition. Conrad was born in the Ukraine and ran away to join the merchant marine. As the chronologies put it, 'a period of biographical mystery
ensues'. After twenty years at sea, he eventually took British citizenship and
settled down to marriage and a life of authorship in English. He set *Under
Western Eyes* (1911) in the anarchist world of pre–First World War Geneva,
among Russian revolutionaries plotting imperial ruin.

He had toured the Alps as a sixteen-year-old. Later, spending time
in Geneva undergoing hydrotherapy, he imbibed the city's atmosphere
of Russian intrigue. Models for *Under Western Eyes* can be found in
Dostoyevsky's *Crime and Punishment* (1866) and *The Demons* (1872), both
of which contain anarchistic or politically motivated murders. Dostoyevsky
himself had spent an impoverished winter in Geneva in 1867–68, gam-
bling and writing *The Idiot* (1869). Both writers modelled their fictional
characters on the nihilist Sergei Nechayev, who was arrested in Zürich and
extradited to Russia.

Under Western Eyes opens with a prominent political assassination in
St Petersburg. The student Razumov turns the assassin over to the police

while managing to keep his cover as an accomplice. Later, he turns up in Geneva and meets the assassin's family and a covert network of exiled anarchists. Lionised by this clique of left-wingers, Razumov gradually works his way into their confidence. He is a plant, a double agent, a sleeper, one of the first in a long line of undercover spies in twentieth-century fiction.

Conrad pictures Geneva as a cold escape from tyranny, 'a respectable town of refuge to which all these sorrows and hopes were nothing'. This 'sleeping town of prosaic virtues and universal hospitality' is merely a backdrop to a tale of betrayal and allegiance. His émigré anarchists shuttle between the Boulevard des Philosophes and assignations on the Promenade des Bastions. His characters watch each other. And Swiss police watch them. The tale's English narrator, a 'teacher of languages', is himself a kind of spy, the western eyes of the title. Geneva is a city of intrigue, biting wind and even colder people. Its inhabitants are characterised as smug keepers of democracy's flame:

> In the very middle of it I observed a solitary Swiss couple, whose fate was made secure from the cradle to the grave by the perfected mechanism of democratic institutions in a republic that could almost be held in the palm of one's hand.[40]

These Russian anarchists congregate at the Château Borel, based on the Villa La Grange, still standing on Geneva's south shore. After meeting them, Razumov looks across the lake towards the Jura and the vineyards below, at 'the very perfection of mediocrity attained at last after centuries of toil and culture'. Unlike Rousseau and the Romantic poets, Razumov is immune to the beauty of the lake. A prig and a moralist, he has fallen into his double-agent role almost by accident:

> there was but little warmth; and the sky, the sky of a land without horizons, swept and washed clean by the April showers, extended a cold cruel blue, without elevation, narrowed suddenly by the ugly, dark wall of the Jura where, here and there, lingered yet a few miserable trails and patches of snow.[41]

Dostoyevsky, very much a xenophobe and a Russian patriot, had also found scant comfort among the Swiss, lamenting in his diary their tendency to smugness: 'Everything here is vile, rotten, everything is expensive.'[42] Conrad's Russians scorn the very democracy they are murdering to attain.

He manages nonetheless to capture the city's émigré microclimate. Give or take a profession, it is not too different today:

> revolutionist members of committees, secret emissaries, vulgar and unmannerly fugitive professors, rough students, ex-cobblers with apostolic faces, consumptive and ragged enthusiasts, Hebrew youths, common fellows of all sorts that used to come and go around Peter Ivanovitch – fanatics, pedants, proletarians all.[43]

Razumov's role as double agent sits uneasy with him under the scrutiny of the assassin's family and these watchful revolutionaries. His silence is interpreted as aloofness and modesty, but is in fact dissent from their firebrand views. At any moment he could be unmasked as an agent. Conrad is careful to associate Razumov with Rousseau. 'To write was the very thing he had made up his mind to do that day,' thinks Razumov, wandering along the quay:

> To his right, beyond the toy-like jetties, he saw the green slopes framing the Petit Lac in all the marvellous banality of the picturesque made of painted cardboard, with the more distant stretch of water inanimate and shining like a piece of tin.[44]

Almost unconsciously, Razumov makes for an island in the stream, 'a tiny crumb of earth named after Jean-Jacques Rousseau', and drinks a glass of milk on a bench. It is here that he has his epiphany and begins to write his true story. Conrad's own divided nationality, his bilingualism, his inherited dislike of Russia are behind Razumov's torn soul. Rousseau too blew hot and cold about his Swissness. His island is perhaps the most visible place to sit down and write in all of Geneva, off the dogleg bridge, smack in the middle of the Rhône as it sweeps out of the lake in a hurry to get to France:

> he pulled out of his pocket a fountain pen, opened a small notebook on his knee, and began to write quickly, raising his eyes now and then at the connecting arm of the bridge. These glances were needless; the people crossing over in the distance seemed unwilling even to look at the islet where the exiled effigy of the author of the Social Contract sat enthroned above the bowed head of Razumov in the sombre immobility of bronze. ... His fine ear could detect the faintly accentuated murmurs of the current breaking against the point of the island.[45]

Ile de J.J. Rousseau in Geneva, where Conrad's Razumov takes up his pen

Razumov has clearly allied himself with Rousseau here, the philosopher of the Enlightenment. The notes he writes are his report to his handlers in St Petersburg, 'his first communication for Councillor Mikulin'. Eventually, Razumov reveals his true affiliation to the revolutionaries and to the assassin's sister. Conrad brings on the storm, as Mary Shelley did a century earlier in the same location at the crisis point of her harried protagonist in *Frankenstein*. Conrad situates his anarchist Geneva outside the old town, along the lake and in the new precincts by the Plainpalais. His Geneva is a city of night, its nihilists and anarchists like wandering ghosts, its hues those of Whistler:

> We walked slowly down the street, away from the town; the low garden walls of the modest villas doomed to demolition were overhung by the boughs of trees and masses of foliage, lighted from below by gas lamps. The violent and monotonous noise of the icy waters of the Arve falling over a low dam swept towards us with a chilly draught of air across a great open space, where a double line of lamp-lights outlined a street as yet without houses.[46]

Conrad's roots – like Eberhardt's – are difficult to disentangle. He was a Pole brought up at the edge of the Russian empire, exiled in England after a formation at sea, a mariner who became a landlubber. His sympathies in *Under Western Eyes* are clearly not with the anarchists and yet he knows their milieu well. His story of spies, double agents, assassinations and international terror has a curious modern resonance. Some do it with poison, some do it with bombs: Conrad does it with words.

Isabelle Eberhardt grew up on the edge of Geneva's *petite Russie*, learning early its tricks of disguise and survival. Like many Geneva travel writers who followed in her footsteps – Ella Maillart and Nicolas Bouvier come to mind – she itched to be away from its confining streets into a larger air, the powder country of the Sahara. Like Conrad's Razumov she became a double agent of sorts: rooting for the desert peoples while reporting back to Lyautey. Like Razumov, uneasy in her own skin, she discovered herself as a writer under the auspices of Geneva. Today she has a street named after her in the Grottes area, a cul-de-sac behind the tracks of the train station. Her conversion and adherence to a secret Sufi brotherhood, her cross-dressing and hashish smoking, her fondness for a bit of rumpy-pumpy in the dunes, make her a peculiarly modern heroine, one hard to pin down. I don't think Geneva will be erecting a statue any time soon.

While the Russians were going to pot and keeping the secret police of several countries on their toes, Switzerland also played host to the original hippies. A band of heliotherapists, vegetarians, dancers and flower children hid away in the mountains, where they were not afraid to take off their clothes and dream of utopia. As the world moved towards the first of two world wars, they thought they had found the land of milk and honey.

5

THE INFINITY POOL

Getting back to the garden with Wells, Lawrence and Hesse

Back to nature on the Brissago Islands, 1930s

where men and women are happy and laws are wise, and where all
that is tangled and confused in human affairs has been unravelled
and made right.
H.G. Wells

Sometimes on Sunday afternoons I visit the vegetarian restaurant in Dornach and check out the old eurhythmic dancers. Over tea and bio rhubarb tart, I notice their bone structure. They sit on after a light lunch with nothing much to do but mind their digestive systems. Long willowy figures, draped in expensive Weleda pastels, have a Grecian quality, as though they'd stepped off a frieze. All is health and maintenance here at the tail end of the Jura, where it meets the tectonic plate of the Black Forest. The Rhine runs between them on the fault line. We are cultivating our chakras at the golden dawn of the twenty-first century. When the dancers get up to go to the loo, they sashay across the restaurant with a spring to their step. The tea goes straight to their kidneys.

I could never get going with Rudolf Steiner, founder of the Anthroposophists, whose headquarters is on the hill above Dornach. What is it about seers and bad prose? At least Jesus Christ had good editors and knew how to keep the story forward looking: miracle here, crucifixion there. But the latter-day visionaries – Madame Blavatsky, Krishnamurti, Ouspensky – have lost the plot altogether. *The Book of Mormon* always strikes me as a rewrite by a Hollywood mogul after a weekend on peyote. And doe-eyed, fourteen-year-old Krishnamurti picked up on the beach at Adyar by Charles Webster Leadbeater? What's going on there?

Leadbeater's grooming of Krishnamurti in 1909 brought about Steiner's break with the Theosophical Society. Leadbeater was a big-bearded Victorian cleric who published *The Astral Plane* in 1895. He used psychometry, the technique of divining character by handling objects. By touching Krishnamurti's head, apparently, Leadbeater could tell that he had a very big aura. 'His tastes ran mainly to boys and tapioca pudding', as one critic put it.[1]

The slightly raffish, metropolitan atmosphere of Theosophy gave way in Anthroposophy to nature-worship and the simple life. Many Theosophists were vegetarians, dress reformers or anti-vivisectionists, but in what amounted to a parody of German thoroughness, Steinerism provided a complete way of life which included all these things in a coherent pattern. The polymath found himself giving guidance on every aspect of life, from the colour of auras to the colour of kitchen cupboards, as he extended his influence from the spiritual lives of his followers to the food on their tables.[2]

When Steiner established his headquarters at Dornach outside Basel, his was one of a number of loosely linked spiritual sites already flourishing in Switzerland. Heliotherapy (nude sunbathing), hydrotherapy (spas), aromatherapy (smells), vegetarianism (muesli) and assorted crystals and candles were already well established. Mumbo-jumbo was on the move. Steiner's educational theories have stood the test of time, however, and are less fluffy. Anthroposophical medicine (massage, eurhythmie, plant-based treatments) and Big Pharma stare at each other across the Rhine at Basel, opposing attempts at health and well-being – or wellness, as it's now known. Wellness is big business in Switzerland and has been for over a century. The poor paddled at Bognor and Butlins, but the rich prefer their infinity pools in the Alps.

The Czech writer Franz Kafka, always a bit of a hypochondriac, went in search of Steiner in 1911 at the Victoria Hotel in Berlin:

He eats two litres of emulsion of almonds and fruits that grow in the air.

He communicates with his absent disciples by means of thought-forms which he transmits to them without bothering further about them after they are generated. But they soon wear out and he must replace them. ...

He listened very attentively without apparently looking at me at all, entirely devoted to my words. He nodded from time to time, which he seems to consider an aid to strict concentration. At first a quiet head cold disturbed him, his nose ran, he kept working his handkerchief deep into his nose, one finger in each nostril.[3]

The first time I visited the Goetheanum, Anthroposophy's enormous, imposing concrete headquarters, I signed on for a guided tour. It turned out to be an hour and a half long, in German. I learned from it that anthroposophists don't hold with right angles, so everything in their architecture is slightly off kilter. The site at Dornach was chosen because of the energy lines where the Jura and Black Forest meet. Dating from 1928, it is one of the first structures built in reinforced concrete. It replaced an earlier wooden building – equally impressive – that burned down.

The original wooden Goetheanum at Dornach, headquarters of
Rudolf Steiner's Anthroposophy movement

The corner stone of the original Goetheanum was laid down 'at an
afternoon ceremony in September 1913 amid a howling gale and prema-
ture darkness'.[4] Spiritual believers had come from seventeen countries to
build it:

> *artists and intellectuals, artisans and amateurs, lay members and lead-
> ers, all working together to produce a wooden palace over sixty-five thou-
> sand cubic metres in size, erected on stone foundations and roofed with
> Norwegian slate.*[5]

Among the workers was Andrei Bely, author of *Petersburg* (1913), one of the
four masterpieces of twentieth-century literature, according to Vladimir
Nabokov. Summoned home for military service in 1916, Bely describes
his journey from Dornach to Russia in *Notes of an Eccentric* (1918). He
believed he was under surveillance by Allied counter-espionage agents and
remembered hearing rumbling gunfire from nearby Alsace as he worked
on building the Goetheanum.

Houses around the giant scarab-like structure have the trademark window frames and roofs, abjuring right angles. There's an expensive bio shop,

a massage centre, arts and crafts galleries exhibiting pastel-inflected art and lumpy unpolished sculpture – like the work Steiner produced himself. It's a warren of alternative living. The road follows the camber of the hill, lined with affluent-looking houses. Like the new mountain spas, the houses are all clean slate and clean lines. The people inside them attempt to lead clean lives. Lush gardens run wild according to the best Steiner farming principles. The air seems rarefied.

Anthroposophy was a turn-of-the-century reaction to German patriarchal militarism in the same way that the hippy movement took umbrage at American wars in Asia. During the last decades of the nineteenth century, Switzerland became a refuge for disaffected sons, wayward women and wanton youth – the children of the educated middle class. They took off their clothes and ran naked through the Alpine valleys. Denizens of *fin-de-siècle* Swiss communes were the original hippies.

The fishing village of Ascona on Lago Maggiore is a corner of the world blessed by nature. Nearby Locarno has been a pilgrimage site since 1470, when the Madonna del Sasso appeared to a Benedictine monk. The mountain rising from the lake is pitted with caves – *grotti* – still used to store wine casks and as makeshift drinking dens. Clement air from the south brings a breath of *la dolce vita*.

The founders of the Monte Verità commune were the son of a rich Belgian industrialist, Henry Oedenkoven, his music teacher partner Ida Hoffmann, from Montenegro, and the Gräser brothers, Karl and Gusto, wild boys from the far reaches of the Austro-Hungarian empire. They bought land – Oedenkoven did, and the others tagged along – costing a hundred and fifty thousand Swiss francs. As with many communes, disagreements surfaced almost immediately.

The Gräser brothers were oddity personified. Karl believed that 'all metals should be left in their native rocks, as ores'. His partner wore date stones instead of buttons. Gusto Gräser was a *Naturmensch*, part of the nineteenth-century equivalent of the back-to-nature movement. He was a vagabond whose agricultural policy was to throw fruit stones on the ground where he thought trees were needed. No sweat – nature did the rest. A haunting photograph of an emaciated Gusto Gräser, wandering through the Munich ruins at the close of the Second World War, shows only himself and the Frauenkirche left standing.[6]

They set up a sanatorium and built basic huts. They were vegetarian sun worshippers, reform minded as regards clothing and marriage. The women wore their hair pre-Raphaelite style. The wild men adopted the

Anti-war activist Gusto Gräser in the Munich ruins in 1945

apostolic look – toga, wraparound skirt and tunic with nothing on underneath. Over time, vegetarians, pacifists, nudists, Freemasons, feminists, Theosophists and bohemians of all stripes made their way up Monte Verità in search of enlightenment or out of simple curiosity. Hermann Hesse visited and was buried up to the neck in soil as a cure for alcoholism. Isadora Duncan sunbathed nude on the roof of her Bauhaus hut, to the delight of onlookers. For twenty years at the beginning of the last century, Monte Verità was an experiment in alternative living.

Before the First World War curtailed his continental trips, writer, socialist and pacifist H.G. Wells wrote two books inspired by the fringe happenings in Ascona. He was a bit of a windbag for social improvement. *A Modern Utopia* (1905) follows a pair of wayfarers, the narrator and a botanist, dropped as though by magic into the Ticino landscape. Their observations on Utopia – Switzerland – are intercut with philosophical musings on the role of women, work, race and marriage.

> With that absurd nearness of effect one gets in the Alps, we see the little
> train a dozen miles away, running down the Biaschina to Italy ... Down
> the mountain we shall go and down the passes, and as the valleys open
> the world will open, Utopia, where men and women are happy and laws

are wise, and where all that is tangled and confused in human affairs has been unravelled and made right.[7]

Wells' utopian vision bears a remarkable resemblance to twenty-first-century Switzerland. He has the uncanny knack of being prescient:

Such great tramways as this will be used when the Utopians wish to travel fast and far; thereby you will glide all over the land surface of the planet; and feeding them and distributing from them, innumerable minor systems, clean little electric tramways I picture them, will spread out over the land in finer reticulations, growing close and dense in the urban regions and thinning as the population thins. And running beside these lighter railways, and spreading beyond their range, will be the smooth minor high roads ... Cycle tracks will abound in Utopia, sometimes following beside the great high roads, but oftener taking their own more agreeable line amidst woods and crops and pastures; and there will be a rich variety of footpaths and minor ways.[8]

Trams, light railways, cycle paths: Switzerland here is the good life, meeting the needs of a leisured citizenry. Our time travellers approach Andermatt from the south and cross the famous Devil's Bridge. They encounter a *Naturmensch* on the road. Perhaps Wells had in mind Gusto Gräser, whose distinctive hairy figure was well known on the mountain roads at that time. Booking into a Lucerne inn, they marvel at Swiss cleanliness and clock-work precision:

It is one of several such establishments in Lucerne. It possesses many hundreds of practically self-cleaning little bedrooms, equipped very much after the fashion of the rooms we occupied in the similar but much smaller inn at Hospenthal, differing only a little in the decoration. ... and when I look out of my window in the early morning – for the usual Utopian working day commences within an hour of sunrise – I see Pilatus above this outlook, rosy in the morning sky.[9]

Wells' Utopia could be any Swiss metropolis: functional, clean, peaceful, trams on time and cycle paths busy. Switzerland's participatory democracy, its frequent referenda on anything from smoking to immigrants, catches the author's eye:

Gräser towards the end of his life in the 1950s

> From a number of beautifully printed placards at the street corners,
> adorned with caricatures of considerable pungency, we discover an odd
> little election is in progress. This is the selection, upon strictly demo-
> cratic lines, with a suffrage that includes every permanent resident in the
> Lucerne ward over the age of fifteen, of the ugliest local building.[10]

Wells revisited his fantasy Switzerland on the eve of the Great War. In
World Set Free (1913) he imagines, years before the Treaty of Versailles or
the United Nations, a futuristic conference of world leaders taking place
in 1959. They convene at what appears to be Monte Verità, in the great
grass meadow where communards danced nude under the moon and wor-
shipped the sun during daylight hours:

> On the mountain-side above the town of Brissago and commanding two
> long stretches of Lake Maggiore, looking eastward to Bellinzona, and
> southward to Luino, there is a shelf of grass meadows which is very beau-
> tiful in springtime with a great multitude of wild flowers. ... This desolate
> and austere background contrasts very vividly with the glowing serenity of
> the great lake below, with the spacious view of fertile hills and roads and
> villages and islands to south and east, and with the hotly golden rice flats
> of the Val Maggia to the north.[11]

Rudolf Laban and his dancers at Monte Verità

Humanity, however, was not saved and the great debacle of civilization ensued – and yet another war after that. The remains of the old heliotherapy beds are still there in the long grass, and the sun hasn't budged. 'The hotly golden rice flats of the Val Maggia' is an inspired phrase, and wonderful risotto is still served up all along the valley. Wells saw Switzerland as a land of peaceful plenty, a refuge from a world going to hell in a handcart. He observed those Swiss qualities of soulless organisation – everything in order – and God's grandeur in the landscape. They were qualities attractive to a boy who had pulled himself up by his bootstraps in middle England.

Wells is not the only English writer who came under the sway of Swiss utopian experiments before the First World War. In September 1913, D.H. Lawrence visited Ascona en route from Bavaria to Italy, a walk he recounted in *Twilight in Italy* (1916). He had left England with Frieda Weekly, née Frieda von Richthofen. She was six years older than him, already married and the mother of three young children. He was the 'stripling lover', a coal miner's son from Nottingham, and she the 'mother goddess', daughter of a baron. Frieda became Lawrence's muse. A year after his Alpine walk, confined to England by the war, Lawrence must have missed the sunny south:

> *When I went from Constance, it was on a small steamer down the Rhine to Schaffhausen. That was beautiful. Still, the mist hung over the waters, over the wide shallows of the river, and the sun, coming through the morning, made lovely yellow lights beneath the bluish haze, so that it seemed like the beginning of the world.*[12]

Another disreputable exile, Norman Douglas, is right to claim Lawrence as one of our great painters of landscape in words. Lawrence took against bourgeois Zürich and the huckster-innkeeper quality he perceived in Switzerland. *Twilight in Italy* is filled with his mood swings:

> One gets this feeling always in Switzerland, except high up: this feeling of average, of utter soulless ordinariness, something intolerable. Mile after mile, to Zürich, it was just the same. It was just the same in the tram-car going into Zürich ... The horrible average ordinariness of it all, something utterly without flower or soul or transcendence, the horrible vigorous ordinariness, is too much.[13]

He walked the right bank of Zürich Lake to a village with a silk-weaving factory, employing Italian migrant workers. In the mid-nineteenth century, Canton Zürich was the second-largest silk producer in the world, renowned for its black taffeta. Lawrence appears to have caroused and bedded down in Pfäffikon:

> They could only give me boiled ham: so I ate boiled ham and drank beer, and tried to digest the utter cold materialism of Switzerland.[14]

He teams up with factory workers rehearsing a play in the back room. He finds them lively, loud and warm, in contrast to the 'cold German-Swiss' with their 'ugly dialect'. Later, repairing to a more convivial Italian-frequented inn, he describes it as 'a warm, ruddy bit of Italy within the cold darkness of Switzerland'. The miner's son from Nottingham (he uses the same combination of adjectives, 'warm, ruddy', to describe his father) has happened upon Italian anarchists escaping conscription on the eve of the First World War:

> He gave me a copy of a little Anarchist paper published in Geneva. L'Anarchista, I believe it was called. I glanced at it. It was in Italian, naïve, simple, rather rhetorical. So they were all Anarchists, these Italians.[15]

It's a Sunday and Lawrence is on the road to Lucerne. His boots are chafing. He has another little rant to himself about the 'Sunday nullity':

> There was fat agricultural land and several villages. And church was over. The church-goers were all coming home: men in black broadcloth and old

chimney-pot silk hats, carrying their umbrellas; women in ugly dresses, carrying books and umbrellas. The streets were dotted with these black-clothed men and stiff women, all reduced to a Sunday nullity. I hated it. It reminded me of that which I knew in my boyhood, that stiff, null 'propriety' which used to come over us, like a sort of deliberate and self-inflicted cramp, on Sundays. I hated these elders in black broadcloth, with their neutral faces, going home piously to their Sunday dinners. I hated the feeling of these villages, comfortable, well-to-do, clean, and proper.[16]

As consolation to the Swiss, Lawrence had an even more bad-tempered view of the English:

Curse the blasted, jelly-boned swines, the slimy, the belly-wriggling inver-tebrates, the miserable sodding rotters, the flaming sods, the sniveling, dribbling, dithering palsied pulse-less lot that make up England today. They've got white of egg in their veins, and their spunk is that watery it's a marvel they can breed. They can nothing but frog-spawn – the gibberers! God, how I hate them! God curse them, funkers. God blast them, wish-wash. Exterminate them, slime.[17]

At one point he impersonates *Naturmensch* Gusto Gräser: 'I said I was from Graz; that my father was a doctor in Graz, and that I was walking for my pleasure through the countries of Europe.'[18] Lawrence blows hot and cold about mercantile Swiss towns and inns. Despite the ranting, his quick sketches of landladies and innkeepers capture a unique spirit of place. In a sentence or two he can sum up a locale like no one else:

Everywhere are the hotels and the foreigners, the parasitism. Yet there is, unseen, this overshadowed, overhung, sordid mountain population, ledged on the slopes and in the crevices. In the wider valleys there is still a sense of cowering among the people. But they catch a new tone from their contact with the foreigners. And in the towns are nothing but tradespeople.[19]

Ascending towards Andermatt and the Gotthard Pass, he describes per-fectly the 'winter's broken detritus' of the high mountains, where winter and snow lend a makeshift aspect to human settlement.

I went through the little, hideous, crude factory-settlement in the high val-ley, where the eternal snows gleamed, past the enormous advertisements for

*chocolate and hotels, up the last steep slope of the pass to where the tunnel
begins. Göschenen, the village at the mouth of the tunnel, is all railway sid-
ings and haphazard villas for tourists, post cards and touts and weedy car-
riages; disorder and sterile chaos, high up. How should anyone stay there!*[20]

He spurns Andermatt with characteristic spite and spleen, settling for a
Gästezimmer in Hospental, in the lee of the pass, well out of the way of civilisation. It is perhaps as well that his landlady is partially deaf. Lawrence is
appreciative of her dinner and the humble, clean dwelling house, cutting
to the quick of experience in rhythmic lyrical prose. Reading him, I inevita-
bly think of my old English professor at Maynooth, Pete Connolly, praising
the felt life phrase by phrase, sentence by sentence, in his best Leavisite
manner, pencil hovering.

The next morning Lawrence crosses the Gotthard Pass with a
seventeen-year-old clerk from Basel, on a week's holiday. They discuss
Swiss military service. Paying tribute to south-facing Airolo, Lawrence
floors us with another perfect, almost monosyllabic sentence: 'It is as if the
god Pan really had his home among these sun-bleached stones and tough,
sun-dark trees.'[21] He notices strip mining and the ugly housing blocks of
the workers. In their horror at the destruction wrought by industrialisa-
tion, both Lawrence and Wells hark back to Dickens and Blake: 'Life is
now a matter of selling oneself to slave-work, building roads or labouring
in quarries or mines or on the railways, purposeless, meaningless, really
slave-work.'[22] Their environmental and existential despair heralds a money-
grubbing age: 'Down the road of the Ticino valley I felt again my terror of
this new world which is coming into being on top of us.'[23]

Dance was an important part of the *Lebensreform* movement in Switzerland
in the early decades of the twentieth century. The American dancer Isadora
Duncan visited Ascona a number of times. She and her brother Raymond
liked to dress in the Grecian manner. Californian by birth, they were vegetarians based in Berlin and later in Paris. I remember parties at the Duncan
house on rue de Seine in the 1970s when some member of the family would
don robes and dance in the small hours through the dope smoke, in the
freezing rooms. Isadora was an early feminist, infamous in her heyday
for young lovers and a dissolute lifestyle – a bit like Michael Jackson or
Madonna in ours. She died tragically in a car accident, strangled by her

scarf. Ascona locals used to buy tickets to the roof of the Villa Semiramis to spy on the nudists and dancers in the park of Monte Verità.

Hermann Hesse lived for forty-three years across the lake from Monte Verità, in the Casa Camuzzi at Montagnola, following the break-up of his first marriage in 1919. Casa Camuzzi sits atop a peninsula with panoramic views across the Alps and the lake. Beatle George Harrison also bought a last home in Montagnola, near his oncology clinic, and recorded his final tracks there, before heading to California to die in 2001. The rock star and Hesse both shared a taste for orientalism and an eye for property values.

In *Klingsor's Last Summer* (1920), Hesse describes the wonderful stepped garden of the Villa Camuzzi:

> Below him, dizzyingly precipitate, the old terrace gardens dropped away, a densely shadowed tangle of treetops, palms, cedars, chestnuts, Judas trees, red beech, and eucalyptus, intertwined with climbing plants, lianas, wisterias. Above the blackness of the trees the large glossy leaves of the summer magnolias gleamed pallidly, the huge snow-white blossoms half-shut among them, large as human heads, pale as moon and ivory. From the massed leafage, penetrating and rousing, a tartly sweet smell of lemons drifted towards him.[24]

Hesse is best remembered for *Siddhartha* (1922), *Steppenwolf* (1927) and *The Glass Bead Game* (1943), all of which chart spiritual quests. Hesse's father was a missionary of Estonian origin. His mother was born in India and spent her first four years there, the daughter of a noted orientalist. The writer was born in 1877, in the northern reaches of the Black Forest. Like his father, he took Russian nationality. He became a Swiss citizen for the first time at age six when his father was attached to the Basel Mission. Hermann Hesse always looked on his adopted city with affection:

> And the vast and, for someone as small as me, infinitely large open space on Schützenmatte, then still undeveloped land, extending from the Schützenhaus out to Neubad, was my butterfly hunting ground and the scene of our cowboy and Indian games. Many of the recollections from this period are captured in the childhood chapter of Hermann Lauscher. Gradually, on Sunday walks with my father, I got to know the centre of town better, the Rhine with the ferry at Blumenrain and the bridges, the Münster and the Pfalz, the Kreuzgang, the historical museum, which was then in the building over the Kreuzgang.[25]

Swabian by culture and accent, Hesse's stamping ground was the Upper Rhine, its ferries, marketplaces and Black Forest hinterland:

> This region in southwestern Germany/Switzerland is my home, and the fact that the region is crisscrossed by several state borders and one Reich frontier is something I was often made to feel quite acutely in both minor and more major matters, yet I have, in the inmost depths of my being, never been able to consider these borders to be natural ... For me, home meant both sides of the Upper Rhine, whether the area be called Switzerland, Baden or Württemberg.[26]

Young intellectuals of the late nineteenth century were influenced by the ideas of Ruskin and Tolstoy. They wanted to get back to the land, to ape the ways of the peasant, like their counterparts in the 1960s in lumberjack shirts and dungarees.

At the Casa Camuzzi Hesse rented four rooms overlooking the garden with its magnolia and Judas trees:

> a little city and a landscape where years ago I had known intimately every small stream and gully, every fieldstone wall with cracks full of little ferns and wood pinks, a landscape that three times during the war sheltered and comforted me and made me happy and thankful once more.[27]

Separation from wife and family played their part in his retreat. His third son succumbed to a serious illness. Hesse himself underwent psychoanalysis and treatment for alcoholism. *Steppenwolf* is the fruit of his psychological breakdown and the failure of his second marriage in the mid-1920s. Its double motif – man and wolf – and the gothic-horror atmosphere remind us of those other Swiss creations, *Frankenstein* and *The Vampyre*. A deranged world of drugs, jazz and 'Americanised men' characterises Harry Haller's mid-life crisis. Harry thinks of himself as a wolf of the steppes, outside civilisation, prey to animal desires, preying in turn on fellow men and women. He has a bad case of schizophrenia, alcohol abuse and psychobabble, all of which plagued Hesse himself. *Steppenwolf* was written in Basel, in Room 401 of the Hotel Krafft overlooking the river, and finished in Zürich.

Harry wanders the night streets 'above the Rhine', frequenting drinking and dancing dens, encountering barflies, a goodtime girl called Hermine and a dealer-trumpeter called Pablo. Harry doesn't quite go howling down the street, but he suffers from delusions: 'A wolf of the Steppes that had lost its way and strayed into the towns and the life of the herd'. He likes to rant, to vent his spleen, and I've often thought that there is something of the failed priest, the pastor manqué about Hesse:

> For what I always hated and detested and cursed above all things was this contentment, this healthiness and comfort, this carefully preserved optimism of the middle classes, this fat and prosperous brood of mediocrity.[28]

Hesse was approaching fifty when he wrote *Steppenwolf* and it is imbued with the travails of middle age coming to terms with what the young people are up to – the new jazz, new drugs, new dances. It's a last waltz before heading for the mountains. Harry can't help moralising and lamenting the American century becoming apparent after the First World War:

> One half of this music, the melody, was all pomade and sugar and sentimentality. The other half was savage, temperamental and vigorous. Yet the two went artlessly together and made a whole. It was the music of decline. There must have been such music in Rome under the later emperors. ... There was something of the Negro in it, something of the American, who with all his strength seems so boyishly fresh and child-like to us Europeans. Was Europe to become the same? Was it on the way already? Were we, the old connoisseurs, the reverers of Europe as it used to be, of genuine music and poetry as once they were, nothing but a pig-headed minority of complicated neurotics who would be forgotten or derided tomorrow?[29]

Once Hesse got this novel out of his system, he seems to have settled down to alternative living and a happy third marriage in 1931. His reputation as a writer sits uneasy, both in the German- and the English-speaking worlds. In the counter-cultural 1960s, however, his brand of oriental enlightenment was shaken out once more and given an airing. Enamoured of the spiritual seeker, the traveller in touch with nature, Hesse peoples his writing with craftsmen, journeymen, maverick tramps. Read in adolescence, he represents an invitation to the vagabond life, but one returns to him in middle age with a sinking feeling. Graham Greene nails it: 'one can cease to be in love as easily as one can outgrow an author one admired as a boy'.[30]

After *The Glass Bead Game* (1943) Hesse stopped writing novels. He wore homespun linen and started painting with fervour. His gouaches, in a palette of oranges and blues rather like his prose, are almost entirely devoid of people, but capture the light and warmth of the Ticino landscape. The novels he wrote in the Casa Camuzzi, in his distinctive old world copper-plate, give off a golden hue as well.

> I was now a little, penniless, literary man, a threadbare and rather dubious stranger who lived on milk and rice and macaroni, who wore his old suits till they were threadbare and in the fall brought home his supper of chest-nuts from the forest. But the experiment, which was the point of it all, suc-ceeded, and despite everything that was difficult in those years, they were beautiful and fruitful. It was like waking from a nightmare that had lasted for years. I inhaled freedom, the air, the sun, I had solitude and my work.[31]

In summer he retreated with his third wife to the Hotel Waldhaus in Sils Maria, escaping the tourists invading Ticino after the Second World War. And from time to time he would descend on Zürich:

> Zürich, of course, is one of those words that has a different meaning for each person. For me it has meant for years something Asiatic. I have friends there who lived for many years in Siam, and at their house among a hundred memories of India, of the sea, and of distant places, I descended, welcomed by the smell of rice and curry, beamed at by a golden Siamese temple cabinet, observed by the still, bronze Buddha. To wander out from this exotic cave into the elegant modern world of music, exhibitions, and the theater, even to the cinema, was for several days once more a pure delight.[32]

Hesse died in Montagnola in 1962 at the age of eighty-five. Readers in the 1960s saw his luminous work in a trippy light and regarded the old German journeyman-sage as a mentor. Unlike the free-loving communards of Monte Verità, he had survived both world wars.

A.S. Byatt, in *The Children's Book* (2009), is the latest writer to fall under the spell of the Monte Verità commune:

> They danced there. Rudolf Laban later led his chain of naked maenads celebrating sunrise by the lake, in the meadows. Lawrence and Frieda came there, Hermann Hesse and Isadora Duncan. The anarchist Eric Mühsam came and the psychoanalyst Otto Gross, whose father, a crim-inologist, wanted him locked up for lewdness and drugs. Everyone wore sandals, like pilgrims, like apostles, like ancient Greeks.[33]

Heliotherapy beds at Monte Verità

Byatt takes her Fabian characters, Major Cain and his daughter, up to the sun-kissed meadow:

> *Major Cain had discovered that it was new, and austere, giving courses in sunbathing, mud-baths, water and a strictly vegetarian diet, with no eggs, milk or salt. ... A cottage was rented on the mountain slope, looking out over a meadow; a manservant was engaged, with a pony-carriage, and a string of young women were interviewed as housekeeper-companions.*[34]

Daughter Florence is an unmarried mother-to-be. She 'spends her days purifying herself with vegetable juice, and water, and lying in the sun in a linen gown, on a long, slatted daybed'. She meets a golden child, an angel, called, appropriately enough for an alchemist, Goldwasser, and quickly marries him. Ascona is just a way station, a refuge from the approaching Great War.

The old heliotherapy beds, nude dancing and vegetarianism limped on into the 1920s, but impetus waned. Hoffmann and Oedenkoven emigrated to Brazil where they founded further utopias. The First World War swept away the imperial culture against which the communards had revolted. Members of the Dada movement were frequent visitors to Monte Verità. A

The elusive Baron Eduard von der Heydt in Ascona, 1930

cast of political and artistic luminaries passed through Ascona: Lenin, Carl
Jung, Wassily Kandinsky, Paul Klee. But by 1920 it was a spent force.

Baron Eduard von der Heydt, a German banker and art collector,
bought Monte Verità in 1926. Long a patron of Berlin's artistic circles, he
had just separated from his wife Vera. (There is some evidence that the
marriage was morganatic.) The Baron engaged architect Emil Fahrenkamp
and began the construction of the present-day hotel, conceived as a world-
lier utopia than the collection of villas and shacks that had housed the
earlier radicals. The building, recently restored, is a striking piece of classic Bauhaus architecture, with pristine lines and aseptic interiors. Like so
many historic buildings in Switzerland, it is a spa, conference centre and
luxury hotel rolled into one.

The Baron consorted with all and sundry. His wife was Jewish. Hanna
Solf, later a leading anti-Nazi conspirator, visited in the 1920s. Prince Auwi,
the Nazi-supporting son of Kaiser Wilhelm II, was the Baron's friend.
During World War II, Monte Verità housed Jewish refugee children, as it
had housed refugees during the First World War and Russian revolutionaries dating back to the time of Bakunin in the 1870s.

But what should we make of the elusive Baron? Was he gay? Was
he simply a blithe spirit? Blithe spirits do not become bankers, losing
and making fortunes twice over. In period photographs he wears white

Sketch of Emil Fahrenkamp's Bauhaus-style hotel built in 1927 on Monte Verità

homespun shorts and T-shirt, curiously modern and unstructured, and carries a parasol over his deep tan. He looks like someone on dress-down Friday rather than one of the richest collectors of his day. He sits cross-legged like a teenager at a party, in the company of the great and the good between the wars.

After the war, the Baron's relations with Nazi officialdom came under Swiss scrutiny. He had rejoined the Nazi Party in 1933 and took Swiss citizenship in 1937. Swiss authorities accused him of treason (for violating neutrality by passing funds), but he was eventually acquitted. A declassified document from no less a source than J. Edgar Hoover attests to his 'being a German espionage agent remitting funds to other German agents operating in the United States and Mexico'.[35]

Following the Baron's acquittal, Monte Verità became the property of Canton Ticino. His considerable art collection, donated to the city of Zürich in 1945, forms the basis of the present Museum Rietberg. The Von der Heydt Museum in Wuppertal also has a rich collection of mostly oriental artworks. Was a deal struck with the Swiss authorities – acquittal in exchange for art? The museum in Zürich comes clean about the Baron's Nazi allegiance. but it is clear who has benefited: 'The judgement, therefore, was lenient and influenced by concern for his patronage. Had von der Heydt been found guilty, he would have lost his Swiss citizenship and he would probably have left Switzerland and taken his artworks out of the country.'[36] The museum is a big supporter of provenance research.

A certain irony attends a high-level meeting in October 1997 at Monte Verità, convened by the Bergier Commission to report on the so-called Nazi gold, *Raubengeld*, and Jewish dormant accounts. Representatives of the US Jewish community sought to bring to a close a decades-long struggle to unearth the truth about Swiss banking conduct during the war and to seek reparations. And so H.G. Wells' dream of a peace conference among the nudists, vegetarians and nature lovers came eventually to pass. What began as a utopian experiment in the last decades of the nineteenth century ended in a post-war Swiss quagmire of bankers, funny money and dodgy art.

6

KEEPING THE WARS AT ARM'S LENGTH

James Joyce's wanderlust in Zürich

Sketch by Frank Budgen showing himself and James Joyce in Zürich
during the First World War

Think you're escaping and run into yourself. Longest way round is the shortest way home.
James Joyce

When James Joyce and Nora Barnacle first arrived in Zürich, on the morning of 11 October 1904, they were living on borrowed funds. Joyce was wearing another man's boots. Eloping from Ireland, via Paris, they took a room in the Gasthaus Hoffnung at 16 Reitergasse in Zürich. This was where the young lovers consummated their union. *Hoffnung* (hope) often proved elusive during the decades ahead, but they were to stick by each other through poverty, two world wars, family crisis and literary fame. They were to find themselves back in Zürich again and again, always by the skin of their teeth.

The proprietor of the guesthouse behind the station was called Döblin, a name the superstitious Joyce appreciated. Under the impression a job was waiting for him at the Berlitz School, Joyce next morning discovered to his dismay there was no such thing. The Director did his best to find the penniless Irish graduate a teaching position in Switzerland, but without success.

Writing to his brother Stanislaus, Joyce emphasised shortage of funds and the secrecy surrounding his elopement: 'Go about the highways of the city but not to any of my touched friends and make up £1 before Saturday which send me on that day without fail.'[1] The twenty-two-year-old couldn't resist a laddish boast: 'Finalement, elle n'est pas encore vièrge; elle est *touchée.*'

The lovers spent a week in Zürich, kicking their heels. Eventually a vacancy turned up in Trieste on the Adriatic. They were off again. That vacancy too proved as elusive as the Swiss one and they continued down the coast to Pola. It was to be a vagabond life.

A decade later, in July 1914, Austria declared war on Serbia. In August, Great Britain entered the war. As holders of British passports, the Joyces in Austro-Hungarian Trieste grew worried. Joyce's brother was interned as an enemy alien in January 1915. In May of that year, Italy mobilised its army, prompting anti-Italian demonstrations in Trieste. Despite the encroaching debacle, Joyce was gestating the novel that would make his name and send its own salvoes across the literary landscape. In a letter to Ezra Pound, he

informed the poet that he had already completed the first two episodes of
Ulysses (1922).

> And so, on 28 June 1915, leaving behind all their furniture and belong-
> ings, the Joyce family were able to leave for Zürich from the Southern
> Railway Station. Weighed down with suitcases, which fortunately were
> not checked by the Austrian police at the border, they took a train bound
> for Innsbruck through the Brenner Pass. They were to come back for less
> than nine months at the end of the war after Trieste had become Italian,
> but only to depart once more, in 1920, for Paris. Never to return.[2]

Their train was detained at Innsbruck to allow the emperor's train to pass.
Joyce had declared earlier in Trieste: 'Kings are mountebanks. Republics
are slippers for everyone's feet.' Nonetheless, his eleven years in Trieste
under Austro-Hungarian rule – 'Each archduke proud, the whole jimbang
crowd'[3] – had been benign.

The Joyces returned for a nostalgic stay in Gasthaus Hoffnung before
settling into Zürich for the duration of the war. In the interim two children
had been born, Joyce had matured as a writer and the realities of poverty, drink and prostitutes had strained his and Nora's relationship. It had
been a scramble to get out of Trieste, then the principal port of the Austro-
Hungarian Empire. Sales of *Dubliners* (1914) stood at 499 copies. The manuscript of 'Stephen Hero', tinkered with in 1904, had become A *Portrait of
the Artist as a Young Man* (1916). Published serially in *The Egoist*, it was a
succès d'estime. Five publishers turned it down and seven printers refused
to set up the type. Joyce had to wait until the last days of 1916 for book
publication. His novel of growing up in Dublin in the last decades of the
nineteenth century sank virtually unnoticed during the First World War.

Shortly after arriving in Zürich, Joyce was awarded £75 from the Royal
Literary Fund, and so buttoned his lip as regards mountebanks. He was
granted a Civil List fund in 1916 as well as other monies privately donated
to an author who was beginning to attract notice. In 1904 and on this occasion in 1915 he had arrived in Zürich skint. By the time he left for Paris in
1920, he had moved from poverty into a qualified bourgeoisie, at home with
some but not all of the *bürgerlich* habits of the banking city.

Zürich during the First World War was awash with refugees and war
profiteers – a vibrant hodgepodge of pacifists, revolutionaries, anarchists
and artists who kept the Swiss police in shoe leather. Lenin arrived in 1916,
taking a room one hundred yards from the Cabaret Voltaire where the

Dada movement held noisy court. Switzerland had long been a crucible of Russian revolutionary thought, hosting such firebrands as Alexander Herzen, Mikhail Bakunin, Piotr Kropotkin, Rosa Luxembourg and Lenin. Many of them were shielded from Siberian exile by Switzerland's tolerance and judicial system. Lenin was a habitué of the Café Odéon and most likely rubbed shoulders there with Joyce. The political revolutionary was more outspoken about his hosts than the Irish writer:

> *Switzerland is the most revolutionary country in the world... There is only one slogan that you should spread quickly in Switzerland and in all other countries: armed insurrection!*[4]

No wonder the Swiss were keen to see him safely across the border. After the abdication of Tsar Nicholas II in 1917, Lenin boarded a sealed train in Zürich that took him across Germany to the Finland Station. The rest, as they say, is history.

From a provincial town, Zürich had grown to become *the* centre of European modernism. Partly this had to do with the influx of German and other refugees – Joyce, Frank Wedekind, Tristan Tzara, Stefan Zweig and the painters Wassily Kandinsky and Jean Arp. Partly too it was because theatres were closed or restricted elsewhere. Little of this ferment was homegrown. Hugo Ball and Emmy Hennings, the wild spirits behind Dada, were German pacifists. Carl Jung's theories derived from the Viennese Sigmund Freud. The Swiss themselves were suspicious of the backwash of foreigners and showed scant interest in their avant-garde activities. Police files during these years followed émigré movements, as they did during the Second World War.

Zürich was where Joyce got down to writing *Ulysses*. The germ for the novel had come to him during an aborted stay in Rome, and its last line – 'Trieste, Zürich, Paris' – is, as Alain de Botton says, 'a symbol of the cosmopolitan spirit behind its composition'.[5] Leopold Bloom, its urban Jewish protagonist, borrows characteristics from Joyce's friends and acquaintances in the rump of the Austro-Hungarian empire. But Bloom has a bit of Zürich in him too – modernist multi-culti Zürich, the Zürich of the *flâneur* as well as the banker. Joyce's friends in the Swiss city were mostly Jews, Greeks and displaced Austro-Hungarians, as they had been in Trieste.

> *Behind him Zürich, suddenly confronted by this and other manifestations of a revolutionary spirit, sat like some austere grandmother, long since inured and indifferent to the babbling of unfamiliar progeny.*[6]

Café Odéon in Zürich, frequented by Lenin and Joyce

Joyce's Zürich drinking haunts signal his relative affluence. Whereas in Trieste he had frequented sailors' dens in the port, in Zürich a better class of establishment came to the fore: the restaurant Zum Roten Kreuz, the Café Terrasse and the Café Odéon. In *The End of the World News* (1982), Anthony Burgess imagines Lenin and Joyce at nearby tables in Zum Roten Kreuz, both plotting revolution in two different dimensions. Together with Joyce's regular haunt, the Pfauen Café, these locales hosted a medley of polyglot drinking, singing and repartee. As the Swiss writer Dürrenmatt reminds us, the Hapsburgs originated just outside of town, and Zürich can strike the visitor as the most western of the *Mitteleuropa* cities.

Many of Joyce's hostelries still flourish a century later. The Café Odéon, reduced to a third its original size, is usually crowded with shoppers and cappuccino drinkers – bags and dogs at their feet – rather than the radical loudmouths of the early twentieth century. In winter there's a smell of wet cashmere. Gilt mirrors and brassy bar have seen generations come and go through the stained glass doors. Across the road, the Café Terrasse is also crowded. The pastries are good, the décor a bit doily. Gone are the newspapers on batons, that quintessential feature of the central European coffeehouse, but laptops are in evidence. Oompa music on public squares

has been replaced by ringtones at tables. Joyce's bars have weathered revo-
lutions and wars and come up in the world in the meantime.

The Joyce family viewed Zürich as an interlude that stretched to four
years, intending to return to furniture and pictures in Trieste as soon as the
First World War had ended. But nobody knew when that would be. They
occupied a number of furnished apartments in the course of their stay, the
longest at Universitätsstrasse 29. The language at home was a Triestine dialect of Italian, with Slavic undertones. Giorgio was turning ten when they
arrived in Zürich, and Lucia eight. They were put back two years in school,
as they knew no German. Joyce himself had quite good German – enough
to write lovelorn letters to his fancy women – but for Nora the language was
a trial. Market day in Locarno reminded her of Trieste: 'It was quite lively
to hear the men calling out the prices and making as much noise as they
could just like in Trieste.'[7]

Contact with other languages in the smithy of the Austro-Hungarian
Empire had made Joyce intensely aware of his own, its registers, dialects,
history and slang. He code shifted from Triestine Italian to Zürich German
to Modern Greek. *Ulysses* has the cosmopolitan soundscape of the war
years, its language a mixing board, its constituent parts broken down, like
notes, like an opera. On any given day in Zürich you never know what
languages you might encounter. Joyce became an auditor of the world's
sounds, at sea in the flotsam of language, adrift from meaning, aware of
multiple levels and the interpenetration of words. A tram bell. A cry in the
street. The murmur along a bar. Rutting in the next room. Vision reduced,
his ears took up the slack.

It was in Zürich that Joyce's eye troubles turned serious. His glaucoma
required an iridectomy, the first of eleven operations over the next fifteen
years. In 1917 he wrote to Pound:

> On Saturday when walking in the street I got suddenly a violent
> Hexenschuss which incapacitated me from moving for about twenty min-
> utes. I managed to crawl into a tram and get home. It got better in the
> evening but next day I had symptoms of glaucoma again – slightly better
> today. Tomorrow morning I am going to the Augenklinik. This climate is
> impossible for me so that, operated or not, I want to go away next month.
> I am advised to go to Italian Switzerland.[8]

Neither Joyce nor Nora adapted to Zürich's muggy climate after balmy seaside Trieste. In August 1917, Nora and the children went ahead to Locarno

while Joyce remained behind. On Bahnhofstrasse he suffered the episode of glaucoma described to Pound. The eye clinic operated successfully and Nora returned to comfort her husband. In the days following, Joyce wrote one of his more touching poems about loss of youthful vision and vim. 'Bahnhofstrasse' is named for Zürich's main thoroughfare, the most expensive shopping street in the world. He was only thirty-seven.

> Ah star of evil! star or pain!
> Highhearted youth comes not again
>
> Nor old heart's wisdom yet to know
> The signs that mock me as I go.

They wintered in Locarno, staying at the Pension Villa Rossa and later at the Pension Daheim. The nearby fishing village of Ascona was already an artists' colony. But Joyce grew bored in Locarno: he was a city boy at heart. Despite snow and an earthquake, he was able to complete there the three opening episodes of *Ulysses* – the manuscript title page bears the inscription 'Pension Daheim, Locarno, Switzerland'. Nora and the children relaxed into the Italian atmosphere, with its accents of home. Pizza was on the menu. Because of his glaucoma Joyce decided to forgo absinthe, his tipple at the time, for Swiss white wines. He settled on Fendant de Sion, comparing its golden hue to an Archduchess's piss: 'From now on the wine was known as the Archduchess, and is so celebrated in *Finnegans Wake*.'[9]

Glaucoma didn't prevent his other eye wandering. Two women took hold of Joyce's imagination, apart from Nora, during his stay in Switzerland. Both made their way into *Ulysses*, forming the composite figure of Gerty MacDowell showing her drawers to a masturbating Bloom.

Dr Gertrude Kaempffer was a twenty-six-year-old recovering from tuberculosis in Orselina above Locarno, where the Madonna del Sasso basilica commands the valley. When she rebuffed his initial advances, Joyce conducted an erotic correspondence with her from Zürich, using a *poste restante* address, as Bloom does in *Ulysses*. Joyce revealed to her his first sexual experience when he was fourteen while out walking with the family nanny through fields on the edge of a wood. The nanny was taken short and asked him to look the other way. She went off to pee. 'He heard the sound of liquid splashing on the ground ... The sound aroused him: "I jiggled furiously."'[10]

This information proved less stimulating to Dr Kaempffer than to the author of *Ulysses*, and so their correspondence fizzled out.

The second of Joyce's dalliances, Marthe Fleischmann, was closer to home. She lived around the corner from the Joyce flat at 29 Universitätsstrasse. Kitty-corner. Their windows were in sight of each other and he first spotted her as she was pulling the toilet chain. Joyce gives to the hero of *Finnegans Wake* an erotic interest in watching girls pee, and the author's correspondence with his wife Nora confirms this peccadillo. Marthe was attractive, had notions about herself and walked with a slight limp (as does Gerty in *Ulysses*). Joyce cast Marthe as the reincarnation of his youthful muse first spotted on Dublin's North Strand: girlish, birdlike, ethereal, her skirts hiked up. He began a correspondence in French with Marthe, deploying his usual Irish blether about Dante, Shakespeare and the Dark Lady of the Sonnets – and by the way, could we meet? He shaved two years off his age, continued ogling her through the window and sent her a copy of his wee book of poems, *Chamber Music*, named in jest for another piddling floozy.

They arranged to meet on his birthday – 2 February, Candlemas Day. Joyce borrowed his friend Frank Budgen's flat for the assignation. Smells and bells, a Hanukkah candelabra (Joyce thought she was of Jewish ancestry), the whole caboodle:

> By nightfall everything was ready. He had lit the candles both because they were romantic and because he wished to see his visitor in a flattering light. His Pagan Mary both yielded and withheld. He confided to Budgen when they met later on that he had 'explored the coldest and hottest parts of a woman's body'.[11]

Marthe was already a kept woman. She liked her airs and graces, and secreted rosewater hankies in her cleavage. But she wasn't averse to a bit of Joyce's dirty talk about undergarments. Her paramour ('*Vormund*') was an engineer named Rudolf Hiltpold, himself putting it about a bit with sundry mistresses, who soon got wind of the peeping Paddy next door. As Joyce expressed it militarily in a letter to Frank Budgen: 'Result, stasis: *Waffenstillstand.*'

It was Budgen with whom Joyce made a second visit to Locarno in May 1919. He was an ex-sailor, a painter and had modelled for the Swiss artist August Suter. He had an associative, imaginative mind, much like Joyce's. The allegorical figure representing Labour, wielding a hammer under the Uraniabrücke in Zürich, was modelled on Budgen, as was the sailor on a pack of Player's Navy Cut cigarettes. Joyce was continually looking for material to feed his mythopoeic imagination, even manipulating conversations to get it, as August Suter noticed: 'he imperceptively brought on conversation that he happened to need for his work'.[12]

On this second visit to Locarno, Joyce and Budgen encountered the Baroness St Leger, who lived on the tiny Isola di Brissago on Lago Maggiore. Joyce was working on the 'Circe' episode of *Ulysses*. Circe in Homer is a kind of temptress emasculator, with Odysseus as her captive toy-boy and her island as a *dolce far niente*. Joyce thought the Baroness might fit the bill: she had been thrice married. He dubbed her the 'Siren of the Lago Maggiore'.

A siren in winter, perhaps. The Baroness is one of those fascinating figures on the margins of writers' lives. She was born in St Petersburg in 1856 and was rumoured to be the illegitimate daughter of Tsar Alexander II. Her birth certificate gives her parents' names as Nicolas Alexandre and Maryam Meyer. Antoinetta was pretty and vivacious. Her piano teacher had been Franz Liszt. Two husbands quickly palled. Her third husband was the Anglo-Irish Lord Richard-Fleming Saint Leger, from Kingstown (Dun Laoghaire), apparently descended from Richard the Lionheart. They bought the two Brissago islands for 10,000 Swiss francs and the Baroness proceeded to import thousands of plants and turn the hideaway into a botanical paradise befitting the Mediterranean microclimate. Her other passion, like Circe's, was for young men; husband number three soon abandoned her in 1897.

By the time Joyce pitched up in 1919, she was sixty-three and as flighty as ever, coming over the water to greet him standing up in her boat. The poet Rilke, fond of people's castles as he was, had visited the Baroness the same year, so she had no shortage of scribbling admirers. She liked to make puppets and had hundreds of them on the island, which may indicate her psychological makeup.

Penniless in 1927, she was forced to sell her islands to the department store magnate Max Emden. He was German-Jewish and fed up with the retail business. (He was founder of the KaDeVe chain, still ringing the tills in Germany.) Emden is yet another maverick. On a good day he dressed in a kimono and did his yoga and meditation around the Roman baths he had built on the island. Curvaceous lovelies kept him company. There was nude water-skiing and slap and tickle among the guests. He was a department store Gatsby. Our Monte Verità art collector, Baron Eduard von der Heydt (more of a toga man), was an occasional poolside visitor. Emden died in 1940, after fifteen good years in a kimono. The Baroness outlived

PLAYER'S NAVY CUT CIGARETTES
MEDIUM OR MILD

Joyce's friend Frank Budgen in sailor suit

him, saw out two world wars as well as the Crimean War and the downfall of the Russian Empire, and died aged 92 in 1948 – still penniless, in an old people's home in Intragna.

Like many Swiss stories, this one has a sting in the tail. In 2012 the grandson of Max Emden, a Chilean, claimed ownership of Claude Monet's 'Poppy Fields at Vétheuil', valued at over €20 million. The Bührle Foundation in Zürich has the famous painting and is clear about its provenance. Max Emden's only son fled Switzerland for Chile at the beginning of the war and the painting was apparently sold to finance his escape from the Nazis. The German government has not ruled in favour of restitution.

Other details of Joyce's Swiss stay make their way into *Ulysses*. A visit to the Rhine falls near Schaffhausen found a faint echo in 'Circe'. Joyce's foray into am-dram, in setting up a troupe called the English Players, led to litigation with a functionary at the British consulate:

> *Up to rheumy Zürich town came an Irish man one day,*
> *And as the place was rather dull he thought he'd give a play,*
> *So that the German propagandists might be rightly riled,*
> *But the bully British Philistine once more drove Oscar Wilde.*[13]

Fritz Senn, the keeper of the flame at the James Joyce Foundation in Zürich, has uncovered numerous references to his city in *Ulysses* and

Department store magnate Max Emden bought the Brissago Islands and
took up yoga

Finnegans Wake. Zürich served as a refuge from the war and provided
Joyce with an atmosphere, an urban vibe and a cacophony of friends who
fuelled his masterpiece. When the Joyce family returned to Trieste in 1919,
it was not for long. It had become a backwater. Paris was the happening
place, and Zürich had whetted Joyce's appetite for it.

One evening, driving back to Switzerland, I tuned into France Musique
and immediately recognized the voice of Maria Jolas, resurrected from
the Paris of 1979. But it couldn't be, could it? She would have to be a
ghost, pushing a hundred and ten years of age. It turned out, however, to
be her musician daughter Betsy. The resemblance between their voices
was uncanny.

Born in 1893 in Kentucky, Maria Jolas accompanied James Joyce's pure
tenor voice in the 1920s and 1930s, when her husband, Eugene Jolas, was
publishing the Irish writer in the magazine *transition*. 'Carry me along,
Taddy, like you done through the toy fair!' Joyce writes on the last page
of *Finnegans Wake*. In her memoirs, Maria relates that it was *her* father,
carrying her through the Jefferson County Fair in Louisville, Kentucky.

Before the First World War she had seen Gustav Mahler conduct the New York Philharmonic and heard Caruso sing at the Met. In November 1913 she sailed to Bremen on the *Imperator* and drank hot bouillon on deck each morning of the ten-day voyage. In Berlin she studied singing and saw a revival of Frank Wedekind's play *Spring Awakening*.[14]

It was this play that she gave me sixty-five years later in 1979, when she was well into her eighties. I was working as a *surveillant* at an international school in Paris, so perhaps she thought I had need of Wedekind's scurrilous awakening. Maria had founded the first Bilingual School of Paris in Neuilly in 1932, which flourished until the Occupation. Usually around teatime I rose in the creaking lift to her apartment on rue de Rennes. I remember the sound of electric typing followed by her heavy tread on the parquet. She was protective of Joyce in his academic afterlife, but voluble nonetheless. A helmet of white hair, and the big-boned Kentucky frame, made her seem formidable. 'I used to know another Padraic, but he spelled it with a *c*,' she said, referring to the Irish poet Padraic Colum. She had been a militant dissenter to the US war in Vietnam, helping deserters who had drifted into Paris.[15] She roped me in to do some typing for her. Once, after a glass of sherry, she broke into 'The Lass of Aughrim', one of Joyce's favourites. She cited his reaction to the German soldiers in occupied Paris: 'what would they have been like if they were fed?'

Joyce was almost blind in those last months of 1940. He and his family were on the run from yet another war and biding their time with Jolas near Vichy, where she soldiered on with the remnants of her school:

> Then our students left little by little during the summer months. Little by little the anguished families were able to come to us – most of the time on bicycle – and before my departure from Vichy, on August 28, 1940, the last pupil was with his family, the last textbooks were put up in the attic, waiting until the school could open once more.[16]

The Swiss Federal Aliens' Police rejected Joyce's initial application for visas on the supposition that he and his family were Jews. The Swiss writer Jacques Mercanton put the authorities right on this point. Joyce himself privately declared that he 'was not a Jew from Judea but an Aryan from Erin'.[17] The mayor of Zürich, the rector of its university, the Swiss Society of Authors and other notables vouched for him. Cantonal authorities wanted a guarantee of 50,000 Swiss francs, later reduced to 20,000. The Joyce family eventually succeeded in gaining entry permits.

In December 1940 they came into Switzerland by way of Geneva, where Stephen Joyce, the writer's eight-year-old grandson, had his bicycle impounded at the border because of inability to pay import duties.[18] They spent the night of 14 December at the Richemonde Hotel, before moving on to Lausanne. Sean Lester, acting Secretary-General of the League of Nations and a Belfast man, had tea with the Joyce family on the Sunday afternoon, in the marble and ormolu salon of their hotel:

The famous Joyce is tall, slight, in the fifties, blue eyes and a good thatch of hair. No one would hesitate in looking at him to recognize his nationality and his accent as Dublin as when he left it over thirty years ago. His eyesight is very bad and he told me it had been saved some years ago for him by the famous Vogt of Zürich, who had also operated on de Valera [President of Ireland and statesman]. His son, seemingly in his late twenties, came in first. A fine, well-built fellow, with a peculiar hybrid accent in English. He told me he is a singer and has sung in Paris and New York.[19]

The Richemonde sits one block back from the more illustrious Hotel Beau Rivage on Geneva's lakeshore. The Beau Rivage is where royalty stayed, where Empress Sisi of Austria-Hungary died from a madman's stiletto, where Somerset Maugham and other international spies kept their ears open. The Richemonde is equally glitzy: Charlie Chaplin, Sophia Loren and Michael Jackson found rooms with a view there. It's a historic corner overlooking Brunswick Monument – a history not lost on James Joyce. As a boy he had lived on Dublin's North Richmond Street. Great Brunswick Street was where he sang in the Antient Concert Rooms at the beginning of the century. The Joyce family might have felt they were once again at history's mercy.

Finnegans Wake (1939), seventeen years in the writing, had received a puzzled reception the previous year. Needing two magnifying glasses to read and write, Joyce was addicted to Radio Éireann. Since 1920, he, Nora and their two children had been living in Paris, where the writer had achieved fame and squandered some fortune. Now Paris was occupied and they were on the move once more.

They were going to settle in Zürich, where they had some good friends. I said I thought it was an unusual place for him to choose and asked, what about Suisse Romande? His wife then intervened and said that Zürich had always been associated with certain crises in their life: they

had rushed from Austria at the beginning of the last war and had lived
in Zürich very comfortably; they had spent their honeymoon there; it was
there that Joyce's eyesight had been saved and now they were going back
in another crisis. They liked the solid virtues of the people.[20]

It was those solid Swiss virtues that supported them as the world turned
once more towards war. When they returned to Zürich in December 1940,
it must have seemed like déjà vu. Not more bloody Swiss German, Nora
might have thought – it was her fourth language. Friends met them at the
Hauptbahnhof. Staying at the Hotel Pension Delphin on Muhlebachstrasse,
Joyce wrote to the Mayor of Zürich to thank him:

The connection between me and your hospitable city extends over a
period of nearly forty years and in these painful times I feel honoured
that I should owe my presence here in large part to the personal guaranty
of Zürich's first citizen.[21]

The Joyce family celebrated Christmas with friends. He walked out in the
snow in the afternoons with his grandson Stephen, to the confluence of
the Sihl and the Limmat rivers, where today the spot has an inscription
from *Finnegans Wake*: 'Yssel that the limmat?' and 'legging a jig or so on
the sihl'.

On a grey Saturday in April I arrange to meet Paul Doolan for lunch at
the Kronenhalle, where Joyce ate his last dinner. The bistro has priceless
art on the walls – we're seated under a Chagall – and has been feeding
artists from Joyce to Picasso to Dürrenmatt and Frisch for over a century.
Paul is an old friend from my Japan days in the 1990s, and now teaches
history at Zürich International School. When I first met him and his wife
Esther they were footloose and fancy free, but since then three daughters
have come along. We're old Leftie intellectuals and have weathered what
Orwell calls 'the smelly little orthodoxies contending for our souls'. Paul
conducts tours around the city's nooks and crannies and I want him to walk
me around some of Joyce's old haunts.

We order, and talk books, as we usually do, and whine about our respec-
tive schools, their new buzzwords ('protocols' in his, 'concepts' in mine)
and office politics. We teach in vivariums of privilege and try to put some
polish on the wealthy. And we endure: two middle-aged humanists skulking along the edges of a managerial culture. Around a million Saturday
lunch tables a similar tone must sound; only the details differ. Madame

Frank Budgen in birthday suit for this August Suter statue near
Zürich's Uraniabrücke

Meyer comes over to say hello and to see if everything is OK and to crack
a joke about Scotland.

After lunch we cross the street to check on a couple of Joyce's former hangouts. Paul's daughter sometimes has a pricey brunch in the
Terrasse Café. He tells me she's up in the University Library revising
for her Baccalaureate exams – it's where Joyce researched *Ulysses* – and
then a minute later there she is, a trilingual eighteen-year-old in brief
sunshine, out for coffee with her friends. The Pfauen has shut – it used
to have a fine hanging sign – but the Schauspielhaus right next door,
where Brecht's *Mother Courage* got its premiere, is still packing them in.
One of Joyce's old apartments has gone, Paul tells me, bulldozed by the
developers.

We cross under the Uraniabrücke and run into one of Paul's philosophy
students, sitting cross-legged on a wall and reading Freud's *Civilization and
Its Discontents*. We gaze up at Frank Budgen, Joyce's model friend, in the
stony buff. Imagine having to go past yourself like that every day? I say.
Finally we check the dates on the plaque in front of Lenin's old apartment
and I head off on my own down to the confluence of the Limmat and the
Sihl rivers, where Joyce liked to walk.

Together with Thomas Mann and Vladimir Nabokov, Joyce is one of the twentieth century's literary greats. All three were marked by history. As Joyce fled Vichy France for Zürich, Nabokov boarded the boat for America and Mann took refuge in California. They all eventually found peace and quiet to write in Switzerland, sometimes engaging but more often disengaging from the conflicts that surrounded them. Nabokov's final resting place is at Clarens above Lac Léman. Mann is buried at Kilchberg across the lake from Joyce, who died on 13 January 1941, age 59. The great modernist is buried next to Nora in Zürich's Fluntern Cemetery, within a lion's roar of the zoo.

The American century that followed the First World War ushered in a brasher class of writer. Kitted out to ski and party, flush with dollars, monolingual, Hemingway and Fitzgerald brought a breath of victory to Switzerland's valleys. Spilling over from the Roaring Twenties, these writers sought hot water, room service and clean martinis in a string of ski stations and lakeside hideaways. They gave Switzerland a run with their money.

7

LOONY BINS AND FINISHING SCHOOLS

*Hemingway, Fitzgerald and the Chalet School girls
on the slippery slopes*

Four climbers descend the Wildstrubel in Gstaad the hard way, 1912

*Switzerland is a country where very few things begin, but many
things end.*
F. Scott Fitzgerald

A magnum of Roederer champagne and three flutes sat on the tray,
when the dirndl-wrapped waitress brought my eleven o'clock coffee
in the Hermitage Hotel in Schönreide. Leaning over, she kept the
whole thing in expert balance. A few minutes later I heard a discreet pop
from the terrace and a rich murmur of voices.

I was escaping for a few hours from ski camp. After breakfast, the camp
cook, Armand, had settled in at the picture window of the chalet cafeteria
and we chatted in a mixture of French and English. Gstaad sat snug in
the valley among snowfields. The sun was glancing off the peaks of Les
Diablerets, turning them a shiny gold. Armand had just signed up for a
master's degree in French literature at the Sorbonne and was phenome-
nally well read. His favourite writer was Proust.

Earlier in the season he had cooked for a school group from Azerbaijan.
'The teachers were afraid of them,' he said. 'The kids did what they liked.
They would pick at the food and then walk down to Schönreide and order
a sixty-franc steak. They asked me, these thirteen year-olds, "Where's the
whorehouse?" And they were dead serious.'

We laughed at the follies of new money, a perennial subject among
international teachers. I thought of Nabokov's returned Swiss governesses
on the benches of Lausanne: the Russian Revolution had reduced their
circumstances.

> One is always at home in one's past, which partly explains those
> pathetic ladies' posthumous love for another country, which they
> never had really known and in which none of them had been very
> content.[1]

We are all governesses in reduced circumstances in Gstaad. International
teachers have their seasoned anecdotes: minor royalty, nouveau riche
Russians, corporate brats we've taught and chaperoned towards a college
education in the Anglosphere. In that day's *Financial Times* the headmaster
of King's College, Wimbledon, was lamenting that British private schools
are becoming 'finishing schools for the children of oligarchs ... facilities
have never been so glitzy, fees have never been so high, results have never
been so consistent'.[2]

The *beau monde* at the Palace Hotel in Gstaad, 1928

Armand noticed that I was reading *Tender Is the Night* (1934) and pointed me in the direction of the Palace Hotel in Gstaad, where Hemingway and Fitzgerald drank in the 1920s. They were the chroniclers of the low, dishonest decades between the wars, the first writers to draw attention to Gstaad as a playground for wealthy foreigners. Hemingway's lovers in *A Farewell to Arms* (1929) cosy up in a chalet down the valley from Gstaad, escaping from the horrors of the First World War. Fitzgerald's *Tender Is the Night* presents a portrait of the golden couple coming undone in Swiss ski stations and sanatoria. Both books are morality tales conceived and played out on the slippery slopes.

Beside these giants of twentieth-century literature, Elinor Brent-Dyer's Chalet School series for girls might seem minor. But the Chalet School books, published between 1925 and 1970, formed early a certain notion of Alpine luxury – *Kaffee und Kuchen*, galumphing girls with crushes on handsome ski instructors and mistresses of French alike. Muriel Spark's more recent *Finishing School* (2004) reflects the ethos of exclusivity and private education in the Swiss Alps that Fitzgerald's generation began. Sanatoria, wellness centres, finishing schools: gilded service is still there in Gstaad, as are the galumphing girls and the filthy rich. It helps to have the school, the bank account, the loony bin and the ski slope all in the same valley.

It was Ernest Hemingway who first immortalised this snow country in *A Farewell to Arms*. He saw Switzerland as a sanctuary from the horrors of the First World War and wrote parts of the novel in Les Avents, in the Pension de la Fôret de Chamby and in the Posthotel Rössli in Gstaad.

Unlike Byron, Hemingway wasn't a scratcher of other people's woodwork, so there's not much trace of the burly American in the valley today.

Hemingway was an ambulance driver for the Red Cross on the Italian front at the close of the war. Wounded, shipped home, he was back covering the International Peace Conference in Lausanne in 1922 for the *Toronto Star*. In *A Moveable Feast* (1964) he recalls those halcyon post-war days with his first wife Hadley:

> 'Do you remember I brought some wine from Aigle home to the chalet? They sold it to us at the inn. They said it should go with the trout. We brought it wrapped in copies of La Gazette de Lucerne, I think.' ... 'They were such wonderful trout, Tatie, and we drank the Sion wine and ate out on the porch with the mountain-side dropping off below and we could look across the lake and see the Dent du Midi with the snow half down it and the trees at the mouth of the Rhône where it flowed into the lake.'[3]

Henry the ambulance driver and Catherine the nurse in *A Farewell to Arms* are on the run from the war and decide to sneak across the Italian border into Switzerland. Hemingway presents neutral Switzerland as a kind of escapist paradise. They agree to meet at Stresa on Lago Maggiore, before attempting to cross the lake at night. Hemingway couldn't have chosen a more romantic spot, with grand hotels, perfect martinis and the Borromean Islands in the offing:

> I took a good room. It was very big and light and looked out on the lake. The clouds were down over the lake but it would be beautiful with the sunlight. I was expecting my wife, I said. There was a big double bed, a letto matrimoniale with a satin coverlet. The hotel was very luxurious. I went down the long halls, down the wide stairs, through the rooms to the bar. I knew the barman and sat on a high stool and ate salted almonds and potato chips. The martini felt cool and clean.[4]

Military police are poised to arrest him for desertion. The barman has a rowboat, sandwiches and a bottle of brandy. The crossing is thirty-five kilometres with the wind behind them.

Hemingway's Switzerland is a land of plenty, as it will be for Patricia Highsmith following the Second World War. 'They have wonderful rolls and butter and jam in Switzerland,' says Henry. Landing at Brissago on the border, the lovers head for breakfast, delighted at their escape 'out of

that bloody place'. Immigration officers send them to Locarno for temporary visas and they spend the night in the Hotel Metropole. Hemingway's
Americans always seem to find the best hotels, the best martinis and to land
on their feet. But it is a temporary reprieve.

On the slopes above Montreux, Henry and Catherine's war takes a turn
into chalet paradise:

> There was an island with two trees on the lake and the trees looked like the
> double sails of a fishing-boat. The mountains were sharp and steep on the
> other side of the lake and down at the end of the lake was the plain of the
> Rhone valley flat between the two ranges of mountains; and up the valley
> where the mountains cut it off was the Dent du Midi.[5]

Byron's prisoner of Chillon looks out on the same island, longing for freedom. Hemingway paints an idyllic picture. The lovers play cards and war
seems as far away as 'the football games of someone else's college'. They
walk down into Montreux through the terraced vineyards of Clarens, where
Rousseau's lovers had disported themselves. Henry drinks 'dark Munich
beer' and reads the papers while Catherine has her hair done. They take
the electric train back up to their chalet.

> A cold wind was coming down the Rhone Valley. There were lights in the
> shop windows and we climbed the steep stone stairway to the upper street,
> then up another stairs to the station. The electric train was there waiting,
> all lights on.[6]

Henry grows a backwoods beard. Catherine's pregnancy begins to show.
Hemingway seizes the Swiss landscape with characteristic simplicity:

> There was an inn in the trees at the Bains de l'Alliaz where the wood-
> cutters stopped to drink, and we stayed inside warmed by the stove and
> drank hot red wine with spices and lemon in it. They called it glühwein
> and it was a good thing to warm you and to celebrate with. The inn was
> dark and smoky inside and afterwards when you went out the cold air
> came sharply into your lungs and numbed the edge of your nose as you
> inhaled. We looked back at the inn with light coming from the windows
> and the woodcutters' horses stamping and jerking their heads outside to
> keep warm. There was frost on the hairs of their muzzles and their breath-
> ing made plumes of frost in the air.[7]

Zelda and Scott Fitzgerald sketched in 1921–22

Close to Catherine's lying-in, they descend to Lausanne to be near the hospital. 'On the days of false spring', Hemingway brings a swift end to this edenic romance. Catherine gives birth to a stillborn boy. The author very lightly connects the larger picture of war and this tragedy in Switzerland: 'Still there would not be all this dying to go through.' Then Catherine too dies and our deserter walks back to his hotel in Lausanne through the rain. The brief Swiss idyll is over.

For F. Scott Fitzgerald and his wife Zelda, Switzerland was also a tragic ending. Fitzgerald famously wrote: 'Switzerland is a country where very few things begin, but many things end.'[8] In *Tender Is the Night*, Dick Diver first encounters Zürich as a twenty-six-year-old psychiatry student in 1917. He has had a good war as an Oxford Rhodes Scholar; like Bill Clinton during a later conflict. 'Even in this sanctuary he did not escape lightly … the war didn't touch him at all.' Diver's Switzerland is set apart, a suite of high-end clinics indistinguishable from well-heeled resorts, but peopled by profiteers. The pre-war world of Thomas Mann's Davos has been wrestled into the American twentieth century:

> *Switzerland was an island, washed on one side by the waves of thunder around Gorizia and on another by the cataracts around the Somme and the Aisne. … the men who whispered in the little cafés of Berne and Geneva were as likely to be diamond salesmen or commercial travellers. However, no one had missed the long trains of blinded or one-legged men, or dying trunks, that crossed each other between the bright lakes*

*of Constance and Neuchâtel. In the bier-halls and shop-windows were
bright posters presenting the Swiss defending their frontiers in 1914.*[9]

Those 'diamond salesmen or commercial travellers' are making a wartime
killing of their own, and reappear in the work of Swiss detective writer
Friedrich Glauser. Diver too is on the make. He spends two years at
Dohmer's clinic on the Zürichsee, thriving on the new therapy of psychoanalysis and on high fees: 'a rich person's clinic – we don't use the word
nonsense'.[10] In finishing school or health resort there is no such thing as
failure, just the higher nonsense, the gobbledegook of new-age psychiatry
or anything-goes pedagogy.

> *The car had followed the shore of the Zürichsee into a fertile region of
> pasture farms and low hills, steepled with chalets. The sun swam out into
> a blue sea of sky and suddenly it was a Swiss valley at its best – pleasant
> sounds and murmurs and a good fresh smell of health and cheer. ... the
> first modern clinic for mental illness; at a casual glance no layman would
> recognise it as a refuge for the broken, the incomplete, the menacing, of
> this world.*[11]

When Zelda Sayre met Scott Fitzgerald at a Montgomery country club
dance, she was a vivacious, ill-educated flirt from a family with a history
of mental illness and suicide. High maintenance, we might say. It was
1918, the war just over. A decade of parties, drugs and drink, a daughter,
three abortions and infidelities ensued. Fitzgerald was no cultural ambassador. Pugilistic, alcoholic, with taxicab French, the best he could rise to
was *'Très bien*, you son of a bitch!' Their Europe didn't go much beyond
hotels, nightclubs, American-style bars and raked Riviera beaches catering
to wealthy expatriates – upper-crust young people, sophisticates and wan-
nabes.[12] We could draw a straight line between Fitzgerald's Europe and the
later films of Woody Allen. Switzerland is where they congregated for the
new winter sports of skiing and sledding; the Princeton golden boy always
liked to follow the money.

Fitzgerald presents psychoanalysis and mental illness as lucrative, as
Thomas Mann did for tuberculosis. Rich children get educated, get treated
for tuberculosis and madness far from state schools and public wards, in
the mountain valleys of Swiss exclusivity. Fitzgerald mentions all the right
places, like high school seniors dropping college names: Johns Hopkins,
Interlaken, Montreux, Geneva, the Palace Hotel in Zürich where 'a

magnificent Rolls curved into the half-moon entrance'. These are the gilded stations of the sickbay.

Cycling in Montreux, Dick Diver notices the world of wealthy leisure picking up again after the war:

> He was conscious of the groups of English, emergent after four years and walking with detective-story suspicion in their eyes, as though they were about to be assaulted in this questionable country by German train-bands. There were building and awakening everywhere on this mound of debris formed by a mountain torrent. At Berne and at Lausanne on the way south, Dick had been eagerly asked if there would be Americans this year.[13]

Fitzgerald pays homage to the scenic beauty, to the echoing acoustics of the Grand Hotel in Caux, now the Swiss Hotel Management School. Here Doctor Diver first kisses his patient Nicole, whom he eventually marries:

> 'My God,' he gasped, 'you're fun to kiss.'
> ... Two thousand feet below she saw the necklace and bracelets of lights that were Montreux and Vevey, beyond them a dim pendant of Lausanne.[14]

Doctor and patient converge on Gstaad for the Christmas holidays, where the beautiful people are. Hemingway's love nest in 1927 with his new partner, the fashion journalist and trust fund babe Pauline Pfeiffer, had been in the humbler Posthotel Rössli on the village street. Fitzgerald's is the newer and more luxurious Palace Hotel. His characters descend to slum it in the 'old-fashioned Swiss tap-room, wooden and resounding, a room of clocks, kegs, steins, and antlers'. Fitzgerald's picture of expatriate life in Gstaad, private schools and all, holds true a century later:

> The great hall, its floor pockmarked by two decades of hobnails, was cleared for the tea dance, and four-score young Americans, domiciled in schools near Gstaad, bounced about to the frolic of 'Don't Bring Lulu,' or exploded violently with the first percussions of the Charleston. It was a colony of the young, simple, and expensive.[15]

The 'schools near Gstaad' are still there: Institute Le Rosey, The John F. Kennedy International School and Leysin American School. Like

Winter campus of Le Rosey International School, Gstaad, early 1900s

Stevenson and Conan Doyle before them, Fitzgerald and Hemingway relate the delights of the new sports of skiing and sledding. Fitzgerald describes the upper crust making use of people with a 'cold rich insolence'. Dick and Nicole make their way by sled to Saanen along the valley: 'They poured into the municipal dance, crowded with cow herders, hotel servants, shop-keepers, ski teachers, guides, tourists, peasants.' Here Dick realises that being tethered to Nicole is a merger and acquisition by her wealthy family: they get two – caregiver and husband – for the price of one. Like Swiss finishing schools and health resorts, his ethics are inextricably tied to money. 'We own you, and you'll admit it sooner or later. It is absurd to keep up the pretence of independence.'[16] Later, he realises he 'had been swallowed up like a gigolo'.

Dick marries flighty Nicole and becomes a partner in a sanatorium, underwritten by his wife's family fortune. He enters the world of Swiss psychoanalysis: fashionable, tentative, pricey, full of ergotherapy (hot baths and exercise), hydrotherapy, woodwork and bookbinding. 'Articulate among them would be the great Jung, bland, super-vigorous, on his rounds between the forests of anthropology and the neuroses of school-boys.'[17] This spa world survives to this day in the valleys and on the slopes around Gstaad: hot pools and Jacuzzis cling to the snow-covered mountainside, offering a good Swedish thrashing and tickling of the chakras. Alpine health resorts provide the smells and bells of religiosity that a later Swiss writer, Peter Stamm, will gently satirise as ersatz spirituality. Hot pools, lava stones, yoga camps and personal trainers – all fleecing pilgrims at a price – have taken the place of the grottoes, monasteries and hermitages of Christianity.

But Nicole doesn't get well, and they shift from clinic to clinic. In 1929 Zelda entered the Valmont Clinic above Montreux. Its website mentions Rainer Maria Rilke and the Belgian royal family as patients – you don't get more neurasthenic than that. Zelda was transferred to Les Rives de Prangins on Lake Geneva. These were the luxury clinics for which Switzerland was famous, combining the facilities of country club and health resort. Zelda began her long slide into madness. Dr Oscar Forel (his father Dr Auguste Forel is on the Swiss thousand franc note) treated both Lucia Joyce and Zelda Fitzgerald. He urged James Joyce and F. Scott Fitzgerald to give up alcohol, as a contributing factor to mental illness – a tall order, but to no avail.

> The grounds were spacious, the gardens immaculately tended; and it had farms, tennis courts and seven private villas for super-rich patients. 'With the addition of a caddy house,' as Fitzgerald wrote of Dick Diver's clinic in Tender Is the Night, 'it might well have been a country club.' The clientele was international, and many of the patients came from families of distinguished ancestry and great wealth. The cost of treatment at Prangins, during the first year of the Depression, was an astronomical $1,000 a month.[18]

By 1929 Fitzgerald could command $4,000 a story from the Saturday Evening Post.[19] In good times Zelda's extravagance had drawn on Scott's success. Now, in bad times, it did too. His portrait of the Hôtel des Trois Mondes in Lausanne recognises Switzerland as a refuge of sinners, not always repentant:

> throughout this hotel there were many chambers wherein rich ruins, fugitives from justice, claimants to the thrones of mediatised principalities, lived on the derivatives of opium or barbitol, listening eternally as to an inescapable radio, to the coarse melodies of old sins. This corner of Europe does not so much draw people as accept them without inconvenient questions. Routes cross here – people bound for private sanatoriums or tuberculosis resorts in the mountains, people who are no longer persona grata in France or Italy.[20]

Fitzgerald haunted the lake towns in the manner of T.S. Eliot in *The Waste Land*. In 1922 Eliot had completed the first draft of his magisterial poem at Lausanne, following his own treatment for nervous disorders. Fitzgerald drank and philandered. He realised he had come to a bad end in his brush with the rich and careless. His marriage to Zelda was irrevocably cracked and she spent the rest of her life in various sanatoria. In 1948 she burned to death in an institution called Highland, in Asheville, North Carolina, in a room whose doors and windows were chained and padlocked. The Roaring Twenties were long over.

After my coffee I set out on the downhill path to Gstaad. The sky was baby blue and the mountains glittery. Trickles of melt water caught the sun, but I had good boots and the way was signposted. Just past the train station at Schönreide sits the winter campus of Le Rosey, the world's most expensive school – fees in excess of £90,000. Every winter it moves from Rolle on Lake Geneva (state-of-the-art concert hall inaugurated by the Royal Philharmonic Orchestra) to the slopes above Gstaad.

International schools in Switzerland have their roots in the nineteenth-century Grand Tour. Parents parked their kids in Geneva and around the lake while they crossed the Simplon to Italy. The Swiss had a reputation as stolidly dependable pedagogues. You could entrust your daughter to them and open up a trust fund at the same time. Henry James was the first to draw on his roving European childhood for fictional material. Polyglot tutors, governesses, chaperones and pale young men with second-class degrees, their sailor-suited charges in tow, became bit-part characters of the nineteenth-century novel. They were hired wherever the international affluent gathered, like migratory birds around a body of water:

> Clean air and beautiful scenery provided an invigorating environment; the multilingual culture gave a sense of the cosmopolitan; and the country's renowned stability and security reassured anxious parents. Social skills were often honed alongside improving deportment or developing artistic talents. But somewhere along the way, the dream faded. By the 1960s, gender equality, women's liberation and an emphasis on higher education for all prompted a decline.[21]

The Chalet School series, begun in 1925 and running to fifty-nine titles, was where most girls fantasised their way to the Alps. The series remains in print and has a growing fan following. Initially set in the Austrian Tyrol, the books needed to keep one step ahead of wartime German annexation.

Elinor Brent-Dyer's Chalet School series ran to fifty-nine titles

In *The Chalet School in Exile* (1940), Brent-Dyer shows she is on the side of the angels, tackling the *Anschluss* and the baiting of Herr Goldmann head-on:

> *an old man with a long, grey beard, plainly running for his life. A shower of stones, rotten fruit and other missiles followed him. Stark terror was in his face, and already he was failing to outdistance his pursuers.*
>
> *... 'He's a Jew! Jews have no right to live!' declared Hans Bocher sullenly. 'Give place, Fräulein Bethany, and hand over the old Jew to us! Better take care, or you'll be in trouble for this. Let him go! We'll see to him!'*[22]

From the Tyrol the school moved to Guernsey. When the Nazis occupied the island, the series settled in Hereford and then finally in Switzerland – *The Chalet School in Oberland* (1952). This search for safe haven, the last good place, mirrors not only Switzerland's perceived role throughout two world wars, but also Hemingway and Fitzgerald's trajectory. When the going gets tough, there's always Switzerland. The popularity of the Chalet School series with generations of girls (and their brothers!) formed a Switzerland of the mind.

> *Elinor had long wanted to move the School back to Austria, but the political situation there in the 1950s forbade such a move, so she did the next*

*best thing and moved it to Switzerland ... The exact location is subject to
much debate, but it seems likely that it is somewhere near Wengen in the
Bernese Oberland.*[23]

Brent-Dyer (1894–1969) was an internationalist and pacifist who came from
a broken family and a terraced house in South Shields in the north of
England. Her best friend in childhood died of tuberculosis. The Chalet
School is coupled with a sanatorium further up the mountain where
'mostly English ladies come to die of TB'. The proximity of school and sanatorium, children in one and parents in the other, is a feature of the series
whether set in the Tyrol, Hereford or Switzerland. In the Chalet School
books, torrents are always 'raging', laughter is 'hysterical', girls read 'avidly'
and are fluent in at least three languages. Brent-Dyer is credited with
inventing the expression 'smashing!' The three places you could graduate
to after the Chalet School were the Sorbonne, Oxford or the Kensington
School of Needlework.[24]

For royal families in the real world, a Swiss education allowed a degree
of neutral distance from the politics of the Great Game. The crowned
heads of Persia and Thailand, for example, were careful to keep the
English and the French at loggerheads with each other. A Swiss education,
furthermore, guaranteed spoken French, the indispensable lingua franca
of diplomacy and sophistication before the Second World War swept all
before it on a vulgar tide.

The ephemeral education of the finishing school – both Princess Diana
and Camilla, Duchess of Cornwall are finished girls – with its emphasis on
social polish, attracted that mistress of comedy, Muriel Spark. In her final
novel, *Finishing School*, she skewers the pretensions of College Sunrise in
Lausanne and the slick self-confidence of its mixed-race co-ed students.
They have free rein, their parents are crooks of one sort or another, and the
line between academics, etiquette and entertainment is blurred: 'Tilly was
known and registered at the school as Princess Tilly, but no-one knew where
she was Princess of.' Spark's trademark wickedness satirises the relationship
between wealth – however ill gotten – and education: 'Your jumped up parents (may God preserve their bank accounts) will want to see something for
their money.'[25] With its view of the lake and the Alps, College Sunrise seems
more like a luxury hotel. Indeed, many of Switzerland's hotels have morphed from spas treating tubercular patients, to schools, to hotel management
schools and back to hotels again with the changing seasons and the economic climate – from dire health to dire wealth. Spark defines her terms:

The Posthotel Rössli in Gstaad, 1880, where Hemingway wrote part of
A Farewell to Arms

> *'You are listed as a finishing school. What exactly is a finishing school?'*
> *said Israel.*
> *'Generally,' said Rowland, 'it's a place where parents dump their*
> *teen-age children after their schooldays and before their universities or*
> *their marriages or careers.'*
> *Giovanna said, 'Polished off?'*[26]

Like royalty, Fitzgerald and Hemingway thought of Gstaad and its environs as a refuge from the world. Descending through the outlying chalets, noting security systems and quadruple garages set into the hillside, I try to imagine the glamour of that lost decade, overlaid with many a fresh fall of snow. But all I can think about is Fitzgerald's phrase: 'this careless, dominant class'. Above Gstaad the Palace Hotel commands the rise like a Bavarian castle. The Posthotel Rössli, where Hemingway stayed, is the true heritage building in town. It sits on the pedestrianised main drag of bedizened designer outlets and ski equipment stores, diminished, smoked like an old kipper.

Another dirndled waitress seats me at the *Stammtisch* and brings hot chocolate. The panelled interior is decorated with sepia ski photos and antique wood and leather skis that have an orthopaedic look. I flick through

a local magazine: Roger Moore strolls the streets of Gstaad without his tou-
pee. Julie Andrews is secreted up one of the valleys. So is Roman Polanski
– perhaps he knows where the whorehouse is? Tucked away like so many
tarnished rhinestones from Tinseltown, they are our modern Dick Divers,
our Scotties and Zeldas.

During the First World War, Swiss neutrality gave birth to a different
kind of writing from the flash American of the Lost Decade. *Noir*-ish,
double-edged, it was peopled with spies and detectives. While empires fell
and fascism rose, Switzerland became a playground of a different kind. The
good days in Gstaad had come to an end. "'Good-bye, Gstaad! Good-bye,
fresh faces, cold sweet flowers, flakes in the darkness. Good-bye, Gstaad,
good-bye!'"[27]

8

THE PLAYGROUND OF EUROPE

I spy with my little eye: Fleming, Maugham, Glauser and the Krimis

Sean Connery plays James Bond in a 1961 Sunbeam Alpine convertible

*The Swiss well knew that their country was the scene of all manner of
intrigues; agents of the secret service, spies, revolutionaries and agitators
infested the hotels of the principal towns.*
Somerset Maugham

A lascivious sea breeze entered the parent–teacher conference room in Rome as Ursula Andress stepped across the threshold. Those famous breasts wool-clad against the Roman winter perked up in a number of teachers' minds. The snake-length hair was matronly coiled. She was remarkably well preserved and carried herself with an awareness of what hips can do to a room. She must have been touching sixty – a late mother, with all a late mother's care. Her son, Dimitri, was seventeen, shaven-headed, with the sleek bronze looks of the Roman tough. He would nonetheless go on to study Philosophy at Princeton and from there to the piranha pool of minor West Coast celebrity. More than one male teacher might have hummed 'Underneath the Mango Tree' sotto voce. The cold Ponentino swirled through the umbrella pines of La Storta, fluttering paperwork on the desks.

Andress was the original Bond girl, Honey Ryder in *Dr. No*. Born in Ostermundigen, a suburb of Bern from which the capital quarried its greenish-bluey-grey sandstone, she was half-Swiss, half-German. Her father, a German diplomat, had been expelled from Switzerland for unexplained reasons and disappeared during the Second World War. Impressively multilingual, the starlet spoke with a Swiss accent in English and so her early films were dubbed.

Bond himself is a Swiss confection. Born in Zürich to a Swiss mother, Monique Delacroix from Vaud, and a Scottish father from Glencoe, Andrew Bond, the hero was orphaned early, like Superman, Batman and Harry Potter. Superman, hailing from the planet Krypton, is raised by Kansas farmers. Batman loses his parents in Crime Alley in Gotham City. James and Lily Potter suffer the Killing Curse. Bond Senior is a company rep in Switzerland for Vickers armaments manufacturer. Not quite in the same league as Krypton and Gotham City. But for Agent Bond, born to the arms world seems apt. Bond, like Switzerland, is a kind of brand.

Bond's parents were killed in a climbing accident outside Chamonix when the boy was eleven, a back-story invented much later when Fleming's spy series had taken off. Agent 007 grew up to become a suave money-spinner, with a finger in the paperback and movie pies and an eye for merchandising. Like his Rolex Oyster Perpetual Submariner and Mont Blanc pen, Swiss luxury is grafted onto the English notion of a gentleman – even though technically half-Scottish. Fleming created Bond in Jamaica at the rate of 2,000 words a day in February 1952. Like Switzerland itself, Bond is synonymous with wealth, stealth and the good life.

Following trouble with a skivvy at Eton and a spot of gonorrhoea at Sandhurst, the nineteen-year-old Ian Fleming was dispatched to Kitzbühel in the Austrian Tyrol to bone up for the Foreign Service exams. There he came under the wing of Ernan Forbes Dennis, a diplomat and MI6 Head of Station for Austria, Hungary and Yugoslavia – on Her Majesty's Secret Service. Fleming perfected his German at the University of Munich and enrolled at the University of Geneva as an external student in 1929 in order to put manners on his French. He left a very light academic imprint on his two universities.

The young blade drove a black Buick and wore an old Etonian tie: Bond branding had begun. In Geneva he joined the *jeunesse dorée* of the early 1930s. The Crash, then as now, didn't hit them the hardest. By twenty-one Fleming had adopted the debonair persona of the Englishman abroad, incarnated by his fictional hero and by a suite of well-spoken actors since. Fast cars, tailoring and blonde bombshells change, but the clean-cut gentleman has staying power.

Decades later in 1963, in a series of articles commissioned by the *Sunday Times*, Fleming wrote about Geneva as one of his thrilling cities:

> For to me Geneva, and indeed the whole of Switzerland, has a George Simenon quality – the quality that makes a thriller-writer want to take a tin-opener and find out what goes on behind the façade, behind the great families who keep the banner of Calvin flying behind the lace curtains in their fortresses in the rue des Granges, the secrets behind the bronze grilles of the great Swiss banking corporations, the hidden turmoil behind the beautiful, bland face of the country.[1]

Simenon, creator of Detective Maigret, ended his days living in Switzerland for tax purposes; not much wielding of the tin opener there. Elsewhere, Fleming notes 'the banal beauty of Switzerland'. This conception of the country as a façade of rectitude and beauty, behind which high finance goes about its murky business, predominated after both world wars. Switzerland was by turns admired for its tenacious neutrality and suspect for the compromises that neutrality entailed.

Fleming focuses on the pillars that hold up a country 'with only services to sell'. Of course, since 1963 Britain, too, has become an economy of 'tat and service industries'. London, in particular, has learned much in the way of financial services from the Swiss model. We could see Switzerland in the vanguard of where the rest of Europe is heading: a grand old *wagon-lit* for the rich and ailing, producing nothing but luxury items and high-end service.

> *In this century they have turned their attention to hotels and sanatoria (with the defeat of tuberculosis they are cannily switching to the modern managerial diseases resulting from stress and tension) and to the creation of the solidest banking system in the world.* [2]

Fleming pulls no punches. Nor is there an iota of nostalgia for his pre-war student days in Geneva. Like his spy-writer compatriots Maugham, Greene and le Carré, he has a jaundiced view of Swiss wealth and banking. Only towards the end of the twentieth century were the country's wartime dealings – particularly the question of unclaimed Jewish assets – frogmarched into the light.

> *The reason why fugitive money, in its search for safe repose, has poured into Switzerland in such a continuous torrent, particularly since the war, is due to the sympathy of the government for money which is more or less hot (if it was not, it would not be on the run).*

Fleming traces Swiss banking secrecy to the act passed on 8 November 1934, shortly after Hitler's accession to power. This law made it a crime to reveal the name of a Swiss account holder. As a consequence, Switzerland is 'universally acclaimed the safe-deposit box for the world'. It is not surprising that all-comers are welcome:

> *Modern Switzerland has gathered to its bosom a new kind of refugee – the fugitive from punitive taxation. The political refugee still exists in the form of fugitive royal families, Italian, Rumanian, Spanish and Egyptian, together with a handful of sheikhs. These sad orphans of the world's storm, evicted from their palaces, have found shelter in the Palace Hotels along the shores of Lac Leman, and there hold strictly mediatised tea and bridge parties and are courted by the local snobs.* [3]

Switzerland hosting a royal tea party is a bit hypocritical, coming from a
writer ensconced on his Goldeneye estate in Jamaica. But it is the oily
royalty – jumped-up generals, Macbeths, carpetbaggers, sundry keepers of
the desert flame – who find Switzerland's fastness most congenial. The
ambient view of such people has grown benign, not just in Switzerland but
in the world of spectacle. Celebs, royals, glitterati – we forget that they are
often merely thieves in ermine. For well over a century, Switzerland has
kept this class of people in tea and cream cakes.

The arrest of Hannibal Gaddafi and his wife in July 2008 for allegedly
beating their servants in a Geneva hotel illustrates the delicate balancing
act between oily money and the rule of law. There had been earlier vio-
lence in 2005 when Hannibal was studying in Copenhagen. Claridge's
Hotel in London also had to deal with screaming, blood and bodyguards.
Muammar al-Gaddafi reacted to the arrests with characteristic huff. He cut
the Nestlé contract, arrested a couple of Swiss businessmen and withdrew
$5 billion from his Swiss accounts. At the G8 summit in 2009, Gaddafi
called for Switzerland to be carved up between France, Germany and
Italy. Hannibal Gaddafi, living up to both his names, said he would 'wipe
Switzerland off the map'. A couple of years later his father lay in a meat
safe in the Libyan desert and he himself was on the run. It's a tough world.
Hannibal now lives in Oman. We might reasonably ask where the $5 bil-
lion has ended up.

However, the more low-key are salting it away too. Fleming reserves
his spleen for Geneva, the town that taught him French and Social
Anthropology. He sees Geneva as Calvin's town in the way that Mecca
belongs to Mohammed and Las Vegas to Liberace.

> The spirit of Calvin, expressed in the ugly and uncompromising cathedral
> that dominates the city, seems to brood like a thunderous conscience over
> the inhabitants. In the rue des Granges adjoining the cathedral, the great
> patrician families, the de Candoles, de Saussures, Pictets, set a fright-
> ening tone of respectability and strait-laced behaviour, from which the
> lesser Genevese take their example. The international set – the delegates,
> staffs of the various organisations and staffs of foreign businesses – do not
> penetrate even the fringes of Genevese society.[4]

This split between old money and the new international order (global business cheek by jowl with global organisations and NGOs) has been a part
of the Geneva landscape since the émigrés of the late nineteenth century.

Before that the Huguenots fled persecution in France during the second half of the sixteenth century and in turn became the status quo. Many of them were skilled goldsmiths, watchmakers and bankers. Switzerland has a long tradition of owing its prosperity to immigrant skill.

Calvin's belief that 'Christ died on the cross not for all mankind, but only for the elect; that God does not will all men to be saved' has given an edge to Swiss materialism. Wealth can seem to be merited – a view much propagated in the United States as well. Conversely, poverty is self-inflicted. This Protestant ethic married to the spirit of capitalism – 'this holier-than-thou attitude', as Ian Fleming describes it – establishes an absolving link between the storing up of earthly goods and godliness. While new money slowly turns old money, oil wealth is alive and well and living in Geneva.

Fleming's is not a flattering picture of Switzerland but one consistent with the way Swiss writers – Glauser, Dürrenmatt, Frisch and Zorn – see their own country, warts and all. Fleming reveals a qualified affection for Switzerland only towards the end of his article:

> I was partly educated in Switzerland – at the University of Geneva where I studied Social Anthropology, of all subjects, under the famous Professor Pittard. I was once engaged to a Swiss girl. I am devoted to the country and to its people and I would not have them different in any detail. But, as I said at the beginning, Switzerland has a Simenon quality, an atmosphere of still-water-running-deep, which is a great temptation to the writer of thrillers. If I have revealed a wart here and a wen there and poked mild fun at the reserved, rather prim face Switzerland presents to the world, this is because the mystery writer enjoys seeing the play from back-stage rather than from out front, in the stalls.[5]

Ian Fleming's gravestone bears the inscription: 'Having enjoyed all life's prizes, you now decay.' It could be read as hedonistic or as moral: the writer enjoyed it both ways.

❖

Joseph Conrad's *Under Western Eyes* spawned the Swiss spy novel genre in the first decade of the twentieth century. Somerset Maugham moulded his own experiences as a spy in neutral Switzerland during the First World War and turned tradecraft into intrigue. Friedrich Glauser's 1930s detectives started a home-grown tradition of *noir* writing. John le Carré cut his spy

teeth in Bern at the beginning of the Cold War. All of these writers wrote
from the peculiar vantage point of Swiss neutrality, surviving by hook or by
crook through two world wars, surrounded by the great powers.

Somerset Maugham's *Ashenden* (1928) follows the cross-border sleuth-
ing of an English spy playing the Great Game; an Austin Powers for the spats
and cocktail set. Ashenden hops on and off trains between Bern, Geneva,
Lausanne and Zürich. He's on Her Majesty's Rail Pass, first class of course.
Ashenden is a precursor to the shadowy agents of Graham Greene and
John le Carré. All of these writer-spies take the imperial measure of the
Englishman abroad among hostile powers, and turn it into fiction.

It's a polyglot world, rather like Switzerland itself. Maugham, Fleming,
le Carré and Greene – unlike their modern compatriots – move easily
among languages and cultures. Maugham was born in the British Embassy
in Paris and attended the University of Heidelberg in Germany. Le Carré
enrolled at the University of Bern and speaks faultless German. All were
recruited to Her Majesty's Secret Service when young and became paid-up
spies during the twentieth century's wars. Extensive travel and writing junkets masked their clandestine activities. They examined a certain kind of
perfidious Englishness – its pompous, imperial snobbery – against a background of Swiss neutrality.

Somerset Maugham worked for the Intelligence Department, precursor to MI6. The writer and dramatist had fluent French and good German
but also, crucially, Russian. In 1917 he was in Russia before the Bolshevik
Revolution. Very much the man about town, darling of the West End,
Maugham had perfect cover. The American State Department was also
interested in hiring him. Here is Ashenden crossing on the 'stodgy little
steamer' from Thonon in France to neutral Geneva:

> *Lake Leman, on fine days so trim and pretty, artificial like a piece of
> water in a French garden, in this tempestuous weather was as secret and
> menacing as the sea. He made up his mind that, on getting back to his
> hotel, he would have a fire lit in his sitting-room, a hot bath, and dinner
> comfortably by the fireside in pyjamas and a dressing-gown.*[6]

Maugham deploys the same duality as Fleming: behind the pretty landscape lurks a menacing secret. Switzerland is a sanctuary – a pipe, slippers
and hot bath nation. Ashenden has been in Thonon to deliver his reports
and receive instructions. He evinces sang-froid for the Swiss authorities:

The Swiss well knew that their country was the scene of all manner of intrigues; agents of the secret service, spies, revolutionaries and agitators infested the hotels of the principal towns and, jealous of their neutrality, they were determined to prevent conduct that might embroil them with any of the belligerent powers.[7]

Swiss concern to keep the peace among belligerent powers runs through the twentieth century's wars and into the conflict resolution of the twenty-first century. 'Talks in Geneva' can be part of a century-long conversation. Towns around the lake – Geneva, Lausanne, Évian – all have hosted talks in their day. Maugham, like Conrad, manages to give Geneva a cloak-and-dagger charm:

At that time Geneva was a hot-bed of intrigue and its home was the hotel at which Ashenden was staying. There were Frenchmen there, Italians and Russians, Turks, Rumanians, Greeks and Egyptians. Some had fled their country, some doubtless represented it.[8]

The hotel in question was the Beau Rivage, where Charles II, Duke of Brunswick, died in 1873. He bequeathed his considerable fortune to the city on the proviso that it bury him in an ostentatious tomb – Brunswick Monument in a triangular park right next to the hotel. Empress Sisi was stabbed by an anarchist after leaving the Beau Rivage, so the hotel had complex royal, diplomatic and anarchist associations by the time Willy Maugham entered the lobby. The code name Maugham gives Ashenden, 'Somerville', was one the author used himself. Ashenden ferrying back and forth across the lake corresponds to Maugham's routine:

He took a room in the Hotel Beau Rivage in Geneva and filed his weekly reports by taking the ferry across the lake to the French side. Maugham was back in London early in the New Year to see Caroline *open in the West End, and then in March, he resumed his duties in Switzerland, accompanied by his newly divorced mistress, Syrie Wellcom.*[9]

Ashenden is tainted with English snobbery, as was Maugham himself. Two Egyptian princesses are 'dressed with a rich loudness which suggested the Fish-market at Cairo rather than the Rue de la Paix'. A count is 'of great family and indeed related to the Hohenzollerns'. The Beau Rivage becomes the drawing room of the world in the manner of a Henry James

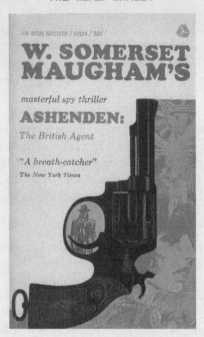

W. Somerset Maugham's agent *Ashenden*, spying for king and country

novel. Ashenden parcels out the day like the gentleman spy he is, confident of Britain's place in the world and himself as a defender of it.

> *He saw his spies at stated intervals and paid them their wages; when he could get hold of a new one he engaged him, gave him his instructions and sent him off to Germany; he waited for the information that came through and dispatched it; he went into France once a week to confer with his colleague over the frontier and to receive his orders from London; he visited the market-place on market day to get any message the old butter-woman had brought him from the other side of the lake; he kept his eyes and ears open.*[10]

Ashenden's runner in London is called R., abbreviated in the manner of later spy novels. The further away from cosmopolitan London they are, the more exotic the characters become. Chandra Lal is an Indian nationalist, a lawyer taking advantage of wartime to advance his country's independence. Maugham describes him as 'a dangerous agitator' and R. calls him 'a greasy little nigger'. 'Little' is an adjective much used by Maugham (himself a bit on the short side) when it comes to foreigners. Lal takes up with a gold-digging dancer called Giulia Lazzari in the 'Tingle-tangle' music halls of Berlin. Lazzari appears to be based on Mata Hari, real name Margaretha Zelle, a Dutch dancer turned German spy who performed in her jewellery and not much else. Ashenden uses Lazzari as a honey pot to trap Lal in Lausanne.

Maugham has an eye for the trains, ferries and lakeshore landscapes of Switzerland, all observed from a first-class carriage. Here and there the style rises above that of the shilling-shocker to a kind of Edwardian grace:

> *Ashenden sat down on the chair in front of the dressing-table and looked idly at the odds and ends that littered it. The toilet things were cheap and tawdry and none too clean. There were little shabby pots of rouge and cold-cream and little bottles of black for the eyebrows and eyelashes. The hairpins were horrid and greasy. The room was untidy and the air was heavy with the smell of cheap scent.* [11]

Maugham's sympathetic movement between female demi-monde and male romance, his understanding of the ticky-tacky theatre world, comes from deep within himself. As a closeted homosexual he toyed with actresses just as the actresses played their paramours. The West End man about town was really a closet within a closet in a long line of homosexual double agents.

Ashenden's attempt to snag Chandra Lal is foiled by prussic acid in the Hotel Gibbons in Lausanne. Indian independence will have to wait for another war. Our heartless spy moves on to cross-border espionage in Basel.

> *Gustav, who lived at Basel, represented a Swiss firm with branches at Frankfurt, Mannheim and Cologne, and by virtue of his business was able to go in and out of Germany without risk. He travelled up and down the Rhine, and gathered material about the movement of troops, the manufacture of munitions ... His frequent letters to his wife hid an ingenious code and the moment she received them in Basel she sent them to Ashenden in Geneva.* [12]

R. in London gets a feeling that 'some hanky-panky was going on' and sends Ashenden to investigate. Gustav's cross-border spying is curtailed by the war and he has invented information to keep the cash flowing. Maugham sketches in the three-corner world of Basel: the station, the trams, clerks and tradespeople. 'He knew that both the Germans and the Swiss guarded the frontier with severity.' Gustav is milking the firm. Ashenden leverages his betrayal by extracting information about another double agent called Grantley Caypor, an Englishman living in Lucerne. Maugham's first assignment as a spy provided the real-life betrayal for this story:

> Maugham made his way to Lucerne where his first assignment was to contact an English operative who had a German wife. The man was suspected of being a double agent who was actually working for the Germans. Maugham not only made contact with this agent, but also convinced him to go to France, where he was seized and shot as a spy.[13]

Ashenden evokes the sights of Lucerne – stone lion, covered bridge, the lake looking 'just as tawdry and unreal as it looked on the picture-postcards'. He recalls an earlier visit as a child. Maugham's style deepens, coming closer to that of le Carré half a century later. Both writers return to Switzerland as a wellspring, where they first gazed at their own duplicity:

> Now, in wartime, Lucerne was as deserted as it must have been before the world at large discovered that Switzerland was the playground of Europe. Most of the hotels were closed, the streets were empty, the rowing boats for hire rocked idly at the water's edge and there was none to take them, and in the avenues by the lake the only persons to be seen were serious Swiss taking their neutrality, like a dachshund, for a walk with them.[14]

Writers as different as Conrad, Maugham, Hemingway and le Carré have attempted to capture Switzerland as a still centre in a changing world. Smug, self-satisfied, prosaic are the words most often deployed. A century of spies slip in and out of hotel rooms in Swiss cities, dining alone, observing guests and inhabitants with professional equanimity.

In Lucerne, Ashenden draws out the German wife of English double agent Grantley Caypor. She speaks with a 'guttural' accent and plays Debussy disdainfully. She views the Swiss with 'Teutonic superiority', deploring the accent and maligning their allegiance: 'after all these Swiss are absolutely pro-German'. Washing her bull terrier's ears, she compares it to 'a nasty little Swiss schoolboy'.

This portrait of Frau Caypor and her exiled Englishman strikes me as a mischievous dig at D.H. Lawrence and his German wife Frieda, née von Richthofen. Married at the beginning of the war, the Lawrences spent much of it under suspicion of spying. The couple eventually left Cornwall under the Defense of the Realm Act. They quit Britain definitively and met Maugham for the first time in Mexico in 1924. The two writers were antipathetic: two radically different Englishmen, brought up poles apart. Lawrence thought Maugham 'a bit rancid' and '*sehr unsympatisch*'.[15] Reviewing *Ashenden*, Lawrence found the stories as rancid as their author.

Caypor pays 'the penalty of his crime'. His wife realises the full extent of her abandonment. The bull terrier 'threw back his head and gave a long, long melancholy howl'. The real-life Caypor was shot for treason. There was an unflinching cruelty in Maugham, which emerges in these Swiss spy stories.

The thriller tradition comes alive in the works of Swiss writers as well. Friedrich Glauser (1896–1938) is the daddy of Swiss *Krimis*, as they're known. The German-speaking world's premier crime fiction prize – the Glauser Prize – is named after him. He wrote a quintet of *noir* novels in the 1930s and died aged forty-two, committing suicide two days before his own wedding. Glauser is one of a few Swiss crime writers to have crossed over into English. The genre has yet to see the kind of mass appeal that Scandinavian *noir* has attained, but conditions are ripe for a Swiss takeover: wealthy façade and criminal underbelly has proven a winning formula.

Glauser led a turbulent life. An opium and morphine addict, he spent long periods in psychiatric clinics and a couple of years in prison. He cultivated connections with the Dadaists in Zürich and spent time in the Foreign Legion. His funny farms are much more sinister than Fitzgerald's gilded palaces. Fitzgerald had a taxi waiting; Glauser was confined for the duration.

His superiors have sidelined Chief Inspector Studer of Bern city police (as they say in Thailand, 'transferred to an inactive post') because 'that business with the bank had cost him his job and he had had to start again from the bottom as a plain detective'.[16] Sergeant Studer is fond of Brissago cigars and the Bern dialect. With Glauser we are very much on the low rungs of society, looking up. His Switzerland, like Dürrenmatt's – a writer he influenced – is a country of shady influence, tight-knit communities, run like clockwork. It was from Glauser's *In Matto's Realm* (1936) that Dürrenmatt borrowed the conceit of a mental hospital as a country in microcosm.

Randlingen – 'Edgeville' in Swiss dialect – Psychiatric Clinic is a gothic world unto itself, and the reader doesn't leave it until Studer has solved its crimes:

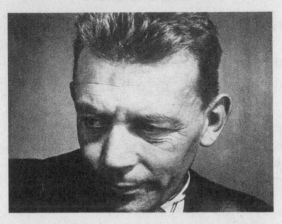

Friedrich Glauser, the father of the *Krimis*, in 1931

*A red-brick building, U-shaped as far as Studer could tell, with lots of
towers and turrets. Surrounded by pine trees, lots of dark pine trees. It
disappeared for a moment, then reappeared; there was the main entrance
and the rounded steps leading up to the door.*[17]

Matto of the title is the spirit of madness. The clinic director has been
murdered and Dr Laduner is in charge. Laduner is fond of occupational
therapy, brightening up the wards and psychoanalysis. It's the time of the
first flush of what Joyce in *Finnegans Wake* called 'The Swiss Tweedledum,
who is not to be confused with the Viennese Tweedledee.' Dr Laduner
represents the correctional impulse in Swiss life – how to tidy up the mess.
In his more extreme moments he seems to anticipate the rise of the Nazi
era.

*The military march faded out and a foreign voice filled the room. It
was an urgent voice, but its urgency was unpleasant. ... foreign states
dare to accuse me of breaking a treaty. When I seized power this land
lay desolate, ravaged, sick ... I have made it great, I have made others
respect it.*[18]

Dr Laduner is listening to Hitler vaunting his achievements on the radio.
Glauser did not live to see the madness of the Second World War. His
salutary picture of Swiss poverty between the wars is a reminder of the Left-
leaning 1930s.

In Matto's Realm (1936), Glauser's noir masterwork

You can't do much on eighty rappen an hour, but he led an orderly life at first, his wife too. Three children. Not enough money. The man went out drinking, the woman took in washing. Two more children. Rotgut schnapps is cheapest, twenty rappen a glass – you can't expect a man like that to drink blanc de Vaud at five francs a bottle, can you?[19]

Glauser knew his psychoanalysis as a patient-victim. His characters are institutionalised, having fallen through the net of sane Swiss society. Glauser's prose has the hectic quality of Dostoyevsky or Gogol. Characters rush along corridors in the dark, into wards, cellars, dayrooms, attics. Their institutional life reeks with the smell of refectory meals, loneliness and pipe smoke. At one point Studer interrupts an analysis session:

They cured them by exploring their dreams and all kinds of obscene stuff came out. Studer's friend Münch, a lawyer, had a book about the method. There were all sorts of things in it you wouldn't even talk about on an evening out with the boys – and what was said then was not for sensitive ears ... So that was analysis ... The real name was different, though, there was another word that went with it ... psychoanalysis, that was it! Psychoanalysis, if they insisted, every profession had its own jargon. In criminology they talked of poroscopy, and no outsider had any idea what it meant – and in Witzwil Labour Camp they called

the warders 'screws'. That's the way it was, every profession had its own
jargon, and psychologists talked of schizophrenia, psychopathy, anxiety
neurosis and psycho ... psycho ... psychoanalysis.[20]

Twenty years after phrenology had burned itself out as pseudo-science, and
seventy-five years before attention deficit disorder, dyslexia, dyspraxia, mas-
saging the amygdala and Ritalin, Glauser knew from experience how each
new generation invents its professional jargon to give a cloak of respecta-
bility to the truth.

His correctional facilities, reformatories, clinics and labour camps are
'like a huge spider stretching its web out over all the land around, and
the inmates' nearest and dearest were caught in its threads, wriggling but
unable to free themselves'.[21] He had reason to see Switzerland as a gilded
cage, an image that runs through twentieth-century Swiss literature from
Glauser to Dürrenmatt to Zorn.

Glauser's *The Spoke* (1937) also makes use of a spider web, this time
describing how international finance enmeshes Switzerland: 'Its threads
run from the big lake in the east to the other in the west, shimmering in the
sun.'[22] The lake in the east is Lake Constance, where Studer is investigating
a hotel murder. There are hidden doors, back staircases, spiked martinis
and a clod-hopping detective. The murder weapon is a sharpened bicycle
spoke. Victims proliferate. Glauser voices his own unhinged mind through
Studer's mordant asides:

> *The dead were well off. They'd put everything behind them: their own*
> *wedding, the christenings, their children's weddings. No more detection*
> *for them, no more playing at being a mole and digging dark passages*
> *underground. They had made their last molehill and were sleeping*
> *beneath it, waiting. Were they really waiting? What for?*[23]

The mole here recalls Kafka's short stories, which Glauser might have read
in 1931.

The Spoke takes us back to a Swiss peasantry in the grip of financi-
ers and loan sharks following the 1929 Crash. As a small population surrounded by more powerful neighbours, the Swiss are easily moved to
paranoia and xenophobia. Glauser's victims are salt-of-the-earth Swiss, his
villains moneymen – themselves often Swiss with foreign connections.
It is a quintessentially 1930s novel with shades of anti-Semitism, predatory international finance, the exploited worker and socialist rumblings.

Viewed from our own post-crisis world, its financial underpinnings look disturbingly familiar:

> These people owe money to Rechsteiner too. It's understandable.
> Farming's never brought in much up here. Their main source of income
> was embroidery; farming came second. But since the economic crisis, all
> the embroidery machines have fallen silent.[24]

Appenzeller farmers are caught in a web spun by bankers, loan sharks and money launderers. High finance and low methods have barely changed in a century. Glauser's fat spiders are prone to spin webs in the shade – 'the post-war world: bankers – German, French, American'. His Switzerland is where dirty money gets washed whiter than white. The motif of money laundering runs through twentieth-century fiction about Switzerland, by Swiss and foreign authors alike.

Other Swiss writers have picked up his *noir* style. Hansjörge Schneider's Inspector Hunkeler works for the Criminal Investigation Department in Basel. The twelve novels featuring the inspector give a flavour of the contemporary border world of Basel: drug smuggling, swimming in the Rhine, the murder of a Turkish woman, stolen art. Schneider's detective has been adapted for television and the author traces his origins as a writer to the need to peel back the smug conformity of post-war Swiss materialism:

> Wanting to become a writer was tied up with wanting to make a revo-
> lution: a revolution against the life of that time, the conditioning of the
> 1950s, the rigidity of the Cold War. First I studied literature at university,
> and after my doctorate the time had come where I could no longer say:
> 'What I'd really like to be is a writer.' I had to take a decision. And so I
> started.[25]

In *Flattermann* (1995), second in the Hunkeler series, a pensioner called Freddy Lerch falls off a bridge into the Rhine at St Johann. Hunkeler's Basel is local, closely observed, laconic; the author is clearly a walker. The endpapers of these handsomely published novels sport a detailed map of Basel. Each case in the series colonises a different area of the city:

> He thought the view was wonderful. The green river, ducks below in the
> slight current, the overhanging linden trees deep green, the bridge above

Basel's riverfront is a favourite beat of Hansjörge Schneider's Detective Hunkeler

to the right with cars in both directions. Behind stood the Münster, rising above the bend in the Rhine, and in the background the Jura hills darkly forested and over it all the blue sky. What a great life! And what was death doing in the middle of it?[26]

Hunkeler dips into the Rhine on hot summer days, death on his mind, fond of the ferries that have been part of Basel's riverscape for a thousand years, plying from bank to bank like Charon on the Styx:

Hunkeler boarded, sat, extracted the fare from the pocket of his togs. Strange, he thought, in or out of water, it had no role to play. The main thing was: water. Man is an amphibian. In the beginning he swims in amniotic fluid and then reaches dry land and laboriously learns to breathe and crawl. Walking upright comes later.[27]

Another contemporary writer with a noir flavour is Alex Capus. In *Almost Like Spring* (2002) Capus imagines the Basel of 1933, when Hitler was sabre-rattling across the border and bank robbery open to a number of interpretations. Capus' narrator has an eye for Basel's Jurassic heritage.

My maternal grandparents were born and raised and spent their whole lives in a village in Basel's hinterland, nestling among the last gentle foothills of the Jura, far from the noise and bustle of the city. The area is famed for its cherry brandy, and the hills afford a fine view of Alsace in the west and the Black Forest in the north. Whenever Germany and France were at war with each other, the sound of artillery fire came rolling across the mountains like thunder and at night one could see the lightning flashes of the guns. However, no foreign soldiers had set foot in Basel's hinterland since the Napoleonic Wars.[28]

Capus' characters too haunt Basel's riverfront, like a shifting tide of detritus. His Bonnie and Clyde outlaws on the run from Germany take to walking along the Rhine in the company of a Globus shopgirl:

They don't take the riverside path but walk along the 20-metre-wide banks of gravel that have formed this winter because the level of the Rhine is unusually low. It's as if the water has emigrated. Lying on the riverbed are encrusted lavatory bowls, rusty murder weapons and old bicycles overgrown with waterweed, and the frozen gravel is slippery and smells of the sea.[29]

The two bank robbers shoot Constable Nafzger in a guesthouse in Kleinbasel. 'His mouth is filling up with blood and everything is going black before his eyes.' Basel's police force is mobilised and the ensuing shootout prefigures the war to come:

The frontier force college in nearby Liestal offers its services to the police. From Basel to Belfort, all crossing points into Alsace are placed on the alert, the Garde Mobile deploy on the French side, complete with steel helmets and carbines, mounted police patrol the German bank of the Rhine and the Reichswehr is called out. The frontier is hermetically sealed for 50 kilometres.[30]

It's the goon squad in full force. Capus' allusion to Bonnie and Clyde suggests that Switzerland too has its folk heroes (William Tell) and its daylight robbery. Throughout the twentieth century, spies and detectives operated in Switzerland against a background of the Russian Revolution, two world wars and the Cold War. These gumshoes all rattled the gilded bars of the climbing frame, the swings and roundabouts of history.

But one writer eventually took up residence in the Swiss playground. A rouble millionaire at seventeen, he escaped from the Russian Revolution to Cambridge, paid for with the jewels hidden in his mother's talcum powder. Émigré Berlin and the booted fascists kept him nimble on his toes and he fled to Paris. There too, approaching war saw him leave the sinking ship at the last minute to board the transatlantic boat. In America he made his fortune and returned for sixteen years to the luxury and discretion of a Swiss grand hotel. His name was Vladimir Nabokov.

9

HIS MASTER'S VOICE

Nabokov in Montreux

Vladimir Nabokov in knickerbocker glory outside the
Montreux Palace Hotel

Exquisite postal service. No bothersome demonstrations, no spiteful
strikes. Alpine butterflies. Fabulous sunsets – just west of my window,
spangling the lake, splitting the crimson sun!
Vladimir Nabokov

One January morning in 2002, I hailed a taxi on Nevsky Prospekt and told the driver to take me to Morskaya Street. It was minus twenty-eight outside and snow squeaked underfoot. I was escaping for a few hours from supervising a school tour. 'Morskaya?' the driver confirmed. 'Morskaya,' I said, imitating him, rolling the *r* and trying to get the stress right. 'Nabokov Museum,' I added, remembering the master's precise injunction about the second syllable.[1] He still had that pedantic effect on me. You minded your *p*s and *q*s around Vladimir. *Vladeemirr.*

It was warm in the taxi, but the ride was short. The driver seemed trustworthy and I unbuttoned my coat, removed my gloves and watched the wide prospect, glad to be away from my responsibilities. I remembered that the teenage Vladimir had been chauffeured to the Tenishev School, Petersburg's most prestigious, in the family Benz, one of only two in Imperial Russia in the second decade of the twentieth century. The other belonged to Peter Ustinov's family. It was the kind of boffin detail about Nabokov I had picked up over the years and cherished like arcane knowledge.

The BMWs and Mercedes of the Russian plutocracy ploughed ahead through snow towards a bridge over the Moika canal. I recognised the horseman at the centre of St Isaac Square as we turned along the quay. Was it in *Speak, Memory*? Was it Bely's horseman?[2] During the strikes and demonstrations of 1905, children had climbed the trees in the square in an attempt to escape the soldiers.[3] The bullets picked them off one by one.

47 Morskaya Street: a wide, three-storeyed townhouse in the grand manner. The building had an Italianate *palazzo* quality that had come down in the world. To the left was an entry, where carriage, sleigh and Benz would have waited. I imagined myself as Vladimir dreaming in exile, his long exile in Berlin, America and finally Switzerland – Vladimir re-exploring the old family pile. We conjured it together, standing in rutted snow with streaks of car exhaust and horse piss run through it. Morskaya Street 2002. Herzen Street under the Soviet. He had been born here, above the abyss, just over a century before, in that upstairs room at the eastern end, his mother's dressing room.

❖

When you leave the motorway for the lakeside road to Montreux, the town takes you by surprise. One overgrown fishing village blends into another: St Saphorin, Vevey, La Tour de Peltz, Clarens. They sound like wines or perfumes or skin creams. They smell of money. You're there before you know it. The streets slope downwards, following old vineyard paths on the hillside, conveying you to the lake. Distracted by the view of the Dents du Midi, reined in by the speed cameras, you need to keep an eye on the road. Only past the forecourt of the station – a gap between tunnels – does the playground character of the town begin to assert itself. Jewellers and casinos, Carpe Diem Nails, a gold medallion in the chest hair of a gigolo or an off-duty croupier. But an espresso machine bangs and clicks, there's a wide selection of international glossies on the racks, and as you swing onto the promenade you begin to think in terms of a drink with a paper umbrella in it.

Parking is a problem. You roll the windows down on both sides. There's plenty of eye candy. The women look kept. The men have the swagger of keepers. Balmy air off the lake adds a chop to the water, carrying smells of frying fish and Chanel No. 5 across the promenade. Palm trees this far north. Then a little red T-model hatchback pulls out just below the Montreux Palace, pumping drum 'n' bass, the shaven-headed driver in shades, and you slide your thirteen year-old Peugeot into the vacant space and let it idle there for a minute, not believing your luck. A Caipirinha, you think. Maybe a mint julep.

The atmosphere of a nineteenth-century spa still clings to Montreux and to the gold coast towns of Switzerland. None is new to the hospitality business; they're all grown-up babes. In A *Little Swiss Sojourn*, William Dean Howells describes the town's charms and seems to pre-figure Vladimir Nabokov's stay here:

> What struck me principally in Montreux was its extreme suitability to the purposes of the international novelist...
> There is a very pretty theatre in the Kursaal, where they seldom give entertainments, but where, if you ever go, you see numbers of pretty girls, and in a box a pale, delicate-looking middle-aged Englishman in a brown velvet coat, with his two daughters. The concert will be very good, and a young man of cultivated sympathies and disdainful tastes could have a very pleasant time there.[4]

By 1960, the writer Vladimir Nabokov was an older man of cultivated sympathies and disdainful tastes. What brought him to Montreux for the final

A determined Nabokov chasing butterflies above Montreux

sixteen years of a wandering life? He was returning to Europe after two
decades soaking up American Cold War democracy. The runaway *succès
de scandale* of *Lolita* (1955) had made him wealthy,[5] following émigré poverty in Berlin and twenty years of postwar teaching in American Ivy League
colleges. But why an ice-cream and casino town like Montreux?

For the first time in his adult life, Nabokov was free from material
dependency – a fancy way of saying he was rich. He'd been a rouble millionaire before, when he was seventeen, and had inherited his Uncle Ruka's
estate – a gay old blade who liked to dandle Vladimir on his knee. But the
revolution swept that largesse from under him. For forty years Nabokov
had kept the day job. *Lolita*'s success and the sale of the movie rights had
released him from the drudgery of teaching in the American college towns
he knew so well. Before America there had been two decades of poverty in
Berlin, giving 'grinds', as we used to call them in Ireland: private language
classes, some tennis coaching, watching the clock in a thousand *bürgerlich*
living rooms. Under the *nom de plume* Sirin ('Firebird'), he became the
premier Russian writer of his generation. The Russian Revolution had long
drawn the curtains on Morskaya Street in St Petersburg. In 1939 in Paris he
began to write *The Real Life of Sebastian Knight* (1941) in English, sensing
that the Nazis were bringing his European period to a close. Like Joyce and
Mann, Nabokov nimbly kept one step ahead of history.

Besides, he was sixty, as old as the century, and felt he had earned
Switzerland. In 1959 Stanley Kubrick was about to direct the movie of

Lolita from his author's revised screenplay, with a fourteen-year-old Sue Lyon in the title role and a music score of Nelson Riddle strings. (Nabokov came round to thinking that the ten-year-old Catherine Demangeot, in Louis Malle's *Zazie dans le Métro* (1960), would have been ideal in the part.) Nabokov had written screenplays before and had been a keen movie-goer throughout the interwar years in Berlin. Kubrick's production of *Lolita* would open up to the reclusive author the Hollywood glamour of the Swiss Riviera, where Chaplin lived, where the *beau monde* kept their hideaways.

Summering in Europe and chasing butterflies, the Nabokovs reunited with family after a twenty-year hiatus. Sister Elena was a Geneva resident, and brother Kirill lived in Brussels. A second sister, Olga, remained in Prague behind the Iron Curtain. Nabokov's other brother, Sergei, had died in Neuengamme concentration camp near Hamburg. Sergei had been openly homosexual, associated with sexual activist Magnus Hirschfeld in Berlin, Jean Cocteau, impresario Diaghilev and artist Pavel Tchelishchev in the gay scene in Paris.[6] Vladimir never had much time for 'poor stuttering Sergei'[7] and was distinctly homophobic.

By mid-August 1961 the Nabokovs were dining with Peter Ustinov, resident in the Montreux Palace. Actor and raconteur, Ustinov was of Russian, Jewish and Ethiopian descent. His Russian forebears had made their fortune in Siberian salt. His father had worked for MI5. The actor had just won an Academy Award for his role in *Spartacus*, and had been considered for the role of Humbert Humbert in *Lolita*. Ustinov could almost have been a Nabokov creation.

At Ustinov's instigation, the Nabokovs moved into two sets of rooms in the original 'tawny and gilt' Cygne wing of the Montreux Palace Hotel.[8] Ustinov tried to restrain his children in case they would disturb 'Mr. Nabokov, who is writing a novel upstairs', but it was the heavy-set Ustinov himself whose treads Nabokov heard.[9] Eventually occupying a suite of rooms on the topmost sixth floor, Vladimir and Véra unpacked their cases for a stay that stretched to sixteen years. Véra continued to live at the Montreux Palace after Vladimir's death in 1977, until shortly before her own death in 1991. It was their longest stay anywhere and perhaps the longest room occupancy in hotel history.

Europe's grand hotels were a familiar habitat for this child of the Russian emigration raised with a retinue of servants. Aged five, Nabokov stayed in the Hotel Oranien in Wiesbaden. At ten it was Biarritz. The Nabokov boys had their teeth braced in Berlin, staying at the Adlon Hotel. Entering the Hotel Negresco's rotunda lobby on the Promenade des Anglais in Nice, the

The original Cygne wing of the Montreux Palace Hotel

adult author vividly recalled running around it as a child, only to discover that it had not been built at the time.[10] Memory was so much his stock in trade that strict truth became immaterial, tricky. In *Speak, Memory* he calls these slips the 'leakings and drafts from another dimension'.[11] Memory and imagination had created their own truth by the time Nabokov booked into the Montreux Palace. He summed up the hotel's usefulness:

> *It simplifies postal matters, it eliminates the nuisance of private owner-ship, it confirms me in my favourite habit – the habit of freedom. ... One of the reasons I live in Montreux is because I find the view from my easy chair wonderfully soothing and exhilarating according to my mood or the mood of the lake.*[12]

He had been visiting the Swiss Riviera for many decades and had made use of Swiss locales in his work right from the start. In 'Wingstroke', a 1923 short story, a triangular relationship involves lust in a Zermatt hotel, against a background of ski slopes: 'he went out onto the enormous enclosed veranda, where a chilled band was playing and people in bright scarves were drinking strong tea, ready to rush out again into the cold, onto the slopes that shone with a humming shimmer through the wide window-panes'.[13] The story reconfigures Nabokov's real-life sojourn in St Moritz with a gay Cambridge pal, Count Robert Louis Magawly-Cerati de Calry. Nabokov would always be fond of arresting names.

In 'Easter Rain' (1926), a story lost for seventy years but unearthed in former East German archives, Nabokov dissects the sentimentality towards Russia of an old Swiss governess: 'in the morning, the mountains on the far side of Lake Leman were all veiled in silky mist, like the opaque sheets of rice paper that cover etchings in expensive books'.[14] This little cameo of exile was drawn from Nabokov's visit to his former governess in Lausanne, Cécile Miauton, the 'Mademoiselle O' of *Speak, Memory*.

Glory (1932), *Laughter in the Dark* (1932) and *Despair* (1934) all have their Swiss scenes in hotels and sanatoria and alpine meadows. Humbert Humbert, the narrator of *Lolita*, has a Swiss father, 'a gentle, easy-going person, a salad of racial genes: a Swiss citizen, of mixed French and Austrian descent, with a dash of the Danube in his veins'.[15] Humbert grows up in the Midi, where 'the splendid Hotel Mirana revolved as a kind of private universe, a whitewashed cosmos within the blue greater one that blazed outside'.[16] From early on, Nabokov liked and exploited hotel settings, the sense they give of a command performance with the guest as conductor. In the novels written in Montreux, characters pass through the same space at different times, like guests in rented rooms.

The novel Nabokov was writing at the start of his stay in Montreux was *Pale Fire* (1962), considered by many his most perfect achievement. He worked steadily on it through a rainy summer, inventing Zembla, Kinbote's imaginary kingdom, which borrows from Switzerland's clockwork idyll. Nabokov admitted making Zembla 'out of the rejects of other countries'.[17] Montreux's microclimate gives a tropical glow to Nabokov's prose in *Pale Fire*: 'intense enjoyment and exquisite heartbreak from the balustrade of a terrace at nightfall, from the lights and the lake below, from the distant mountain shape melting into the dark apricot of the afterglow'.[18] This is as good a description as any of the view from Nabokov's top floor rooms at the Montreux Palace.

In *Strong Opinions* (1973), Nabokov singles out the hotel garden that had become his study:

> A good deal of Kinbote's commentary was written here in the Montreux Palace garden, one of the most enchanting and inspiring gardens I know. I'm especially fond of its weeping cedar, the arboreal counterpart of a very shaggy dog with hair hanging over its eyes.[19]

The success of *Lolita*, novel and film, gave the author a certain celebrity on the Swiss Riviera. American friends who visited him found a Nabokov code-switching from his new-world courtesies back to the European grand manner with a dollop of Russianness. By the 1960s, Hollywood had discovered *la dolce vita* and the delights of wintering in Switzerland. In February 1966 Nabokov began writing *Ada* (he had the habit of composing novels in his head long before noting them onto index cards), following a drive along the shore to the Hotel des Trois Couronnes at Vevey. Véra and Vladimir had arranged to dine with actor James Mason, like Nabokov a Cambridge graduate (Trinity: second-class honours in Russian and French for Vladimir; Peterhouse and a first in architecture for Mason). Mason had played Humbert in Kubrick's *Lolita*. The fourth member of the party was Countess Vivian Crespi, formerly Vivian Stokes, a Newport childhood friend of Jacqueline Kennedy and an 'international socialite'. She had married a son of Standard Oil first time round and Italian nobility on the rebound. This mix of old Europe and Hollywood glamour fed into the worldly characters of Van and Ada, the romantic incestuous couple at the heart of Nabokov's new novel.

He amalgamated the Montreux and Vevey hotels to build his house of cards in the air. Van and Ada's steamy trysts take place at the Hotel Trois Cygnes. The real Hotel de Cygne, built in 1837, became the Montreux Palace in 1906. The hotel has a mural 'seen through its entrance, the huge memorable oil – three ample-haunched Ledas swapping lacustrine impressions'.[20] The swan wall painting is still there in the lobby.

> *The Three Swans overwinged a bastion. Anyone who called, flesh or voice, was told by the concierge or his acolytes that Van was out, that Madame André Vinelander was unknown, and that all they could do was to take a message. His car, parked in a secluded bosquet, could not betray his presence. In the forenoon he regularly used the service lift that communicated directly with the backyard.*[21]

Thus Nabokov, like Van, had his habits. The rear entrance to the Cygne wing leads to a garden encroached on these days by parking bays. Two adjacent exits take the guest onto the junction of Avenue des Alpes and the narrow rue du Cygne, which descends to the lake. Towards the end of *Ada*, Nabokov twice describes this tiny corner observed so well on his daily stroll to the newsagents:

He went for a stroll – and saw that the famous 'mûrier,' that spread its
great limbs over a humble lavatory on a raised terrace at the top of a
cobbled lane, was now in sumptuous purple-blue bloom. He had a beer
at the café opposite the railway station, and then, automatically, entered
the flower shop next door.[22]

Only the dead end of the rue du Cygne remains cobbled today, but the café
opposite the station – The Grand Café Suisse – is still serving excellent
espresso. The mulberry bush does not have 'great limbs'; this is Nabokov
in playful mood, whimsically morphing the vegetation. Photographed for
a *Life* magazine feature in front of the station kiosk, Nabokov joshed with
the proprietor. Joshing was his manner. He purchased his polylingual dai-
lies and glossy weeklies opposite the station, on the covers of which old
Cold War warriors – Solzhenitsyn, Pasternak, Bobby Fischer and himself
– slogged it out for democracy.

When I hover over the rear exit of the Montreux Palace on Google
Street View, with its weeping cedar and fresh tarmacadam, the oncoming
cars magically rush through me as I zoom and navigate. I have become a
Transparent Thing, outwitting time. I can zoom in on Morskaya Street in
St Petersburg with the stroke of a trackpad, or travel to Vyra, the Nabokov
country estate. None of this surfing is a match for his subtle, multilayered
prose, tracking consciousness:

A gingko (of a much more luminous greenish gold than its neighbour,
a dingily yellowing local birch) marked the corner of a cobbled lane
leading down to the quay. They followed southward the famous Fillietaz
Promenade which went along the Swiss side of the lake from Valvey to
the Château de Byron (or 'She Yawns Castle'). The fashionable season
had ended, and wintering birds, as well as a number of knickerbockered
Central Europeans, had replaced the English families as well as the
Russian noblemen from Nipissing and Nipigon.[23]

In *Ada,* Van alludes to his long memory of Switzerland. Having lost
one country – the Russia of his childhood – Nabokov looked on all
countries as temporary backdrops for his imagination, to do with as he
sees fit. Montreux is the magical town of his fancy and Swiss hotels are
a kind of assemble-it-yourself world that pops into life on Mnemosyne's
whim:

'When I was a kid,' said Van, 'and stayed for the first – or rather, second – time in Switzerland, I thought that "Verglas" on roadway signs stood for some magical town, always around the corner, at the bottom of every snowy slope, never seen, but biding its time.'[24]

When not writing his late, magical novels, Nabokov hunted butterflies, played tennis on the hotel courts and walked along the lakeshore promenade. He was a fan of Swiss efficiency. His biographer Brian Boyd recounts how Nabokov's broken American dentures were mailed to Lausanne at eleven o'clock in the morning and returned fixed at nine in the evening. Between braced teeth in Berlin in 1910 and false teeth in Lausanne, a half-century of turbulent history had transpired.

Nabokov cut a dapper figure on the streets of Montreux. He had always been sartorially interesting. His Cambridge undergraduate threads – boating and tennis whites, the canary-yellow cardie – gave way to cable-knit V-neck sweaters in the 1930s, thin at the writing elbow. Once he gave up smoking, Professor Nabokov morphed to the rotund, tweedy elegance of middle age. Montreux photographer Horst Tappe snapped a mischievous, multi-faceted, outdoorsy man of letters: 1950s sack suit, desert boots, the full regalia of the butterfly hunter.[25]

On the esplanade across from the Montreux Palace sits a statue of the master in butterfly-hunting duds, facing the lake and the mountains. Knickerbockers and thick knee socks give him a resemblance to Baden Powell. A butterfly net beside him brings to mind a word I picked up from Nabokov and cherished for years: tarlatan, the green mesh used for catching butterflies or striddlies. Nabokov's statue suggests a fulfilled life, a man pleased with himself. It's not a particularly good likeness, but it captures him in magisterial mode, looking out at a view he probably clocked better than any other.[26]

A break from one hotel to another, at the Grand Hotel in Saas-Fee in the Valais in June 1970, allowed the slim novel *Transparent Things* (1972) to 'burst into life' after a dinner of *raclette* and white wine. Nabokov was still working on it a year later and staying again in the Valais. He asked for a room facing south, but because of construction noise ('a tremendous crater full of excavating machines'; a motif in *Transparent Things*) the manager gave him both a room facing south and another facing north.

Transparent Things is the master's most Swiss novel. The interchangeable resort hotels and mountain slopes of the Swiss Riviera and the Valais, where Nabokov had made his home, form its shifting backdrop. Hugh

Person (You Person), the protagonist, is trapped in time, returning to the same locale over decades, as Nabokov had now been doing in Switzerland since his twenties:

> *This was his fourth visit to Switzerland. The first one had been eighteen years before when he had stayed for a few days at Trux with his father. Ten years later, at thirty-two, he had revisited that old lakeside town and had successfully courted a sentimental thrill, half wonder and half remorse, by going to see their hotel. A steep lane and a flight of old stairs led to it from lake level where the local train had brought him to a featureless station.*[27]

Trux seems a shoe-in for Montreux, and we are back at Nabokov's old stamping ground: steep lane, hotel and featureless station. These days there are statues of Miles Davis and Quincy Jones side by side with Nabokov's on the waterfront – stars at the jazz festival that has become Montreux's calling card. Freddie Mercury, microphone in hand, regales the lakeside. I'm not sure Vladimir would relish such loud company. He was inclined to call modern music 'jungle jingles' or 'primitive', in the same way as his homosexuals are always described as 'mincing'. Jazz from below decks, the workingman's blues, was never his thing.

In *Transparent Things* the distinguished writer R. is a guest of the Versex Palace. Nabokov parodies the august manner of the grand old man of letters, but somewhere in this hall of mirrors he's sending himself up:

> *Yet what a grand sight R. presented – his handsome chauffeur helping the obese old boy on one side, his black-bearded secretary supporting him on the other, and two chasseurs from the hotel going through a mimicry of tentative assistance on the porch steps. The reporter in Person noted that Mr. R. wore Wallabees of a velvety cocoa shade, a lemon shirt with a lilac neck scarf, and a rumpled grey suit that seemed to have no distinction whatsoever – at least, to a plain American.*[28]

In one of the many photos of Nabokov at Montreux, he's wearing 1960s cocoa-coloured Wallabees. He was good at describing staff – waiters, tutors, servants. It is a patrician view, that adjective often used for his sense of hierarchy, his place in the world. Reading him, we get an idea of Switzerland as one big, many-roomed hotel, with the sounds from outside muted and the scenery bright as a chocolate box. Here's what he likes about it:

Nabokov outside the Montreux Palace Hotel

Exquisite postal service. No bothersome demonstrations, no spiteful strikes. Alpine butterflies. Fabulous sunsets – just west of my window, spangling the lake, splitting the crimson sun! Also, the pleasant surprise of a metaphorical sunset in charming surroundings.[29]

On my visits to Montreux I usually sit on a bench on the promenade and look up at the Montreux Palace, picking out the rooms the Nabokovs stayed in. It costs a small fortune to rent them. Yellow scalloped awnings shade the balconies, as though a theatre has been turned inside out, each trimmed with palatial gold monogram. The forecourt is 'cordoned off with blood-coloured ropes',[30] as John le Carré puts it in a completely different context, a *cordon sanitaire* suspended between brass goalposts.

On one visit I sit in the coffee shop and watch a tall flunkey go about his business. He fills out his doorman's uniform – a grey, three-quarter-length morning coat with brass buttons. Beside him a bellboy in a little cocked pillbox hat, one step lower, in lovely livery. Then a big silver BMW with French plates pulls into the forecourt and an elderly man is escorted towards it. He's wearing a check flat cap, the kind that Maghreb men wear in retirement. His bodyguard holds the car door open for him as he laboriously manoeuvres himself and his cane down and in. Is he a retired general, an ex-president, a deposed despot? He could be any of these. The man behind me is talking loudly into his mobile phone in a hybrid of Arabic and English management-speak.

It could be R. from *Transparent Things*, being helped out of the Versex Palace. But I suspect he is some old oily potentate past his best, off for an afternoon nap and perhaps a bit of how's-yer-father with a call girl masquerading as a masseuse. *Barely legal babes*, I say to myself out loud in the coffee shop, rolling it around in my mouth the way we're encouraged to enunciate *Lo-lee-ta*. It has a satisfying assonance and alliteration. Nobody pays me the slightest bit of notice. Mr Management-speak is still talking on his phone. The moral climate of Montreux, I think, is torrid, and immune to such things. I imagine the old patriarch writing his memoirs in Arabic with the help of a ghostwriter, and then breaking off for a spot of mint tea.

During the hot summer of 1977, the summer of punk, I was a street sweeper in Amsterdam. The job was a good one, cleaning the pavements of the Oud-West district, the fruit and vegetable market at Kinkerstraat. My day started at six in the morning but finished by eleven. I headed to the American Bookstore on Spui, where I read Andrew Field's *Nabokov: His Life in Part*, which had just been published. Fifty pages at a sitting, cross-legged on the floor upstairs in the window alcove. I finished it within the week. In those pre-internet days there was little about the master beyond the biographical note. Nabokov, too, claimed never to have bought a book in émigré Berlin, but to have 'read whole tomes little by little in the bookshops'.[31]

I'd been a lone Nabokov fan for years. Lifting my head from Imperial Russia, the 1970s flotsam of Amsterdam swam into view. There was a long-haired couple we called Jesus and Mary who panhandled to feed their heroin habit. They had the addict's dogged stride, those cheesecloth shirts with the sleeves rolled down. The smell of fried *krokets*, mayonnaise on chips, drifted up from a fast food outlet. The new punk hairdos. I dipped back into the hardscrabble world of émigré Berlin in the 1920s, into Nabokov's astonishingly prolific imagination.

Down on Spui a posse of Hare Krishnas swayed and jangled. They always looked as though they'd cacked their pantaloons. It didn't occur to my young self that Nabokov was dying in Switzerland as I read. I could have hitchhiked down the Rhine valley, popped across the border and stalked the hospital at Clarens, hiding out in the expensive shrubbery. *Vlad! Volodya! Lody!*

With age the world grows transparent, we become transparent things: we see through the ploys of our employers; 'our cloudy blackboards' become whiteboards, become interactive; there is more memory than anticipation; we start thinking we've been here before, the whole show is déjà vu. We start to look again at writers who have accompanied us along the way, who have been guides.

For me it was round about 1972 and *The Real Life of Sebastian Knight*, bought in Hamills on the North Road in Monaghan. It stocked *Sweet 16* or *Teen 16* or *16 Sweet Teens*, American import magazines that had a gloss, lick and spittle entirely absent from *The Lourdes Messenger*, say, or the *Catholic Truth Enquirer* or *Our Boys*. Memory tells me the proprietor was Irish-speaking. Broad-planed face, brilliantined hair like a shogun's. Amateur dramatics and cathedral choir: that kind of decent provincial newsagent.

The Real Life of Sebastian Knight's air of continental savvy drew me in. I was a sucker for the *wagons-lits*, French dropped into a sentence. All aboard for the *Conti-nong*! And the niggling sense that something tantalising was going on beneath the writing.

These days I like to drive up to the graveyard at Clarens, park the car to look down on the lake and across at the Dents du Midi. The master's buried there beside Véra, both part of the Russian diaspora, an exile that in many ways gave him a subject. The revolution pulled his childhood in St Petersburg and Vyra from under him. Assassins shot his liberal father, and one of them became Hitler's deputy of émigré affairs. Life thereafter became an invention, a short-time hotel, an enfilade of rooms for hire, a magic carpet. Below, following the old vineyard paths, sits the rococo Montreux Palace Hotel, like a doddering dowager in a bath chair on the lakeshore. A susurrus of leaves, a breath of oxidation from Rousseau's vineyards, traversed by Byron and Shelley, Dickens, Hugo, Twain, James, Eliot, Fitzgerald, Hemingway and Nabokov – all the big boys. Slowly the mountains turn pink as a twelve-year-old's lipstick and then decline to purple – the puce of a good-time-girl's mouth.

I leave you with Nabokov's masterly description in *Transparent Things* of the inadequacy of Swiss hot chocolate:

> You were served a cup of hot milk. You also got, separately, a little sugar and a dainty-looking envelope of sorts. You ripped open the upper margin of the envelope. You added the beige dust it contained to the ruthlessly homogenized milk in your cup. You took a sip – and hurried to add sugar. But no sugar could improve the insipid, sad, dishonest taste.

Armande, who had been following the various phases of his astonishment and disbelief, smiled and said:

'Now you know what "hot chocolate" has come to in Switzerland.'[32]

10

TICINO NOIR

Highsmith plays hide and seek

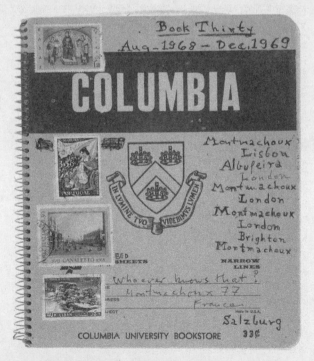

Patricia Highsmith's Columbia University 'cahier'

As long as there's a Switzerland, I don't know when I'll get around to going home again.
Patricia Highsmith

She first arrived in Switzerland after the war as a successful young novelist, a material girl with everything going for her. The last thirteen years of her life were spent as a recluse in Switzerland's Ticino. Alcoholic, her looks gone, her mind poisoned by right-wing phobias – but rich. Patricia Highsmith's almost fifty-year relationship with Switzerland hardly impinged on her work as the mistress of murder, but she did write a final novel set in Zürich. She thought of Switzerland as a refuge from the dirty world, from tax inspectors, and as a place to work in peace. Although she left her considerable fortune to Yaddo writers' colony in upstate New York, she left her papers to the Swiss Literary Archives in Bern. She is a dark moth, winging her way back to Switzerland, looking for a place to call home.

At the end of 1952, thirty-one-year-old Patricia Highsmith had good cause to feel happy. Her first novel, *Strangers on a Train* (1950), was a critical success. She had seen Alfred Hitchcock's masterly film production of it in Munich. Her second novel, *The Price of Salt/Carol* (1952), had sold to Bantam for $6,500. It would become a cult classic on the lesbian daisy chain and go on to sell a million copies. In 2015 it would be made into yet another successful Highsmith film. She was already working on a third novel, *The Blunderer* (1954). Her first three books would in time become *noir* masterpieces. In June she had spotted 'a solitary, young man in shorts and sandals'[1] on the beach at Positano, whose fictional reincarnation as Tom Ripley would make her fame and fortune in the decades to come.

But Highsmith was not constitutionally made for happiness. She was born in Fort Worth, Texas, nine days after her mother divorced. Mother and stepfather abandoned her with her grandmother while they went off to find work in New York. She was an only child. By the age of twelve she knew she was a boy in a girl's body. In 1952 she was in the middle of a quarrelsome on-again, off-again relationship with Ellen Hill, a forty-two-year-old sociologist about whom nobody has a good word to say.

For two years Highsmith had been zigzagging across Europe, dropping one woman and picking up another, hobnobbing with the great and the articulate. She met Peggy Guggenheim and Somerset Maugham in Venice. Maugham made her his signature dry Martini. In Forio on the Amalfi coast, she encountered W.H. Auden 'barefoot with a pansy'.[2] To her

Patricia Highsmith, age 12, on the Staten Island ferry, New York, early 1930s

dismay, the famous conversationalist wittered on about the cost of living – a subject the miserly Highsmith was not averse to herself.

They travelled by car from Paris, across Switzerland, to Trieste, where Hill had a job inspecting refugees. Europe was recovering from the devastations of war, but you would hardly notice it from Highsmith's account. She describes the 1952 road trip in the spiral-bound Columbia University lined notebooks she kept all her life, which she called her *cahiers*. Together with her typewriter, the *cahiers* have taken up permanent residence in the Swiss Literary Archives in Bern.

On a previous spin through Zürich, Highsmith had noted that it was 'very prim and bourgeois and opulent. I am a bit sated on luxury.'[3] Hill footed the bills for the best hotels, as well as providing the car. It was that golden period after the war when everybody who mattered seemed to be on Fulbrights, the dollar was riding high and 'empty young heads were living on some ancestors' money'. Highsmith envied the trust fund babies their easy, careless movements, and the key to Ripley's arriviste pretensions lies in her own insecurities of class and gender. Throughout the 1950s, she used the cheaper trans-Atlantic tramp steamers rather than Cunard liners.

On Christmas Day 1952 they were in Basel, staying at the Hotel des Trois Rois, the city's finest. They had a 'tournedos dinner' in the hotel dining room. Highsmith noted the Rhine flowing 'like a millrace northward'.

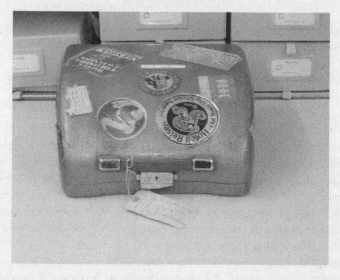

Highsmith's Olympia Deluxe portable, used from 1956 onwards

Basel was closed for the holiday, but she carefully observed the façade of the cathedral and remarked on its 'gabled-like roofs, decorated with yellow lozenges with red dots, like a calico parasol'.[4]

It was the untouched post-war prosperity of Switzerland that appealed to Highsmith, in contrast to the privations of France. This view of Switzerland as a shiny little America appealed to her acquisitiveness, her eye for consumerism. She was an author on the make in a land of plenty. She was also homesick:

> Whenever I get desperately homesick, but still not desperately enough to spend several hundred dollars getting back to America, I go to Switzerland.
>
> In Zürich, walking down Bahnhofstrasse, or lunching at the Möven-Pick, I can imagine I'm right back in America. The waitress at the Mövenpick who speaks English with an American accent. And in fact it was that astoundingly self-confident advertisement in the Swiss tourist bureau and in the Paris Herald Tribune – 'the only country in Europe where all your hosts speak English' – that gave me the final push to come. Ah, that luscious Grade A milk of Switzerland! Those hamburger steaks served with a bottle of California-made ketchup! And a hotel room with a free cake of soap on the basin! And the central heating that really functions! And the taxicabs that I can actually get into

without fracturing a skull! Just like America! And after all, the taxis are American cars.[5]

In Zürich they stayed at the Hotel Zum Storchen, near the Coop, about which Highsmith waxed lyrical:

> But what eases my homesickness quicker than anything else is to visit a big Cooperative Self-Service market, like the one on the square near the Storchen Hotel. All those endless shelves of cans, cellophane-wrapped cookies, breakfast foods, cheeses, delicatessen meats, fresh vegetables, cigarettes and candy are not only like America but – (I whisper it gently) – even better. You have a bigger variety of breads and cookies than we have. Every and better cheeses, infinitely more types of cigarettes to choose from. Obviously Switzerland has adopted a lot of new ideas from America, but there are some that Switzerland has improved upon – like the de luxe type of sandwich shop that the Mövenpick is.[6]

Highsmith's four novels at mid-century – *Strangers on a Train, The Price of Salt, The Blunderer* and *The Talented Mr Ripley* – fizz with the Fifties. She took trouble with verisimilitude: a Pullman interior's 'unlighted cigar that still gyrated conversationally in a bony hand behind one of the seat backs'[7]; the pre-Christmas rush of a New York department store where the section manager 'was dragging dolls from the stock shelves and seating them, splay legged, on the glass counters'.[8] She captures the gloss of American diners, luncheonettes and soda fountains. Her fleeing lovers in *The Price of Salt*, pursued by an undercover detective, anticipate the road trip in *Lolita* and pre-date the Beats. She renders an American city hotel in the lean prose of pulp fiction:

> She wandered across the lobby, looked through the glass into the barber shop where a couple of men were getting shaves. A black man was shining shoes. A tall man with a cigar and a broad-brimmed hat, with Western boots, walked by her. She would remember this lobby, too, forever, the people, the old-fashioned-looking woodwork at the base of the registration desk, and the man in the dark overcoat who looked at her over the top of his newspaper, and slumped in his chair and went on reading beside the black and cream-colored marble column.[9]

The Swiss notebook from 1952–53 gives us a rough draft of Highsmith's cool style, her characteristic way of looking. Here she describes a pre-theatre dinner in Zürich:

> I order a calf's liver in one of the sturdy little Weinstübli of Zürich. In America a piece about the size of my palm would appear – and out comes a large platter with enough liver and onions, string beans and Bratkartoffeln to feed a couple of husky men. And I should mention that the price is little more than half what I would pay in a comparable place in New York or Paris too. Applesauce afterward? By all means. Then comes a soup bowl full of it, and a couple of delicious cookies with it besides. Considering that Swiss-sized breakfast I ate in the hotel the same morning, including about half a liter of hot rich milk, and the Mövenpick lunch when I nearly killed myself sampling about five items, it seems impossible to finish all the apple sauce – but I do. Indirectly the hearty appetite of the other people in the Stübli inspires me. I have been watching a man demolish a Schweinskotelette about the size of his head, while the woman at the table on the left, after a heaped plate of hors d'oeuvres, is now tackling a plate of half a chicken, noodles. This crucial diet, I suspect, probably makes for the famous stolid character of the Swiss people. The Americans drink too much, anyway. I note that the average Swiss drinks Apfelsaft or beer with his food.[10]

Highsmith fancied herself a gourmet, but she was a picky eater. What we're witnessing here are the stirrings of her Europhilia, which would lead to decades of exile in France and, eventually, Switzerland. In the second week of January 1953 the pair had moved to the Kulm Hotel in St Moritz. Highsmith noted 'the staid couples swathed to the neck in racoon rugs' heading to their hotels or to Handsellmann's Konditorei, and the 'hot chocolate, lebkuchen biscuits and obscure martinis'.[11]

She was a hungry girl.

After four stormy months in Trieste, they sailed back to the conditioned air of Eisenhower's America. 'It was a queer, sultry summer, the summer they executed the Rosenbergs,'[12] as another female American writer put it. Ellen Hill, always high-strung, attempted suicide in New York. Highsmith retreated to her birthplace in Fort Worth and wrote The Blunderer, one of her best books.

She began writing The Talented Mr. Ripley in Lenox, Massachusetts. Central to the novel's reworking of Henry James's The Ambassadors is the lure of Europe for young Americans, the freedoms of *la dolce vita* during the McCarthy years. Ripley's frenetic motoring around the Med, shedding his own identity and assuming that of the wealthy, debonair Dicky Greenleaf, has its parallel in Highsmith's high living with Ellen Hill – meals and wheels, Swiss grand hotels, all the food you could eat. Ripley sails to Europe first class, paid for by the father of the man he will kill. His last words in the novel are '*Il meglio albergo. Il meglio, il meglio!*' – 'The best hotel! The best, the best!'

By the time Highsmith returned to live in Switzerland in the early 1980s, the best was behind her. Her later books can be hit and miss, but she was rich from the movie rights. At one point the BBC was considering a $100,000 deal to adapt the Ripley novels as a television series. The famous cool style had begun to wear thin, to become plain speaking in the Texan manner. Alcohol had hardened her *gamine* looks. French tax inspectors and Mitterrand's socialists had her scurrying to Switzerland's Italian-speaking Ticino. Here she lived out the last thirteen years of her life in miserly wealth, poor health and alcoholism.

She bought a tall stone house in the hamlet of Aurigeno in the Valle Maggia, behind Locarno. On a sunny day the deep cleft can be sparkling and magical, but for much of the year it is lightless and forbidding. In a late story about a land dispute between a local priest and a farmer, 'A Long Walk from Hell', she described her situation: 'a land of mountains that block the sun, a land of granite outcroppings, of trees that cling to the slanting hillsides, but nevertheless grow straight up'.[13]

She intended to divide her time between homes in France (two of them, as well as a cottage in Sussex, England) and Switzerland, to com-ply with favourable tax arrangements. In 1988, she wrote to an old lover, Marijane Meaker:

> When you make a lot of money you get suspicious. Did I tell you that Bloomsbury liked my latest Ripley so much they gave me an advance that in American money comes to about $115,000? I never got that much for a book. You know, in the U.S. no one really recognises me, but in Europe I'm often recognised and treated like a celebrity.[14]

Aurigeno had 105 inhabitants at the time of Highsmith's arrival in 1981. Ticino villages had fed emigration to California during the nineteenth

century. Ticinese farmers, initially attracted by the Gold Rush, began sup-
plying dairy products to San Francisco. As Switzerland prospered, the canton's valleys and lakeshore sheltered second homes, wealthy foreigners and
artists. Golo Mann and Max Frisch had houses up the valley. The Locarno
film festival brought a sprinkling of Tinseltown. 'The Ticino is also a mysterious place,' wrote Highsmith, 'composed of a lot of granite said to have a
magnetic effect, draining one's energy.'[15]

Her house had been built with Ticino's traditional grey granite in 1680.
'People come to the Ticino for the light,' said her editor Daniel Keel, 'and
she put herself into the darkest, most cramped house, no room, no quality
of life; she didn't give her guests anything, but she didn't give herself anything either. It was the most uncomfortable house in the world with the
mountains right up against it, which cut out even the two hours of sunlight
a day the town got.'[16]

Even Highsmith disliked it:

> I had the feeling of living in a submarine. The submarine is my house ...
> The walls are a meter thick at least. The lower cellar's two rooms are like
> dungeons with arched ceilings lined with round stones the size of oranges
> and grapefruit. Four pieces of granite project from the walls of each dun-
> geon to hold lengths of red chestnut wood, now sagging with time. These
> crosspieces were to keep cheese and hams out of reach of mice and rats.
> I have never seen a rat or a mouse here, but once I found a snake in the
> second cellar.[17]

She had always been interested in houses. Guy, the protagonist of *Strangers
on a Train*, is a prize-winning architect. Ripley plays lord of the manor in
modernist swank in France. Highsmith was drawn to the clean spare lines
of the Bauhaus. Her own houses, however, were singularly uncomfortable
and badly chosen.

> The village sits on one side (the side with less sun in winter, as it happens)
> of the Valle Maggia, and has two main streets parallel to each other,
> paved but one-lane, causing cars to move slowly. There is no bakery or
> butcher, but a small grocery shop exists for staples. One trattoria serves
> as bar-café, and provides hot meals if you get there on time to meet their
> chef's hours. There's wine, of course. Everyone drinks wine here and also
> grappa. A village man sells his home-made grappa for twenty-five francs
> per liter, and very good it is, either neat or tossed into a cup of espresso.[18]

Patricia Highsmith with cat in Palisades, New York, 1958.

Highsmith was self-taught in German and peppered her speech with phrases to the point of irritation. 'Pat grabbed at any opportunity to speak German,' recalls Marijane Meaker, who thought it was 'a melancholy affection for the father she never really knew'.[19] A neighbour in Switzerland 'thought that German was Pat's best language – and it was bad'.[20]

Her former agent, Schartle Myrer, had this to say about Highsmith's antipathy for America and her put-on Europhilia:

> She was totally secretive about her past – I asked a few questions about Texas, which she refused to answer. She really didn't want anyone to know about her American origins and always avoided it. She tried to assume a superior European view even in that first meeting [1959], which was rather pathetic. Highsmith had absolutely no grace – poor woman, she thought having an espresso machine made her sophisticated.[21]

After six years in Aurigeno, Highsmith moved a few kilometres down the valley to a modern house in Tegna, commissioned from architect Tobias Amman. On her first trip through Switzerland in January 1953 she had written:

Someday, perhaps, I shall have a house built of rock, a house with a name – Hanley-on-the-Lake, Bedford on the River, West Hills, or plain Sunny Vale. Something. So even without my own name on the envelope letters will reach me, because I and only I shall be living there. But that can never make up for these years of standing in line at American Express offices from Opera to Haymarket, Naples to Munich.[22]

Casa Highsmith has a functional foursquare look, with the 'French windows' she repeatedly notes as a marker of class. She showed photos of it to Marijane Meaker, saying 'I designed it myself, which I hope qualifies me as an artist, since I don't have my sketchbooks with me. I had help from a prominent architect whose name probably isn't familiar here.' Meaker thought the 'windows seemed like lookout slits in the side of an old fort'.[23] They faced a garden where Highsmith liked to potter – as does Ripley. In a radio interview she mentions planting American corn and *fraises des bois* or wild strawberries. Her go-to coffee-table book was *A Color Atlas of Forensic Pathology*. Her few visitors were eager to leave.

One of them was Australian writer Robert Dessaix, whose narrator is coming to terms with an AIDS diagnosis:

I thought she might have interesting things to say about death, having described it from every conceivable angle. ... 'Be under the clock in the main square at one,' Patricia Highsmith had said to me on the telephone in a kind of diffident drawl ...

It was an oddly suburban sort of house in concrete brick, not at all the sort of house I'd thought Patricia Highsmith would choose to live in. It had nothing of the tasteful charm, for instance, of Tom Ripley's 'Belle Ombre' about it, although she must have been much wealthier than she'd made Ripley out to be. Then again, her novels are often very suburban (in a sense), cluttered with the details of ordinary lives in ordinary settings. And she herself – what was my mother's phrase? – did not take much trouble with herself. Long, grey-brown hair, a brownish cardigan – the boutiques and salons of Locarno were clearly not her stamping-ground. Owlish is the word that comes to mind, perhaps because of the slightly hooded eyes.[24]

In a letter to editor Liz Calder at Bloomsbury, Highsmith described her routine: 'When I get up in the morning, I first of all make the coffee and then I say to my cat, we're going to have a great day.' Highsmith's day, in point of fact, began with a shot of vodka from the fridge. She marked the bottle so she could keep track of her drinking. *Then* she made the coffee. Meaker describes the moment in 1963 when she realised Highsmith was an alcoholic:

> *By now she was apparently drinking all day, beginning with breakfast. By evening, she was sullen, quiet, looking most unhappy when she appeared for dinner in the usual shined shoes, pressed trousers, blazer, white shirt, and ascot.*[25]

When she ate, it was the comfort dishes of Fort Worth, Texas: American bacon, fried eggs and cereal. 'She would never eat,' reported one of her lovers, 'she would cook *lapin à la crème* for her two Siamese cats, but would not touch it herself.'[26] A favourite supper was corned beef hash with an egg on top. Another guest recalls 'being absolutely starving and looking in the fridge and all there was was peanut butter and vodka. I hardly saw her eat.'[27]

At the Giardinetto Pizzeria in Tegna, she nursed a pash on the proprietor. She made sorties to nearby Locarno and Ascona. The covers of the Columbia University cahiers record hectic travels to film festivals and writers' junkets. Six films had been adapted from her books and there were options for more. The roster of directors and stars is impressive: Alfred Hitchcock, Claude Miller, Claude Chabrol, Wim Wenders, Alain Delon, Gérard Départieu and Denis Hopper. Twenty years after her death, films based on her work are still being produced.

Wenders described how his film *The American Friend* came about:

> *And then she pulled this fat typewritten manuscript out of the drawer of her writing table and gave it to me. (Well, it must have been a copy.) And she said: 'Even my agent hasn't read this one yet. So I'm certain the rights are not sold yet. Maybe you want to read it.' Did I want to read it!? The title said:* Ripley's Game. *I had finished it before I was home in Munich on the train. And I wrote to her: 'Yes, absolutely. I want to acquire the rights to make a film after this novel!' And it became* The American Friend. *My first working title was:* Framed. *Did I know that she was Texan? Sure. I knew she was from Fort Worth.*[28]

Her anti-Semitism and bigotry had become entrenched with the years. In the 1960s, Highsmith used the terms 'nigro' and 'nigger' with impunity, granting 'Negro' only ironically. She thought being a Texan gave her special licence in race matters. This descendant of antebellum slave owners from Gadsden, Alabama harboured no particular empathy for the plight of African Americans. In November 1961, when Martin Luther King, Jr was leading protests against segregated lunch counters and restrooms in Georgia department stores, Highsmith was grumbling about Northerners not understanding 'the colored'. She disparaged Lorraine Hansberry, the first female playwright to make it to Broadway with *A Raisin in the Sun*. Hansberry was black, and a closet lesbian. Writing to Kingsley in 1969, Highsmith didn't hold back:

> I regret to say I have now joined the batch of Whites (I hardly dare spell it with a capital) who have sort of had enough of the Blacks. Soul Food. Black Studies. What are they going to teach, is the question (sic) of my friend Alex Szogyi, Professor of Romance Languages at Hunter College. More money they want. The mind boggles. Or it buggers the imagination. Now the Blacks are trying blackmail, I learn. And some of my best friends, and some of my closest relatives in Texas, call me a nigger-lover. It is indeed difficult to live.[29]

In 1988 Highsmith, a member of Amnesty International, taxed her old friend Kingsley with sending a copy of *Mein Kampf* to Switzerland. She had borrowed Hannah Arendt's *Origins of Anti-Semitism*, 'which should provide a sane balance for Hitler'.[30]

Meeting her old lover again in 1992, after a gap of twenty-eight years, Meaker was appalled by the virulence of Highsmith's racism:

> 'Do you live in some little Nazi coven?'
> 'I'm not surrounded by neo-Nazis, just easy-going Ticinese, old Italian families, and new families of workers. I notice the products from Israel are shunned in the supermarkets, and the Jaffa orange juice disappeared this year. People say, why should I buy something from that country? And when they know I'm an American they ask me why America gives these people so much money. Everyone knows Israel imprisons without habeas corpus, throws families who are not terrorists out of their houses at gunpoint ... that Jew editor Otto Penzler removed my dedication To the Palestinian people from People Who Knock on the Door without a by-your-leave request? Penguin and European countries left it in!'[31]

'Lean, louche and androgynous' – Highsmith photographed by
Rolf Tietgens in 1942

The Swiss Literary Archives contain a cache of Highsmith's pseudonymous
letters to newspapers railing against minorities of every stripe. Other letters
are addressed to US President Jimmy Carter, US Secretary of State James
A. Baker III or Senator Bob Dole. They reveal a mind much exercised by
the Israeli-Palestinian problem, but also careful to protect its sanctuary in
Switzerland and hoping to acquire citizenship. Highsmith used a revolv-
ing set of pseudonyms: Eddie Stefano, Janet Tamagni, Prissila Appleby,
A Proudfoot Grasshopper. At one point she upbraids Vice President Dan
Quayle on his spelling mistakes, calling them Quayle droppings – 'I liked
his about "wishing he'd studied Latin harder, so he could talk with the folks
in S. America."'

Highsmith was cavalier about her lesbianism. She had friendships with
gay men and multiple botched affairs with women. Characters in her fiction are often androgynous, sexually smudged or just plain oddball. From
her Barnard days she was sexually driven and promiscuous, although
chase seems to have been all; she had the only child's unwillingness to
share. In her youth she had been highly attractive to men and women
alike. Photographer Rolf Tietgens, a dalliance in 1942, confessed that he
was attracted to her because 'you are a boy, you know'. Terry Castle tells
us 'just how dizzyingly attractive she was as a young woman. Lean, louche,

androgynous, with jet-black hair, a foppish forelock, and full, pouting lips: a real Texas Cherubino ... a boyish, flirty, compulsive seductress – a sort of sapphic Dennis the Menace.'[32]

Ronald Blythe, remarking astutely that she desired women but didn't like them, described a night with Highsmith in the early 1960s:

> We would sleep in the same room and talk; she needed some kind of close-ness. We weren't lovers, but we did sleep together once or twice. We talked about gay love and the unsatisfactory nature of some of our romantic friendships – she knew all about my sex life ... sex with her was like being made love to by a boy. Her hands were very masculine and big and she was hipless like an adolescent boy.[33]

In a short 1989 essay 'Of Time and the Country Life', Highsmith appreci-ates the different rhythms of the Ticino and is clear-eyed about the effect on women:

> In the small towns in this area, it is not the done thing for women to con-gregate in the local bar or café at 9 p.m., women presumably always hav-ing something to do at that time, and at home too. In brief, the married woman with children in the Tessin countryside is at the beck and call of husband and all the children, possibly even the elderly in-laws, round the clock. She is car-driver, cook, shopper, house-cleaner, seamstress, hostess, nurse.[34]

She wrote every day at her trusty, much-travelled 1956 Olympia Deluxe typewriter. On *Desert Island Discs* she described her writing day in a cagey, cool voice, completely diffident, its Texan inflections tempered by European swagger: eight typewritten pages per day, mostly written in the afternoon over four or five hours. She needed three drafts to get it right:

> I don't write very smoothly in first draft ... I write action passages fast, but what comes after might need a mood change. I retype my books two and a half times. I like retyping for neatness and polish, not style. Style does not interest me in the least – emotion is worth more than the intellect.

Her chosen desert island book was *Moby-Dick*. All parsimony and industry, she reminds me of the Scotch-Irish on her mother's side, the Stewarts. On her father's side she was Prussian – no levity there either. This didn't prevent her from noting similar qualities in the Swiss: 'Ah, the tidy, thrifty, law-abiding Swiss! Uptight! Why else did the Swiss have the highest drug-abuse rate per capita in the drug-abusing world – meaning the world?'[35]

Small g: A Summer Idyll (1995) remains Highsmith's only completed novel set in Switzerland, published posthumously. The title refers to a neighbourhood bar in Zürich with the designation 'partly gay clientele', or 'gay at night'.

She wrote *Small g* during the last two years of her life when she was sick, drinking and smoking heavily as usual. It begins with a fatal mugging and ends with the funeral of a closeted lesbian. The protagonist is a forty-five-year-old commercial illustrator (as were Highsmith's parents) improbably named Rickie Markwalder. He likes them young: 'He was a nice old uncle to them, ready to lend a hundred francs and forget about it. To listen to someone's troubles, pour another drink, offer a bed in a crisis.'[36]

The novel follows a coterie of barflies and milliners in a district behind the train station in Zürich. Highsmith had always enjoyed depicting soaks and ne'er-do-wells. In *Strangers on a Train* the double crime surfaces after the two protagonists tie one on over highballs. *The Talented Mr. Ripley* opens in Raoul's on Fifth Avenue, with a gin and tonic, and quickly moves on to brandy. Highsmith's characters are usually a little cranked up before the reader gets to them. At the end of her life, Highsmith's intake was a finger or two of vodka to get going, Dewar's Scotch during the day and a steady intake of Pilsner Urquell. Terry Castle unsparingly described Highsmith in her later years: 'she typically manages to look both petrified and pickled, like an alcoholic basilisk.'[37]

Highsmith makes a number of passing references to drugs, specifically to Platzspitz Park, or Needle Park, where Zürich authorities tolerated open-air drug dealing and shooting-up until 1992.

> *The park had become such a slum really, a dealer's paradise, a public toilet too, that the police had been ordered to clear them all out, take the addicts by busloads back to their homes, often in small towns. But a great many of them had made their way back to Zürich for their drugs, and they were still hanging around, nearly three hundred of them daily drifting in Zürich's streets, according to a recent news bulletin that Rickie remembered. Street hold-ups, muggings at knifepoint, had come back, Rickie knew. Not to mention that he could see a few almost any time of the day or night in the St. Jakob's church area, sleeping in a nook somewhere,*

Performance artist Tabea Blumenschein in the summer of punk

*or sitting on the pavement propped against the building, too far gone to
stand up to beg.*[38]

Small g reflects Zürich's dark side, but also Highsmith's own take on it.
One of her last infatuations was with Berlin performance artist Tabea
Blumenschein, thirty years Highsmith's junior. Tabea sported spiky blonde
hair, a sailor's cap and a moustache. She could play a *Gauleiter* with a
whip. 'I have just bought Tabea a flick knife, not allowed in Berlin, and got
it to her via Hamburg TV crew Friday,' wrote Highsmith. It was the second half of the 1970s in Berlin; David Bowie was making his three classic
albums at Hansa by the Wall. Tabea took Highsmith to lesbian discos and
gave her the Rolling Stones' *Sticky Fingers* and Lou Reed's *Transformer*.
Not to be outdone, she bought Tabea a Stiff Little Fingers album.

What attracted Highsmith to the figure of the con man in fiction was
her own early exclusion. The Fort Worth lesbian writer of genre fiction was
never quite welcomed into the high-end locales she aspired to: Washington
Square, Snedens Landing on the Hudson River, Aldburgh in Suffolk, posh
French Fontainebleau, Switzerland's Riviera. Her characters ape expensive social polish rather than achievement. They murder for it.

She thought that living abroad 'sharpens perspective. You see the class
differences in America when you live in England.'[39] In a brief piece about
foreigners living in Switzerland she was characteristically impersonal and
disingenuously shallow:

I have now lived in the Ticino for a few years, a region which may be less formal than Zürich or Berne areas, but still the pavements and gutters of Locarno are not littered with discarded paper cups, broken bottles and empty cigarette packets ...

The dark marble floor shines, unlittered. It is like a well-cared-for living room, in fact.

Switzerland is something like a club. Perhaps not everyone would want to join, but for those who like order and the quiet life, Switzerland is the place to be.[40]

She had finally been admitted to club class.

Her editor Daniel Keel visited her a few months before her death in February 1995. She had asked for chocolate cake, which he picked up from Sprüngli in Zürich's Bahnhof. Their work done, Highsmith opened the box and both of them stared at the cake. It was coffin-shaped. Keel was mortified, and knew that she knew. A macabre moment, typical of her work.[41]

Still seeking Swiss citizenship, in the last few weeks she decided to leave her papers to the Swiss Literary Archive in Bern. Three days before she died, she continued to fiddle with her will. She died alone in the hospital in Locarno.

Up the road from her house, and across the train tracks from Highsmith's final resting place, another writer of a different calibre also found a kind of refuge in Tegna. Hannah Arendt summered there for many years. The great witness to Nazi evil has a memorial seat in the Barbatè guesthouse garden, facing the lovely tropical trees and Highsmith's forbidding blockhouse in the valley. I sometimes conjure a conversation between these two writers, these mistresses to the banality of evil – one a right-wing Texan lesbian who disliked Jews, the other a German-Jewish philosopher. I'm not sure they would see eye to eye.

Highsmith's ashes are immured in the columbarium of the little Catholic cemetery in Tegna. She hated Catholics. Friends and admirers, many of them Jews belonging to the New York publishing world, the post-war cinema world, packed the church. They brought flowers. Highsmith hated flowers. She was a great hater. They came to remember an anti-Semite of long standing. This mean-spirited, tight-wad crime writer bequeathed her millions to Yaddo writers' colony in upstate New York, where over forty years before she had written her first novel, *Strangers on a Train*. Rumour has it that millions are gathering dust and compound interest in the Bahamas and the Cayman Islands. This 'jaded, butch, Scotch-soaked lady novelist',[42] whom nobody much liked, was laid to rest.

11

TRUFFLES MISSING FROM THE
BONBON BOX

Dürrenmatt's detectives

Still from the first 1958 Spanish-Swiss-German film adaptation of
Dürrenmatt's *The Pledge*

Rundown aristocrats, arteriosclerotic politicians (unless still in office),
debilitated millionaires, schizophrenic writers, manic-depressive
industrialists, and so on, in short, the entire mentally disturbed elite of
half the Western world.
Friedrich Dürrenmatt

The yummy mummies behind me on the bleachers of the indoor pool on Lake Neuchâtel were rooting for their kids. It was a swimming competition of the Swiss Group of International Schools on a Saturday afternoon in mid-November. I was the stroke judge, keeping an eye out for flutter kicks and false starts. But my mind wasn't on the job. The evening ploughed ahead, relay after relay, and an expensive dinner date was in the offing. They always get their pound of flesh, these private international schools. I've spent a lifetime working in them. You can talk all the pedagogical puffery you want, but when it comes down to it we're lackeys for hire in capitalism's late flourish. Nineteenth-century Swiss nannies kept the royal houses of Europe and Russia on the go with hot water bottles, broth and needlework. The royals have gone and in their place are Citibank, Novartis and sundry middle-eastern nabobs. Heated perfumes in the tepid air: Gold Coast princesses, embassy chattel, tiger moms and Russian babes.

Beyond the plate glass of the pool lay the lake. Lights twinkled on its northern shore and a late ferry cruised to port. The western lakes of Switzerland – Lake Neuchâtel and Lake Biel – are more muted and subtle in their scenery than the more frequented Lake Lucerne, Lake Geneva and the two either side of Interlaken. The dramatic landscape is toned down. La Tène was out there in the darkness, the early Celtic settlement three thousand years old – Iron Age. They could flutter kick all they wanted. In the long time of history the SGIS swim meet was just a chlorine blot on the landscape.

Dinner was at La Maison du Prussien, a boutique hotel and restaurant tucked away at the bottom of the Gorge du Vauseyon just outside Neuchâtel. I'd checked into my room earlier. It took me three spins around interlocking roundabouts to find the turn-off down to the Seyon river, tumbling with November floodwater to the lake. The hotel owes its name to the Prussians making yet another foray for *Lebensraum* in these parts.

Frederick William III of Prussia once ruled the Principality of Neuchâtel. It was restored to him in 1815 after Napoleon the Corsican had tried to nick

Swiss architect Mario Botta's Centre Dürrenmatt above Neuchâtel

it. It was as a principality that Neuchâtel joined the Swiss Confederation in that year. La Maison du Prussien, built five storeys high to catch the light in 1797, was one of a number of mills, sawmills and *fabriques d'Indienne* – cotton mills – along the deep gorge. It became a brewery, a bakery and a straw-hat manufactory in short order. Now, in the second decade of the twenty-first century, it serves excellent champagne and an inventive truffle-themed menu. The spacious old-world rooms are named after former millers; mine was called Meunier Abraham. It seemed a pity to spoil the décor with a pile of orange exercise books, each with a *Romeo and Juliet* essay waiting to be marked. I was tempted to throw them out the window into the millrace below. Trains clattered above at regular intervals, setting off a murder of crows in the sketchy trees.

In the mid-nineteenth century, Neuchâtel republicans successfully revolted against Prussian rule and sent Fritz packing. By one of those strange ironies of monarchical rule, the line of primogeniture ran through the principality of Monaco. The heir to Neuchâtel's princely lands is the Irish historian and scion of the Guinness family, Patrick Guinness of Leixlip Castle. I lived in Leixlip as an undergraduate and remember gazing down on the castle from the top of the 66 bus, hoping to spot Mick Jagger or David Bowie. The brewery baron was known for hob-nobbing with rock aristocracy. Celts have always been resident around the lake. We might consider it our lost homeland. Those Prussians are just blow-ins

compared to the Irish. This is what I was thinking poolside, as Speedos did
their lengths. I whiled away the afternoon looking across at lost ancestral
lands.

The La Tène archaeological site is situated on the northwest shore
where the short River Thielle flows into the lake. The river was good for fishing and now forms the cantonal boundary between Bern and Neuchâtel,
but is also one of those curious language boundaries – a shibboleth. West
of the lakes the language is French; on the eastern shores German is the
lingua franca, so to speak. You might think the French speakers would be
Catholic and the German-speakers Reformist. You'd be wrong – it's more
complicated than that.

Two and a half thousand years ago, on this swampy neck of land between
the lakes, La Tène culture prospered. Post house remains in orderly rows
have been preserved underwater. The wealth of gold, bronze and ironwork
artefacts, with their distinctive convoluted designs, is what characterises
the period. I learned about it in art class at school. You can draw a direct
line from La Tène to the illuminations of early Irish manuscripts to James
Joyce's *Finnegans Wake* to the gold Celtic squiggles on our school blazers.
Convoluted, but direct.

Just up the lakeshore from the swimming pool is the Laténium
museum. It's built down into the mud, descending four floors through
history to the early lakeside settlement and its trove of metalwork. Lakes
define Switzerland because you have to get across and around them. They
act as barriers – to religion and to language. The Jura Mountains rise
on the western flank of Lakes Biel and Neuchâtel, marking the boundary of Burgundian culture. Pre-Roman, pre-Allemanic, pre-Prussian,
pre-Napoleonic; the oldest mountains on the European landmass. The
museum houses the preserved skeletons of boats lifted from the lakebed
where long ago they plied the current.

Early next morning I was the only guest downstairs in my hotel. I like
these tinkly Swiss breakfast rooms in the off season: you can collect your
thoughts. I read Friedrich Dürrenmatt's *The Inspector Barlach Mysteries*
right through breakfast and then went up to my room and graded those
Romeo and Juliet essays in short order. Checking out, I asked about the
Dürrenmatt house. He lived for much of his life above Neuchâtel and his
fictional crimes have a habit of taking place in the hinterland. I felt like a
spot of literary gumshoe. When I cleared the town, I climbed through the
trees, past a botanical garden, parked in a clearing and walked down to
the house, now a museum. Dürrenmatt did well on Broadway: celebrity

Film *noir*: Dürrenmatt's *The Judge and His Hangman* in a 1961
BBC production

architect, stunning view of the lake from his panoramic terrace, coffee shop
cum bookshop.

Dürrenmatt was the son of a village pastor from Konolfingen in the
Emmental region, in the canton of Bern. Perhaps he got his moral cur-
mudgeon quality from his father. I imagine Swiss pastors as the epitome
of moral probity. Dürrenmatt is one of two twentieth-century Swiss writers
whose work puts their country under the microscope; the other is Max
Frisch. They often get confused: Frisch became tired being asked for
Dürrenmatt's autograph by air hostesses on his many transatlantic plane
journeys. Dürrenmatt was born in 1921, Frisch in 1911. Both were witness to
Switzerland's wartime and post-war prosperity. Both are known abroad as
dramatists. But Dürrenmatt's talent is polymorphous – at home on stage,
in literary fiction, in genre-bending detective stories. He liked to take his
country to task, a literary pastor thumping the pulpit, and so he has an
ambiguous relationship with Swiss readers.

Barlach is Dürrenmatt's fictional Detective Inspector of Bern City
Police. A sick, hard-drinking veteran of the machinery of Swiss justice, he
is a good man in a labyrinth, a thorn in the side of his less scrupulous
superiors. *The Judge and His Hangman* (1950) sees the inspector attempting to get to the bottom of a policeman's murder in the hills above Lake
Biel. The who-done-it involves business interests, crooked politicians and
equally crooked cops. In *Suspicion* (1951) a former concentration camp
doctor, practising in a Zürich clinic for the wealthy, describes Barlach as a

'sad knight without fear or blemish, who set out to fight evil with the power of the spirit'.[1] In both short novels Barlach tilts at the windmills of Swiss vested interests:

> And there's a whole heap of crimes no one pays any attention to, because they are more esthetic than those blatant murders that get written up in the newspapers, but it all amounts to the same if you care to take a close look and exercise a little imagination.[2]

Set in and around Bern, Neuchâtel and Biel, the Barlach mysteries bring these watery regions alive. Swiss writers identify strongly with their region as much as with their country and this can sometimes hamper wider recognition, especially so as regions come in three different languages. Dürrenmatt's characters slip from German into French and back again, with unease, the way driving around the lakes involves gear shifts from one language to the other. Dürrenmatt describes the locality south of the Jura bordering Lake Biel: an old settled landscape of vineyards, a thoroughfare for Celtic settlers between forbidding mountain ranges, and where Rousseau sought his last refuge in Switzerland on the island of St Pierre:

> They drove downhill in the direction of Ligerz, into a land that opened out far below, at a tremendous depth. All around them, the elements lay spread out far and wide: stone, earth, and water. They were driving in the shade, but the sun, which had sunk behind the Tessenberg, was still shining on the lake, the island, the hills, the foothills of the mountains, the glaciers on the horizon, and the immense towering heaps of cloud floating along in the blue oceans of the sky.[3]

This deep landscape rubs up against a shiny post-war business world. Dürrenmatt's tightly knit plot veers into metaphysical fantasy, peppered with acerbic asides on his countrymen. A policeman's murder links to a nearby clandestine meeting of industrialists, arms dealers and the mysterious 'foreign power'. Dürrenmatt writes a state-of-the-federation novel as well as a detective thriller.

> Let's face it: the Swiss have no education, no cosmopolitan character, not a trace of European consciousness. There's only one remedy: three years of military service.[4]

Dürrenmatt pokes fun at the cosiness of the economic miracle, as Rousseau had characterised the remittance economy of Swiss mercenaries and their new-fangled sophistication. Under the post-war prosperity, artists are co-opted by entrepreneurs hand in glove with the state, their hands in each other's pockets. Wealth operates as a gagging order. Secrecy obscures the bottom line. We are familiar with twenty-first-century corporate capitalism – if you can't beat 'em, privatise 'em – but its first flush was in post-war Switzerland:

> *Decoration. We live in a cultured society, Lutz, and we need to advertise that. The negotiations have to be kept secret, and artists are good for that. Everyone dining together, a nice roast, wine, cigars, women, conversation, the artists get bored, huddle in little groups, drink, and never notice that the capitalists and the representatives of that foreign power are sitting together.*[5]

Dürrenmatt's detective mysteries were written at the height of the Cold War when Switzerland was concerned with bolstering its arsenal of fighter jets and tanks. Its principal arms supplier was Great Britain, later to be replaced by the United States. Switzerland's military-industrial complex recalibrated its neutrality to a new set of circumstances and to 'members of a foreign embassy', as Dürrenmatt's state councillor puts it. Crime in *The Judge and His Hangman* extends its tentacles into the arms industry under this new world order. Cosy with the Germans during the war, Swiss expediency – if not allegiance – has shifted. 'For us, it's a question of money: for them, it's political principle,' says the police chief with unintended irony. Like the later spy writing of John le Carré, recruited in Bern at about this time, Dürrenmatt's detective mysteries suggest Cold War manoeuvring behind the local crime scene, but also greed. Profit from a 'foreign embassy' trumps dead bodies; a hand played surreptitiously and successfully during the war is still a winning suit.

Suspicion, the second of the Barlach mysteries, makes overt links between wartime medical experiments at Stutthof concentration camp and a clinic called the Sonnenstein, 'one of the most expensive private hospitals in Switzerland'. The Sonnenstein caters to the terminally rich. Dürrenmatt has learned from Glauser and Brecht the allegorical trick of having a clinic represent the sickness of a whole country – a device later Swiss writers also found useful, as did the author of *One Flew over the Cuckoo's Nest*. Glauser's insane asylum in Bern, with its hushed-up murders and spider web of intrigue, confines the poor, the victims of the 1920s and 1930s. It mirrors Switzerland's situation between two world wars. Dürrenmatt's Inspector Barlach is ailing. In the first sentence of *Suspicion* he 'checks into the Salem' with an incurable disease. He says to his visiting boss, 'They let the big scoundrels go and lock up the little ones' – a comment with a particular resonance in the late 1940s as it has in our own day after the 2008 economic crash. 'But the real prey, the big beasts, the ones most worth hunting because they most deserve it – they're officially off limits, like animals in a zoo.'[6] The zoo, of course, is Switzerland.

Bern is equally claustrophobic, comfortable for some, a labyrinth:

> But that's what Berne has always been, a nice little hole in the wall for policemen to nest in. This place has been one infestation of tyranny from the beginning ... Fifty years I've been living in this fat sleepy hick town of a capital, I can't begin to tell you what it means for a writer, a man of words (not of letters!), to starve and vegetate in this place where all you get for mental food is the weekend book review section in the Bund.[7]

Between Glauser's 1930s and Dürrenmatt's 1950s, wealth has trickled down but also gushed upwards. In his Salem hospital room, Inspector Barlach spots the resemblance in a *Life* magazine picture between a concentration camp doctor and a contemporary practitioner working in the most expensive private hospital in Switzerland. 'Most of the face was hidden behind a surgical mask.' The allegory – concentration camp underwrites contemporary wealth – is clear. Dürrenmatt has Switzerland wriggling under the microscope again:

> Even if it's a crime to think what we're thinking, let's not be afraid of our thoughts. How can we overcome them – presuming they're wrong – unless we examine them, and how can we do that unless we admit them to our conscience?[8]

Dürrenmatt's subject is the examination of conscience. The pastor's son coming of age in wartime Switzerland holds his father's generation up to the mirror. Not a new theme following a war, but new for a neutral country.

In the second section of *Suspicion*, Barlach himself is imprisoned in the clinic, at the mercy of ex-Nazi Dr. Emmenberger and his morphine-addicted assistant. The clinic is straight out of a Hammer movie, with its resident dwarf and sliding wall revealing a Grand Guignol operating theatre. The plot turns gothic and the monster is in charge; Mary Shelley's *Frankenstein* is not far away. Dürrenmatt is fond of such medicalised set pieces. *The Pledge* ends with a deathbed confession in the cantonal hospital. Dürrenmatt's best known play, *The Physicists*, is set in Les Cerisiers, an up-market insane asylum in a lakeside town suspiciously like Neuchâtel, 'the once attractive little place with its castle and old town':

> *rundown aristocrats, arteriosclerotic politicians (unless still in office), manic-depressive industrialists, and so on, in short, the entire mentally disturbed elite of half the Western world.*[9]

In a chapter of *Suspicion* titled 'The Hell of the Rich', the clinic becomes a metaphor for Switzerland as the retirement home of Europe: drip-fed the best but dying at heart. Dr. Emmenberger acts in a Faustian pact with his wealthy patients:

> *the names of the politicians, the bankers, the industrialists, the mistresses, and the widows, celebrities all of them, and those unknown crooks who have raked in millions at our expense and at no cost to themselves. So here's where they die, in this hospital. Some of them make blasphemous jokes about their own decrepitude, others revolt and spit out wild curses against their fate, against the fact that they own everything and yet have to die, and still others whine the most revolting prayers in their rooms full of silk and brocade, begging to be spared the substitution of paradise for the bliss of living down here.*[10]

Dürrenmatt's morality tale pits extreme wealth and mortality. The land of milk and honey dreamed up at the beginning of the century by H.G. Wells has curdled with money. Contemporary Switzerland may be as close as we get to heaven for those who can pay, but Dürrenmatt suggests that it comes at the price of turning a blind eye.

The moral conscience of the tale comes from the mouth of a boulevard littérateur called Fortschig, who is killed by a dwarf for exposing the evil doctor:

> *That a human being, a Bernese, went about his bloody trade under an assumed name in an extermination camp near Danzig – I dare not describe in detail with what bestiality – appals us; but that he should be permitted to direct a clinic in Switzerland is a disgrace for which we can*

find no words, and an indication that these may very well be our own
latter days … for our reputation is at stake, the harmless rumour that we
are still honestly muddling through the sinister jungles of these times –
(perhaps earning a little more money than usual with watches, cheese,
and some weapons of not very great significance).[11]

Vera B. Profit (a name Dürrenmatt might have dreamed up himself) suggests that the Sonnenstein is partly based on a clinic in Berlin where mentally ill patients were systematically liquidated from 1940.[12] Dürrenmatt
locates his Sonnenstein on the Zürichberg where Dr Bircher-Benner – of
muesli fame – treated his patients with a diet of fruit and nuts in monastic
conditions. (Bircher's clinic now belongs to Zürich Financial Services.)
Dürrenmatt means to point the finger at Swiss materialism – 'that unfortu-
nate tendency to regard morality as unprofitable and to equate profit with
morality'.[13] He suggests that the whole of Switzerland is a health farm for
the wealthy, where an ageing population is served up the best that life has
to offer. The search for prolonged life at any cost becomes the ultimate
expression of materialism.

> *If the camp near Danzig was the hell of the Jews, the Christians, and the*
> *Communists, this hospital here, in the middle of dear old Zürich, is the*
> *hell of the rich.*[14]

Dürrenmatt's Huis Clos situations turn farcical. The nurses are fit for
assisted suicide. Reproduction masterpieces adorn the walls as kitsch panacea for the dying – guests? Inmates? Customers? Cocooned in cotton wool
and tortured by an ex–concentration camp doctor, these terminal cases are
a blistering judgement of the Swiss post-war economic miracle.

Dürrenmatt achieved even wider international fame with his novel *The*
Pledge (1958), adapted for the screen for the second time in 2001 by Sean
Penn, starring Jack Nicholson as investigating detective Matthäi. Its subject
is that most contemporary of crimes: child abuse. An eight-year-old girl is
brutally murdered in Mägendorf, a quiet lakeside village near Zürich. She
is the third victim.

Dürrenmatt frames his story with a chance encounter between a writer of
detective fiction and Dr. H., former chief of police of the canton of Zürich:

> *Last March I had to give a lecture in Chur on the art of writing detective*
> *stories. My train pulled in just before nightfall, under low clouds, in a*

dreary blizzard. As if that wasn't enough, the roads were paved with ice.
The lecture was being held in the hall of the Chamber of Commerce.
There wasn't much of an audience.[15]

This leisurely opening points the way to a fast-paced thriller. *The Pledge*
shows small-town Switzerland seething with elemental revenge. Men are
farmers, hunting and fishing types. Their womenfolk don't yet have the
vote (granted only in 1971). Church bells ring. The village bar is called The
Stag. The reader might even be tempted to see the murdered girl as Heidi,
that emblem of Swiss innocence:

> *The farmers and workers stood again as before, silent, threatening,*
> *motionless under the sky, which was putting on the first shining lights*
> *of the evening; street lamps swayed over the square like pale moons. The*
> *Mägendorfers were determined to seize the man they took to be the mur-*
> *derer. The police cars stood like large dark beasts, at bay in this human*
> *tide. Again and again they attempted to break loose, the motors roared*
> *and howled, then subsided, discouraged, and were turned off again. No*
> *use. The whole village – the dark gables, the square, the crowd in its*
> *uncertainty and rage – staggered under the burden of the day's event, as*
> *if the murder had poisoned the world.*[16]

Investigating detective Matthäi confronts Dr. Locher in the first of the
thriller's two clinics. They try to profile the psychology of the murderer.
Dürrenmatt sets his elemental crime at the heart of a bell-ringing nation:

> *Bells ringing all around, the whole country seemed to be clanging and*
> *chiming; and somewhere in Schwyz canton I got held up by a procession.*
> *One car after another on the road, and on the radio, one sermon after the*
> *other. Later the sounds of guns banging, whistling, clattering, booming*
> *away in shooting booths in every village. A monstrous, senseless commo-*
> *tion – the whole of eastern Switzerland seemed to be on the move.*[17]

This hunting and shooting description of a Swiss Sunday has a Wild West
quality. Matthäi sets a trap for the serial murderer, using an eight-year-old
girl as bait, in a gas station on the Graubünden highway. She wears red.
The big bad wolf plies the child with chocolate truffles and 'drives a black
American car'. Guns, gas station and US car: is Dürrenmatt suggesting the
post-war Americanisation of federal life?

A visit to a second clinic eventually solves the crime. The Chief of Police is summoned to a deathbed confession from Frau Schrott, 'waxen, unreal, but still curiously animated'. Dürrenmatt presents this old doll as hailing from patrician military stock:

> My grandfather was Colonel Stänzli who led the retreat to Escholzmatt
> in the Sonderbund War, and my sister married Colonel Stüssi of the
> Zürich General Staff in the First World War, who was General Ulrich
> Wille's best friend and knew Kaiser Wilhelm personally.[18]

Her sister 'owns half the Bahnhofstrasse'. Dürrenmatt seems to suggest that the crime is due to the sclerosis of Swiss values. On the one hand, Heidi the victim in her red dress; on the other, this old-money crone whose second marriage was to her 'chauffeur and gardener and general handyman',[19] a toy-boy thirty-two years her junior. Shades of *Lady Chatterley's Lover*, that other allegory of social classes in bed with each other. Bertie the handyman has 'limited mental capacity' and loves to eat, 'especially noodles, all sorts of pasta in fact, and chocolate. That was his passion, chocolate.'[20]

As with the two earlier detective stories, Bertie the handyman and old-money Frau Schrott are emblematic of something rotten in the confederation. He drives her vintage pre-war Buick. 'There were truffles missing from the bonbon box,' she says.[21] This marriage of convenience between old military money and the simple-minded chauffeur with his passion for chocolate becomes an allegory for wartime Switzerland: chocolate and arms. Dürrenmatt discouraged such readings, but they are clear for all to see.

Mrs Rose in *The Physicists*, Dürrenmatt's most enduring play, is a similarly benevolent sugar mamma:

> When I first met him, he was a fifteen-year-old schoolboy. He had rented
> an attic room in my father's house. He was an orphan and miserably poor.
> I made it possible for him to enter college and later to study physics ...
> To provide for my family, I went to work in a chocolate factory. Tobler's
> Chocolate.[22]

Toblerone keeps the marriage sweet. Bertie the child-killer, for his part, takes his justification from God, although not very convincingly. '"Mumsie," he replied, "please let me do it just this one time; it's commanded by heaven,

I have to obey, and she has a red skirt, too, and blond braids.'"[23] God shines light on this marriage of convenience. The priest waits with Extreme Unction, that panacea for the sins of the world.

Dürrenmatt employs a wicked humour throughout these parables of post-war Switzerland. The retirement clinics where his plots tick along are kept going with money from the dead.

Dr. H. the Chief of Police likes to eat in Zürich's Kronenhalle restaurant under a painting by Miró. Dürrenmatt enjoys juxtaposing high art and lowbrow business:

> The place was full – everyone who was anybody in Zürich and interested in a good meal was there. Waitresses scurrying around, the food on the trolley steaming, and the rumble of traffic sounding in from the street. I was sitting under the Miró, all unsuspecting, eating my liver dumpling soup, when the sales representative of one of the big fuel companies came up to me.[24]

The atmosphere of wellbeing here belies the undercurrent of crime: chief of police and fuel company representative in a consumer paradise. In the final chapter of *The Pledge*, Dr. H. returns with his family to Chur, where the bonbon box is taken out again:

> In Chur we had trouble parking. The pastry shop was crammed full of people from Zürich and their screaming children, all stuffing their bellies and sweating. But finally we found a table, ordered tea and pastry. But my wife called the waitress back again.
> 'And please bring us half a pound of chocolate truffles.'[25]

Dürrenmatt's most scathing comment on Swiss material smugness is an essay, originally a speech for Václav Havel, dramatist, dissident and president of the Czech Republic. 'Switzerland – A Prison' was delivered in 1990 following the Velvet Revolution. Dürrenmatt has chosen his occasion with mischief and an eye to history.

> Thus Switzerland can be juxtaposed with your tragic grotesques as another kind of grotesque: a prison, albeit very different from the kinds of prisons into which you were thrown, dear Havel; a prison in which the Swiss have taken refuge.[26]

Friedrich Dürrenmatt, Switzerland's scourge

Switzerland has historically provided safe haven for refugees. Dürrenmatt sees it as safe haven for the Swiss themselves, a mountain redoubt as General Guisan conceived of it during the Second World War. The writer builds his prison metaphor by alluding to immigrant labour:

> On the one hand, there are not enough free prisoners to keep the prison clean, to polish the luxury cells, the hallways, the prison bars themselves, so people have to be let in from outside who will renovate, restore, reconstruct, and maintain the prison just in order to make a living, while prisoners, who also earn a living but are free look down on these outsiders as prisoners who are not free.[27]

The Swiss blow hot and cold about Dürrenmatt's portrayal of their country as asylum, wealthy funny farm and prison. It spoils an image of themselves as squeaky-clean, their history above reproach. He knows all the sore points:

> The opinion is becoming more and more prevalent that the real purpose of the prison is not to guard the freedom of the prisoners but to guard banking secrecy ... the alleged founding of the prison seven hundred years

ago, even though at that time the prison was not a prison but a widely feared robber's nest.[28]

Dürrenmatt in 1990 is prescient about how western democracy will get into bed with big business and consumer capitalism. His essay points to Switzerland as a bellwether for the rest of Europe:

Only their way of manipulating people is infinitely more subtle and refined than the brutal methods of the post-totalitarian system. ... this omnipresent dictatorship of consumption, of production, of advertising, of commerce, of consumer culture, this endless flood of information.[29]

Dürrenmatt has been proved right in the quarter century since the fall of Communism. His invective is an attack not just on Swiss smugness, but on the whole free world enterprise:

In our country, too, politics has retreated from ideology into economics. ... Our streets are battlefields, our atmosphere is exposed to poisonous gases, our oceans are oil spills, our fields are polluted with pesticides, the third world has been plundered, worse than the orient was by the crusaders – no wonder the Middle East is extorting us now. ... The free market economy is an industrial battlefield, driven by competition, a war for markets.[30]

Dürrenmatt appropriated Glauser's metaphor of Switzerland as a sanatorium confining the wealthy mad, run by a conspiracy of psychoanalysis hand in glove with militaristic authority. Swiss private clinics and Switzerland itself became a poultice, a panacea. Bring me your mad, bad and rich and I will offer a gilded cage and room service at a price. This view of Swiss wealth as a source of illness resurfaces in Fritz Zorn's *Mars* (1977), where the rich-boy narrator conflates the golden coast of Zürich with his own cancer.

In a recent novel by Jonas Lüscher, *Barbarian Spring* (2014), the motif surfaces again. A Swiss industrialist is recovering in a clinic from his traumatic experience of Tunisia in the early days of the Arab Spring and the financial crisis. Swiss business plays its familiar, profitable part in these two recent events. Preising, the aptly named businessman, heads Prixxing, a communications company. Prixxing is the new face of the Swiss economy, just as the arms dealer Oerlikon-Bührle was the old. Preising is in Tunisia on a junket, guest of an exclusive resort owned by business partner Slim

Malouch. The paradise on earth begins to show its true colours. Prixxing
turns out to rely on child labour. The tale turns sleazy. Preising escapes,
with the help of the Swiss embassy, and lives to savour once again the
Zürcher Geschnetzeltes mit Rösti at the Restaurant Kronenhalle in Zürich,
a nod to Dürrenmatt's detectives who retreat to the same high-end cosy
restaurant.

When the Berlin Wall fell in 1989, Eastern Europeans swelled the
glitzy cities of the West. I remember Czech, Hungarian and East German
coaches parked at dawn on the Place Pigalle in Paris. They had travelled
all night to see the bright lights. The American cartoonist Gary Trudeau
quipped: 'They came, they saw, they did a little shopping.'

I started this chapter on Dürrenmatt in the Maison du Prussien in
Neuchâtel and ended it in Bangkok under military dictatorship, the ump-
teenth one of Thailand's history. In this context Dürrenmatt doesn't have
too much to complain about. His critique of Switzerland speaks of the
freedom to speak. His sharp, clockwork crimes are curiously tame, like
luxury items – a fine Mont Blanc pen or a gold watch assembled high in
the Jura where he lived, in a house overlooking the lake. Viewed from this
street stall by Siriraj Hospital where the king of Thailand lies ailing – a
king who began his long life in the lap of Swiss luxury and ends it in intensive care – Dürrenmatt's morality dramas and detective stories seem lovely,
bejewelled comments on how the rich get by, on how Switzerland made it.

Switzerland's neutrality during the Second World War had a powerful
effect on the country's prosperity and on how belligerent nations viewed
the little federation. Our next writer cut his spying teeth in Switzerland and
knows the dark side of allegiance. Money talks and spies listen. Dürrenmatt
kept his ear to the ground, but it was John le Carré who developed Cold
War themes on a global stage. Wealth, arms dealing, betrayal, Big Pharma,
crime, money laundering, tax avoidance and banking collusion are all, like
the poor, still with us. No one has explored them more variously than the
spy who came in from the cold.

12

HARD BOILED IN BERN

Le Carré's bolthole

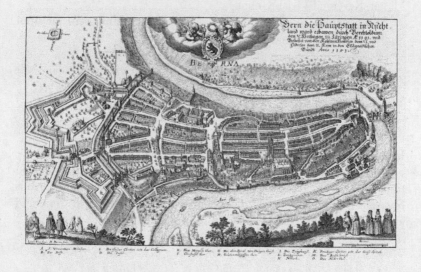

1638 map of Bern

The Bellevue Palace Hotel, an enormous sumptuous place of mellowed
Edwardian quiet, which on clear days looks across the foothills to the
glistening Alps, but that evening was shrouded in a cloying winter fog.
John le Carré

rivate schools used to have mottoes – a scrap of high-flown Latin
below a crest with a predator rampant. Now they have mission state-
ments. Schools are in thrall to corporate life; from dorm to boardroom
is really only a growth spurt and a change of uniform. On chalk hills, down
darkling lanes, England's private schools must be chokker with Chinese
and Arabs in Church brogues paying full whack – with a supplement for
intensive English.

Sherborne's colours are royal blue and gold. The motto is *Dieu et mon
droit*, the same as the reigning monarch's; no arguing there. It has a roster
of old boys going back to Alfred the Great. Scratching around among the
staff of the post-war years, we see it has had its fair share of spymasters. The
very word gives pause.

The father of computer science, Alan Turing, who worked at Bletchley
Park, and two former heads of the Secret Intelligence Service – MI6 – were
Old Shirburnians. David Cornwell, better known as John le Carré, admits
that his spymaster George Smiley was part based on Chaplain and Assistant
Master, Reverend Vivian Green.

The Guardian obituary for Rev. Green makes him seem far from
Smiley's English reticence:

> *He had a wonderfully secure sense of who he was, something that allowed
> him, even as chaplain, to be seen either in leather trousers or, at the very
> least, in discordant tie and shirt; and he was happy, in later years, to
> admit to a great admiration for Miss Piggy from the Muppet Show.*[1]

It sounds as though evensong got off to a rollicking start. Cornwell was
enrolled at Sherborne from 1945 to 1948. His con-man father, Ronnie, had
trouble paying the fees. Cornwell disliked the school and feigned a nervous
breakdown to escape, but he has returned to its playing fields time and
again as to an old nightmare that is forever England:

> *We were still being taught that the best career would take us to Rhodesia
> or Kenya, or that we should go and rule India; and I think that even as a
> child I was overwhelmed by the arrogance of these assumptions.*[2]

Vivian Green, in loud checks, one of the models for George Smiley

What the blacking factory did to Dickens, this encounter with England's plutocracy did to le Carré. He is the heir to Dickens in other respects too: the larger-than-life comic muse, his vivid, sometimes one-trick characters and class-defining dialogue. Le Carré wrote *The Spy Who Came in from the Cold* (1963) – the most successful espionage novel ever – in six weeks, in Königswinter on the Rhine near Bonn. Locales and types recur: posh schools, Swiss grand hotels, innocents embroiled in international wheeling and dealing. But each new novel of late has tackled a different Goliath. Walls, entire countries, empires have fallen by the wayside, while le Carré has scripted post-war unease on the side of the spy in the works.

He persuaded his father to send him to the University of Bern, where he turned up in 1948 when he was sixteen and lied about his age. He'd begun learning German at Sherborne. 'It was love at first sight,' he declared some seventy years later. 'It was the German language that provided me with my bolt hole.' He went on to study Modern Languages at Oxford and taught German at Eton; 'Germans, like Brits, are branded on the tongue.'[3] The language gave le Carré another culture, like a second passport. 'He needed to be able to close the door on his Englishness, love it as he might, and carve a new name somewhere fresh,' he writes of Magnus Pym, his alter ego in *A Perfect Spy*.[4] Le Carré's most long-lived creation, George Smiley, has a German childhood:

Germany was his second nature, even his second soul. In his youth, her
literature had been his passion and his discipline. He could put on her
language like a uniform and speak with its boldness.[5]

'Somewhere fresh' was Bern. Interviewed by Jon Snow, le Carré is clear
and forthcoming: 'I was recruited informally when I was a young student
in Switzerland. It was the element somehow that I felt born into.'[6] Bern in
1948 was a diplomatic crossroads. Le Carré has described it as 'the spiritual
home of natural spies'.[7] In common with zoned Berlin and Tangiers, his
Bern has an atmosphere of intrigue and treachery behind the chocolate-box
exterior.

Ben Macintyre describes the Swiss spy theatre when Nicholas Elliott
was MI6 head of station and the Cold War was hotting up:

But beneath a placid, neutral surface, the place was riddled with spies.
Swiss efforts to discourage espionage during the war failed utterly: Allied,
Axis and freelance agents had converged on the country as a base from
which to launch intelligence operations into enemy territory. The Soviets
had run at least two linked spy networks based in Switzerland, the Rote
Kapelle (Red Orchestra) and the Lucy Ring, extracting top-secret infor-
mation from Nazi Germany and funnelling it to Moscow ... Switzerland
became a magnet for defectors, resisters and rats leaving the sinking Nazi
ship, all clutching their secrets. During the war, the Soviets ran their
own networks, and the British and Americans ran theirs, in wary coopera-
tion. But with the coming of peace, Soviet and Western intelligence forces
would turn on each other.[8]

Jean Ziegler, Swiss parliamentarian, *bête noire* and author of *The Swiss, the*
Gold and the Dead, cites Friedrich Dürrenmatt on their native country:
Switzerland is like a girl who works in a brothel but wants to remain a virgin. According to Ziegler, the Swiss live with a self-concocted myth about
themselves, which their mountain fastness has a way of echoing back at
them: 'The bank vaults of Zürich, Basel, Bern and Lugano have become
a sewage system into which flow streams of filthy lucre from all over the
world.'[9] Switzerland was already established as a launderette at the conclu-
sion of the First World War. Conrad, Glauser, Maugham and Dürrenmatt
had developed their views of Swiss neutrality long before le Carré came on
the scene:

> *Switzerland's financial sharps in Zürich, Basel, and Berne fenced and*
> *laundered the gold stolen from the central banks of Belgium, Poland,*
> *Czechoslovakia, Holland, Luxembourg, Lithuania, Albania, Norway,*
> *Italy and elsewhere. It was they who financed Hitler's wars of conquest.*[10]

Philip Roth has called le Carré's *A Perfect Spy* (1985) 'the best English novel since the war'. Rick Pym is a charm merchant exploiting British wartime shortages – 'chocolates, nylons, dried fruit and petrol'. Magnus Pym has inherited his father's talent for double-dealing. Le Carré's father had died in 1975 and *A Perfect Spy* is a coming to terms with the world of 1930s fences and confidence men. Rick and Magnus Pym take two pre-war trips to Switzerland, setting the template for later visits:

> *those pre-war winters in Switzerland become fused in my memory as*
> *one place. Even today I have only to sniff the leather interior of a grand*
> *car and I am wafted willingly away to the great hotel drawing-rooms of*
> *St. Moritz in the wake of Rick's riotous love of festival. The Kulm, the*
> *Suvretta House, the Grand – Pym knew them as a single gigantic palace*
> *with different sets of servants but always the same court: Rick's private*
> *household of jesters, tumblers, counsellors, and jockeys.*[11]

Pym's memory of the 'single gigantic palace' that is Switzerland recurs throughout le Carré's writing. Rick the playboy spiv turns up in different disguise in a score of novels. In *A Perfect Spy* le Carré joins the dots between a 1930s world of seaside crooks first outlined by Graham Greene (another paid-up member of MI6), wartime racketeering and Cold War sleuthing.

Pym, like le Carré, finds himself in post-war Bern, 'that lovely candle-lit city with its clocks and wells and cobbles and arcades'.[12] He has fallen for his own game – a confidence trickster masquerading as the Duchesse Rothschild, 'the last of the great Czech line'. She tells a tall tale of family art, Swiss bank accounts and border smuggling. Pym is in Bern as chargé d'affaires for his father in order to fleece her. She ends up fleecing him.

During the war Switzerland had been a lucrative market for loot of all colours and provenance. Stolen art, antiquities, jewels, much of it Jewish in origin, made its way across the borders from countries under Nazi occupation, where Jewish property had been commandeered. In Amsterdam it was rough diamonds. In France it was art masterpieces. Later it was rings and gold teeth extracted from concentration camp victims.

Allen Dulles, CIA Director under Presidents Eisenhower and Kennedy, was stationed in Bern during both world wars. During the First World War he handled political intelligence in Bern and in 1919 was a member of the American delegation to the Versailles peace conference. During the Second World War, as head of OSS Switzerland (forerunner of the CIA), Dulles operated from his Bern office at Dufourstrasse and from home at Herrengasse 23. Arranging for the streetlights at the rear of the splendid building to be removed, he received his shifty informants. 'With the exception of the code-breakers at Bletchley Park,' Thomas Powers estimates, 'no intelligence operation of the Second World War achieved more than did Dulles' tiny office in Bern, staffed with a miscellany of Americans stranded in Switzerland by the war. What Dulles did he did largely by himself.'[13]

> One of my most important German sources during my days in Switzerland in World War II almost had a serious mishap because his initials were in his hat. One evening he was dining alone with me in my house in Berne. My cook detected that we were speaking German. While we were enjoying her excellent food – she was a better cook than a spy – she slipped out of the kitchen, examined the source's hat and took down his initials. The next day, she reported to her Nazi contact ...
>
> My source was the representative in Zürich of Admiral Canaris, head of German military intelligence. He frequently visited the German legation in Berne.[14]

During the late 1940s Soviet mole Kim Philby was in and out of Bern, meeting with SIS Head of Station Nicholas Elliott at the British embassy from 1945 to 1953. Philby's wife Aileen was a self-harmer, suffering from Münchausen's syndrome, and receiving treatment in a clinic in Switzerland. Elliott was one of the last people to meet Philby and extract his confession, before he defected to Moscow in 1963. Ben Macintyre's A Spy among Friends, with an afterword by le Carré, uncovers the lethal mix of friendship and betrayal of the post-war years. When the first two Cambridge moles, Guy Burgess and Donald Maclean, defected in May 1951, the Soviet embassy in Bern provided fake passports and onward passage to Zürich and eventually Moscow.

Le Carré made use of these events in his Tinker Tailor Soldier Spy and always claimed it was Philby who blew his cover to the Soviets. Elliott was on the selection board when le Carré was first interviewed for the Service:

When I became a new entrant, he was a fifth-floor grandee whose most
celebrated espionage coup – the wartime recruitment of a highly placed
member of the German Abwehr in Istanbul, smuggling him and his wife
to Britain – was held up to trainees as the ultimate example of what a
resourceful field officer could achieve.[15]

Sixteen-year-old Magnus Pym is resourceful: working 'black' at the zoo,
staying at the Salvation Army hostel and enrolling at Bern University under
false pretences: 'He lied first about his qualifications and then about his
age, for the one could not have been earned without the adjustment to
the other.'[16] Pym frequents the English church in Elfenau, 'the diplomatic
fairyland' with its 'weekly shot of the English banality'.[17] At night he haunts
the station:

In the immediate post-war years it was still an ill-lit Edwardian staging
post, with stuffed stags in the concourse and murals of freed peasants wav-
ing flags, and a scent of Bockwurst and fried onion that never went away.
The first-class buffet was full of gentlemen in black suits with napkins
round their necks, but the third class was shadowy and beery, with a whiff
of Balkan lawlessness and drunks who sang out of tune.[18]

Pym makes friends with Axel, a German from Carlsbad with a chequered
war. Like the gold making its way through Swiss vaults at the time, his true
provenance is hard to tell. Together they wander the streets of the capital
and knock on Thomas Mann's dressing room door. Fact and fiction, as
always with le Carré, play footsie:

Thomas Mann peered at Pym, then at Axel so pale and ethereal from
his fever. Thomas Mann frowned at the palm of his own right hand as if
asking himself whether it could take the strain of an aristocratic embrace.
He held out his hand and Pym shook it, waiting to feel Mann's genius
flow into him like one of those electric shocks you used to be able to buy at
railway stations – hold this knob and let my energy revive you.[19]

Pym meets his contact at the English church, 'where the flag of Saint
George fluttered victorious in the neutral Swiss breeze'. Jack and Felicity
Brotherhood are Secret Service brave and squaw. The pass occurs over
mince pies after a walk in the woods. Pym is willing. His test mission is
to translate armaments catalogues for twenty francs – 'funny little Swissie

firms that are manufacturing things we don't much like'. As Dürrenmatt intimated, Swiss Cold War arms deals were much sought after by both sides. Pym graduates to providing names of students at the Cosmo Club, a left-of-centre hangout at the university. It's only one small step to shopping his new friend Axel.

> There were the stories Axel had told him when he was delirious and spill-ing his drinking water with both hands. There were the stories he had told him in Davos when they went to visit Thomas Mann's sanatorium. There were the crumbs he had gleaned for himself on his occasional pre-cautionary inspections of Axel's room. And there was Brotherhood's clever prompting that dragged things out of him he hadn't realised he knew.[20]

The Swiss deport Axel as an illegal alien. Pym leaves for Oxford. Winners and losers. 'By the time he reached Basel he knew that Bern had sunk with all hands.'

Cornwell's activities on behalf of Her Majesty's government stood him in good stead. In due course he was formally recruited by MI5 and spied on Leftist groups, as he describes Magnus Pym doing during his time at Oxford. Cornwell put his German to good use in Bonn and Hamburg at the height of the Cold War. Kim Philby had blown his cover long before. By 1964 it was time to go anyway. *The Spy Who Came in from the Cold* had made le Carré famous. Divided loyalties – spying or writing? – played their part. Writing won.

George Smiley is back at the hardboard chicane of the Circus towards the end of *Smiley's People* (1979). Dutch elm disease is ravaging England. The bloody unions are on a rampage. Ireland is playing up and the Commies are entering the Great Game's last set with two sets all. George to serve, blinded by the sunset. His long career in espionage comes to a showdown with his nemesis Karla. The place of assignation is Bern.

Smiley checks into le Carré's base of operations when he's in town:

> the Bellevue Palace Hotel, an enormous sumptuous place of mellowed Edwardian quiet, which on clear days looks across the foothills to the glistening Alps, but that evening was shrouded in a cloying winter fog. He had considered smaller places; he had considered using one of Toby's safe flats. But Toby had persuaded him that the Bellevue was best. It had several exits, it was central, and it was the first place in Berne where any-one would think to find him, and therefore the last where Karla, if he was

looking out for him, would expect him to be. Entering the enormous hall,
Smiley had the feeling of stepping onto an empty liner far out at sea.[21]

Le Carré's writing has been able to conjure the sights and smells of Bern
for over half a century. His choice of detail is always emblematic of the
broader picture: 'The streets were cobbled; the freezing air smelt of roast
chestnuts and cigars.' His Bern is nostalgic, opulent, suffused with the
past: 'So many nights, he thought. So many streets still here. He thought
of Hesse: *strange to wander in the fog ... no tree knows another.* The
frozen mist curled low over the racing water; the weir burned creamy
yellow.'[22]

The Elfenau diplomatic district, with its CD plates and patrolling police
cars, is a well-trodden beat for le Carré. 'They descended a gentle hill, passing the British Ambassador's residence on their right, and his Rolls-Royce
parked in the sweep.' Bern's Soviet Embassy gives us a feel for lost empire,
the 1970s balance of power, typists and Tass:

> *Twenty-four diplomats, fifty other ranks – ciphers, clerks, typists, and*
> *some very lousy drivers, all home-based. The trade delegation's in another*
> *building, Schanzeneckstrasse 17. Grigoriev visits there a lot. In Berne we*
> *also got Tass and Novosti, mostly mainstream hoods. The parent residency*
> *is Geneva, U.N. cover, about two hundred strong. This place is a side-*
> *show: twelve, fifteen altogether, growing but only slow. The Consulate is*
> *tacked onto the back of the Embassy. You go into it through a door in the*
> *fence, like it was an opium den or a cat house. They got a closed-circuit*
> *television camera on the path and scanners in the waiting-room.*[23]

Grigoriev is embassy counsellor. Smiley's team tail him on the promenade
fronting Bern's Cathedral while he watches chess being played with giant
pieces. The team muscles him into a car. Smiley himself is waiting in an
apartment behind the university. 'Grigoriev was a hooked fish.' Under
pressure from a few dirty photos, he spills what he knows of the Karla
Directorate in Moscow.

Le Carré returned to a Swiss theatre of operations with 'The Unbearable
Peace', a non-fiction piece in *Granta* in spring 1991. Its subject is Swiss
General Jean-Louis Jeanmaire, convicted of passing military secrets to a
Russian diplomat in Bern in the early 1960s and sentenced to twelve years'
solitary confinement. Le Carré's assignment is an interview with that rare
bird, an eighty-year-old Swiss traitor and ex-con.

Swiss General Jean-Louis Jeanmaire: Cold War traitor or patsy?

The writer's dissection of General Jeanmaire's character and motivation seems to be of the Swiss psyche itself:

> For those who know Switzerland only for its slopes and valleys, Swiss militarism, if they are aware of it at all, is a harmless joke. They make nothing of the circular steel plates in the winding mountain roads, from which explosive charges will be detonated to seal off the valleys from the aggressor; of the great iron gateways that lead into secret mountain fortresses, some for storing military arsenals, others for sitting out the nuclear holocaust; of the self-regarding young men in officer's uniform who strut the pavements and parade themselves in teashops at the weekend. They are unaware of the vast annual expenditure on American tanks and fighter aircraft, early-warning systems, civil defence, deep shelters and (with 625,000 troops from a population of 6,000,000) after Israel the largest proportionate standing army in the world, costing the Swiss taxpayer eighteen per cent of his gross national budget.[24]

This is the Cold War arms world alluded to in Dürrenmatt's fiction, but viewed from le Carré's post–Cold War vantage point. The old spy writer's subject matter has suddenly shifted, and a new game is in town. There's nothing like a traitor in the ranks and a witch-hunt, le Carré suggests, to bring about an increase in the military budget. The Americans in 1975 were itchy about the Soviets finding out about their Florida early-warning system and state-of-the-art US technology fitted to Swiss tanks. Le Carré's analysis of arms and money signals a new phase in his work when *glasnost* was in the air. He turned his attention to global capitalism hand in glove with the military-industrial complex. No better place to start than Switzerland.

General Jeanmaire's contact was the Soviet military attaché Colonel Vassily Denissenko. Deni was a charming hero of Stalingrad and had bedded Jeanmaire's wife, Marie-Louise. She was Russian born, her father a Swiss professor of languages, exiled in Switzerland after the Bolshevik coup. The first meeting between Jeanmaire and Deni was in 1959 at a routine military exercise. Jeanmaire and Marie-Louise met dashing Deni again at the Schweizerhof Hotel in Bern. Thus the 1960s got underway, a ten-year cocktail party in and around Bern – the Hotel Kreuz, the Tabaris nightclub, sundry railway-station buffets and apartments. Jeanmaire at one point handed over classified documents: the Swiss 'organisation plan of staff and troops at corps and division levels', the *Mobilization Handbook* and other top-secret papers. It wasn't until 1975 that authorities became aware of General Jeanmaire's relationship with successive Soviet attachés. Why so late? And who tipped them off?

> And if the tip-off did indeed come from the CIA, who tipped off the CIA?
> Was the source reliable? Was it a plant? Was it Russian? British? French?
> West German? Swiss? In the grimy market-places where so-called friendly
> intelligence services do their trading, tip-offs, like money, are laundered in
> all sorts of ways. They can be slanted, doctored and invented.[25]

What the facts lack is plausible motive. By even the tamest Swiss standards, the General was not a fellow traveller. He was no fondue Socialist. Whatever gifts Denissenko gave – a television, trinkets – were trifling. The quality of intelligence, too, was negligible: 'All he ever gave the Russians was peanuts, not least because peanuts were all he had.'[26] Le Carré smells other possibilities: was Jeanmaire thrown to the lions to 'silence American apprehensions and re-establish Switzerland's self image as a responsible and efficient military (and neutral) power'?[27] Was Jeanmaire just a patsy?

Official records of the trial in June 1977 have not been released and Swiss secrecy, as is often the case, is the soft cosh of peace. The Swiss press painted Jeanmaire as traitor of the century. His case fed the self-image of a country beleaguered by hostile foreigners: they change uniform and colour with the passing of the seasons, but are always at the gates. Sentenced to eighteen years for treachery, he served twelve.

Zürich's Dolder Grand Hotel, and the model for le Carré's 'Meister Tower'
on the right

*It had made a big spy out of a small one. Such a huge sentence must
betoken a huge betrayal. The witch was burned, a great leak had been
stopped and America need no longer equate Switzerland with a communist country.*[28]

Le Carré followed his reportage on General Jeanmaire with *The Night
Manager* (1993), his first novel wholly completed after the fall of the Iron
Curtain. In the interim the Soviet Union had come apart like a tin toy.
Humpty-Dumpty couldn't be put back together again. Or could he? Le
Carré knew that great powers play a long game.

The novel opens magnanimously in the Hotel Meister Palace, modelled on Zürich's Dolder Grand. The Salvation Army hostel in Bern is
long gone, and the lobbies and salons of Switzerland's luxury hotels are
heretofore where deals get done. Jonathan Pine, the eponymous manager,
is a study in close observation, in keeping your eyes peeled:

*The doors swung open again, disgorging everyone at once, so that
suddenly an entire leftover delegation of the English affluent society was ranged under the chandelier, each of its members so sleekly
groomed, so sun-rich, that together they seemed to share a corporate
morality.*[29]

Our party occupies the Meister Tower, a three-bedroom palace tacked onto the Edwardian hotel, 'a pastel experience in what Jonathan confidingly calls Swiss Franc Quatorze'. Fifteen thousand francs a night, continental breakfast included. The first Gulf War is underway and our baddie is British arms and drugs dealer, Richard Onslow Roper.

The opening chapter sketches the Lear jets and room service world of people with money to burn. The novel quickly moves from sedate Switzerland to a James Bond props cupboard of gun-toting men and alluring women, fast cars and luxury island hideaways. *The Night Manager* presents Switzerland as luxury brand – discreet, napped by snow, exclusive. Behind the new wealth are the new television wars, and le Carré is expert at delineating the fuzzy borders between terrorism, government skulduggery and the carpet bagging of resurgent capitalism. His moguls and bling kings haunt the playgrounds of the rich – Davos, Klosters, St Moritz. The resort names seem like brand names. 'What is black money, when is it grey, when does it go white?'[30] While the old moralist highlights the complicity of the British state in financial shenanigans – 'we'd go anywhere for money' – his pointing the finger at Switzerland is equally devastating. Like le Carré, Jean Ziegler pulls no punches: 'Switzerland remains one of the most efficient international laundries for billions in drug money and the profits of organised crime.'[31]

Le Carré's fine-tuned ear for dialogue comes to the fore. Jed, a kept beauty, consults the hotel menu and wonders about the Swiss national dish.

> 'What's roasty, *anyway?*' *says Jed.*
>
> '*I think you're looking at rösti,' Jonathan replies in a tone laced with superior knowledge. 'It's a Swiss potato delicacy. Sort of bubble and squeak without the squeak, made with lots of butter and fried. If one's ravenous, perfectly delicious. And they do it* awfully *well.*'
>
> '*How do they grab you?' Roper demands. 'Likee? No likee? Don't be lukewarm – no good to anyone. ... Hash browns, darling; had 'em in Miami. ... What do you say, Mr. Pine?*'[32]

Mockney meets the jetsetter, the parlance of New Labour. We are a long way from the laments about cockney tourists in Switzerland by travellers such as William Brockenden in 1833: 'I had no idea that the gentilities of Wapping had ever extended so far from the Thames.'[33] Le Carré's grip on the way different social classes play snakes and ladders is unerring. Their talk sparkles.

The night manager is one of those deracinated Englishmen le Carré specialises in. Pine becomes a 'plant' behind enemy lines. Allen Dulles explains: 'The only way to disguise a man today so that he will be acceptable in hostile circles for any length of time is to make him over entirely. This involves years of training and a thorough concealing and burying of the past under layers of fictitious personal history which have to be "backstopped."'[34] Dulles was writing in the early 1960s. 'Backstopping' a plant these days would involve a thorough scrubbing of the electronic trail we all leave behind us, and the fabrication of a new electronic identity. The selfies need to match.

Set for the most part in Kenya (le Carré still pronounces it 'Keen-ya'), *The Constant Gardener* (2001) has a number of key scenes in Switzerland's Engadin and Basel. His target this time is globalism, that *fin-de-siècle* buzzword already tarnished. Le Carré has described globalism as 'a board room fantasy' where 'the shareholder is the excuse for everything'.[35] His particular target is the way Big Pharma plays dangerously with lives in the developing world in order to pump up shareholder value. The benign public face of the drug dealers peels away to reveal business as usual underneath. This theme comes under renewed scrutiny now that globalism has fallen flat on its face. In a 2013 documentary *Fire in the Blood*, Dylan Mohan Gray depicts the devastating policies that pharmaceutical companies pursue in order to protect, by hook or by crook, their monopoly on AIDS drugs.[36] Recent investigations by the Cochrane Collaboration show how Roche withheld vital information on clinical trials for its drug Tamiflu, now shown to be ineffective.[37] Techniques of obfuscation, delay, selective evidence and confidentiality agreements, used in response to the scandal of unclaimed wartime assets, hamper the search for truth in these cases too. There seems to be little appetite for truth; merely greed. It pays to keep mum.

In *The Constant Gardener*, British High Commission man Justin and his activist wife Tessa, who is murdered, stumble on the truth about treatment trials. 'I try to get two innocent people into a Hitchcockian muddle and fight their way out'[38] is how le Carré describes his working method. The aptly named Justin journeys to Basel. Home to such Fortune 500 companies as Novartis, Ciba-Geigy, Roche and Bayer, Basel is a Big Pharma town. During the war, proximity to Germany led to lucrative deals. The first Nazi gold deliveries were credited to the Bank of International Settlements based in Basel. Its airport gives you a choice of exits – Swiss or French. A hop across the Rhine and you're in the Black Forest. This three-corner business park is a goose that lays the golden egg. Basel's large international school caters to the sons and daughters of well-travelled, well-heeled research chemists, company executives and bankers.

Le Carré develops a Jack and the Beanstalk metaphor to convey his theme of the small man speaking truth to power. Before confronting the giant, Justin recuperates in the mountains from an earlier fight:

> *Switzerland was a childhood dream. Forty years ago his parents had taken him on a walking holiday in the Engadin and they had stayed in a grand hotel on a spit of forest between two lakes. Nothing had changed. Not the polished parquet or the stained glass or the stern-faced châtelaine who showed him to his room. Reclining on the daybed on his balcony, Justin watched the same lakes glistening in the evening sun, and the same fisherman huddled in his rowing boat in the mist.*[39]

This seems to be the Waldhaus in Sils-Maria, with views of Lake Silvaplana and Lake Sils, another of le Carré's opulent palaces. He captures 'that fabled valley of the upper Rhine where pharma-giants have their castles':

> *First up a cobbled hill to the medieval city with its bell towers, merchant houses, statues to free thinkers and martyrs of oppression. And when he had duly reminded himself of this inheritance, as it seemed to him, he retraced his steps to the river's edge, and from a children's playground gazed upwards in near-disbelief at the ever-spreading concrete kingdom of the pharma-billionaires ... And at their feet lay whole railways, marshalling yards, lorry parks and wharfs, each protected by its very own Berlin Wall capped with razor wire and daubed with graffiti.*[40]

Justin is on the trail of KVH, a company based in Basel, manufacturers of Dypraxa, a fictitious tuberculosis drug. Despite flawed clinical trials and deaths in Africa, Dypraxa has been rushed to market. Le Carré states in an afterword: 'as my journey through the pharmaceutical jungle progressed, I came to realize that, by comparison with the reality, my story was as tame as a holiday postcard'.[41]

Two of Basel's giant pharmaceutical companies, Novartis and Roche, refused to comment on the novel. A spokesman admitted: 'I don't think anybody from management has had the time to read through the over 500 pages yet.'[42] The dearth of management reading has a lot to answer for. Le Carré researched his novel undercover:

In The Constant Gardener *in particular, it was quite extraordinary to go*
to Basel, to get among the young pharmaceutical executives in a private
way, promise them that I would never divulge their names, and listen to
them pouring out their rage against the work they were doing, the people
who were making them do it. But they were still taking the penny, and
they were still doing what they were doing. They were still contributing
to the invention of diseases, they were fiddling with compounds to turn
them into new patents when they actually had no greater effect than the
previous patent, they were joining the lie that every new compound put
on the market costs six or eight hundred million dollars.[43]

Justin crosses the Rhine to an immigrant no-man's land by the border. The
description splices the St Johann district of Basel with Grenzacherstrasse,
where Roche has its headquarters. St Johann is home to a Novartis Campus
straddling the French–Swiss border, in an area since tarted up. It's Pharma
Central:

Justin crossed the bridge and, as in a dream, wandered a dismal wasteland
of rundown housing estates, secondhand clothes shops and hollow-eyed
immigrant labourers on bicycles. And gradually, by some accident of
magnetic attraction, he found himself standing in what at first appeared
to be a pleasant tree-lined avenue at the far end of which stood an
ecologically-friendly gateway so densely overgrown with creeper that at
first you barely spotted the oak doors inside, with their polished brass
bell to press, and their brass letter box for mail. It was only when Justin
looked up, and further up, and then right up into the sky above his head,
that he woke to the immensity of a triptych of white tower blocks linked
by flying corridors. The stonework was hospital clean, the windows were
of coppered glass. And from somewhere behind each monstrous block rose
a white chimney, sharp as a pencil jammed into the sky. And from each
chimney the letters KVH, done in gold and mounted vertically down its
length, winked at him like old friends.[44]

On a warm February evening in Bern I cross the Aar, two hundred and thirty
meters below. The river turns sharply where the Bellevue Palace Hotel commands the bluff. To the right is the Casino where the seventeen-year-old
Cornwell shook Thomas Mann's hand. Facing the river is the Esplanade
where Allen Dulles imagined a waiter 'spying for an Iron Curtain country'.[45] Snow tops the Bernese Oberland. Groups of young people on the

benches are rolling joints, canoodling. Black Mercedes limousines with diplomatic plates litter the hotel forecourt. A young doorman does his duty. I ask him where I can have afternoon tea. He gestures to the Bellevue bar where for a century Bern's diplomats and spies have consorted.

The manager takes my coat. We confer about teas and settle on Assam. It comes in a silver pot, accompanied by a little mandarin tart. 'Elevator operators, like waiters and hotel people generally, remember faces. In certain countries, employees of this sort, bartenders, doormen, are police informants.'[46] The bar is studiously masculine, like a gentleman's club. A pianist tinkles the ivories, just as he did for Smiley. A man leans over a laptop, Bluetooth device in his ear. He could be secretly filming me, relaying my presence to Moscow or Beijing. A few shelves of books labelled 'Politics and Espionage', a copy of le Carré's *Our Kind of Traitor* sitting snug beside a biography of Bill Clinton.

A marble stairwell descends to the toilets, scene of Dima's escape in *Our Kind of Traitor* (2010). Russian money-launderer turned Queen's evidence, Dima is the epitome of suave vulgar oligarch – the Wild East, as le Carré calls it. Luke the spook spirits him away to safety:

> *As Luke buried himself a little deeper in his leather chair, and raised the lid of his silver laptop a little higher, he knew that if there had ever been such a thing as a Eureka moment in his life, it was here and now ... the apéro is getting underway. A low baritone burble issues from the Salon d'Honneur, starts to grow, and drops again.*[47]

Tonight the Salon d'Honneur is filled with burbling Kuwaiti diplomats. Oleaginous politicos who will inherit the earth. The Bellevue is where the cream of Bern rises, rich but not necessarily thick, where le Carré stays when he comes to town, where Dulles and Smiley haunted the bar, where intrigue played out through two world wars and their long cold aftermath.

Our Kind of Traitor opens with a tennis match in an island hideaway and closes in two Swiss hideaways – the Bellevue's five-star opulence and a Wengen chalet. The novel has all le Carré's trademarks: laundered loot, rich trappings and government duplicity. In a 2011 *Democracy Now* interview, le Carré hints at a possible genesis for this late sortie by an old activist. He cites the scandal of Labour Party mandarin Peter Mandelson, caught partying off Corfu in 2008 on the yacht of Russia's richest man, Oleg Deripaska. Deripaska had pulled himself up from the Caucasus by his bootstraps and made his billions in aluminium. Mandelson as EU Trade

Commissioner had been responsible for setting aluminium tariffs. The FBI
wanted the Russian for questioning. Other guests on the yacht were hedge
fund manager Nathaniel Rothschild, shadow Chancellor George Osborne
and newspaper magnate Rupert Murdoch – rich pickings on the eve of
the financial crisis. George Osborne and Tory fundraiser Andrew Feldman
allegedly solicited Deripaska for donations. *The Independent* newspaper
sketched the story succinctly:

> *They drew attention to the power games of a globe-spanning elite of men
> and women. They shed light on how decisions that can change the world
> are made on the yachts of the Mediterranean and Caribbean, the ski
> slopes of Switzerland, in the fashionable restaurants of New York, London
> and Moscow and the casinos of Montenegro.*[48]

Le Carré transposed this scandal to *Our Kind of Traitor*, where a crucial
scene of skulduggery is video-recorded on a luxury yacht in 'an ancient
crowded harbour with expensive sailing boats'. From the boat's stern
'hang the flags of Switzerland, Britain and Russia'. The Russian Prince is
'waiting for the Americans to drop some thoroughly unreasonable money-
laundering charges'. One of the guests on the yacht is a 'Shadow Minister,
tipped for stratospheric office at the next election', a leading member of
Her Majesty's Opposition:

> *handsome in the way that young men of the eighteenth century were
> handsome in the portraits they donated to Luke's old school when they
> left it: broad brow, receding hairline, the haughty sub-Byronic gaze of
> sensual entitlement, a pretty pout, and a posture that manages to look
> down on you however tall you are.*[49]

We are back at Sherborne School, and the Head Boy caught with his pants
down. *Our Kind of Traitor* ends in a chalet in Wengen, where turncoat
Dima is sequestered with his family pending a deal with the spooks in
London (including posh boarding schools for the kids). Le Carré keeps his
own chalet in the mountain resort and knows its forest tracks well:

> *Ollie was referring to the village of Grindelwald, which lay at the oppos-
> ing foot of the Eiger massif. To reach Wengen from the Lauterbrunnen
> side by any means except mountain railway was impossible, Ollie had
> reported: the summer track might be good enough for chamois and the*

odd foolhardy motorcyclist, but not for a four-wheeled vehicle with three
men aboard.[50]

As crown witness, Dima will expose the launderers' dirty linen. His handlers spirit him across the saddle of Kleine Scheidegg:

> *Ollie dowsed the jeep's lights altogether, and they slunk like thieves past*
> *the twin hulks of the great hotel. The glow of Grindelwald appeared*
> *below them. They began the descent, entered forest and saw the lights of*
> *the Brandegg winking at them through the trees.*[51]

Le Carré's protagonists have been hiding out in Switzerland for half a century, as undercover or double agents. Custard-coloured primroses push up
through the motorway embankments at Morges along the lakeshore from
Lausanne. Probably nuclear shelters behind them. Vaults of dodgy gold?
After reading le Carré, one wonders what various bumps and protrusions
in the Swiss landscape conceal. The old spymaster has revisited again and
again a terrain where his seventeen-year-old self cut his spying teeth. He
keeps checking into its grand hotels, drawn to them like treachery itself.
Switzerland is where the boy from Sherborne first set out to walk on the
shady side of the street.

13

ON THE ROAD

Carry on up the Khyber with Maillart, Schwarzenbach and Bouvier

Annemarie Schwarzenbach and Ella Maillart on the trip detailed in *The Cruel Way*

It is the Switzerland of Asia, a buffer-state without colonies or
access to the sea.
Ella Maillart

When I went to pay for Nicolas Bouvier's one-volume *Oeuvres* (2004), clocking in at 1,400 pages, the grey-haired lady behind the counter at my local bookshop in Sète turned misty eyed. We travellers, she admitted, always took Bouvier with us in our backpacks. It was the thinking woman's *On the Road*. This cult following grew to literary fame only towards the close of Bouvier's life. He died in 1998, fêted as a great wanderer and chronicler. He is in a line of footloose Swiss writers on a spiritual quest for adventure they didn't find at home. This is the story of three of them, heading east to Afghanistan long before the hippy trail, half a century and more in advance of yoga and chakras, wellness and mindfulness, the Buddha of suburbia and the Zen of corporate chic.

My bookseller recommended Ella Maillart. Maillart's journeys led me to Annemarie Schwarzenbach, with whom I fell a little bit in love. It's hard to look at any photo of Annemarie and not to come under the spell of her icy androgynous beauty with its *noli me tangere* hauteur. I could Google her image all day. Her photographs and the cult of personality have put her writing in the shade. These three Swiss travellers – Ella, Annemarie and Nicolas – are the sons and daughters of Rousseau's wanderlust. What is it about Switzerland that sends its writers out on the road?

Ella Maillart led a long life of action. Born in Geneva in 1903, she was the daughter of a Swiss furrier and a Danish mother. The lake entranced her early and she took to sailing, representing Switzerland at the Paris Olympics of 1924. Later, she was the only woman member of the Swiss National Ski Team, at a time when women didn't have the vote in Switzerland and when skiing was still thought of as somewhat of an English pastime.

She began her travels in the South of France, soon headed to Weimar Berlin and then to Russia, where she studied film and became a fluent speaker of the language. By 1930 she was in the Caucasus, later in Russian Turkestan. She wrote an account of her travels as *Among the Russian Youth* (1932). Travel and writing were inextricably linked for the rest of her long life. 'I write with my foot,' she admitted.[1]

In 1939 she teamed up with Annemarie Schwarzenbach (1908–42) for a cross-country drive in a Ford Roadster 'Deluxe' 18 horsepower from Geneva to Afghanistan. Schwarzenbach was a writer, photojournalist and antifascist scion of one of Switzerland's blue-blooded families. Her father was

Annemarie Schwarzenbach and Ella Maillart en route to Afghanistan

a wealthy silk industrialist (he provided the car) and her mother an aristocratic horsewoman descended from Bismarck. Renée Schwarzenbach had
wanted to be a boy and passed this conflicted identity on to her daughter. The mother was imperious and manipulative – the kind who burns
your papers after you die. She dressed Annemarie as a boy from an early
age. Annemarie was strikingly good-looking and photogenic. Outspoken
against the rise of Hitler and National Socialism, she was eager to escape
the strictures of the family estate on Lake Zürich. Her reactionary family
included fervent supporters of the little failed painter from Austria; they
saw Annemarie as the black sheep. She took up a position against Nazism
early in the 1930s, at a time when many in the German world and further
afield were enamoured.

For Roger Martin du Gard, Annemarie had 'the face of an inconsolable
angel'.[2] The American writer Carson McCullers promptly fell in love and
dedicated *Reflections in a Golden Eye* (1942) to her: 'She had a face that I
knew would haunt me to the end of my life.'[3] Trousered, lounging against
the bonnets of vintage cars, louche-eyed, Annemarie looks like a cross
between David Bowie as the thin white duke and a leggy thirteen-year-old
boy between the wars. In 1930 she encountered Klaus and Erika Mann,
the wayward children of Thomas Mann. Both left-wing gay intellectuals
decades ahead of their time, the 'terrible twins' introduced Annemarie
to the politicised decadence of Berlin's cabaret, the world of Isherwood
and Dietrich, as well as to morphine. Her unrequited love for Erika Mann

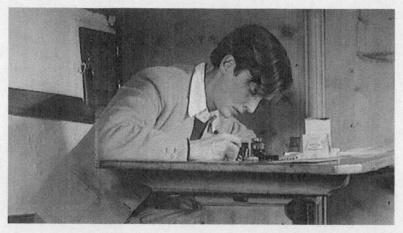

Schwarzenbach writing in her house in Sils-Baselgia in 1942

marked her short life. Annemarie's first novel *The Friends of Bernhard* (1931) and her *Lyric Novella* (1933) are set in this cabaret semi-closet on the eve of Hitler's accession to power. She was another gay writer who switched the pronouns.

She took to the road as a photojournalist and travelled to Turkey, Syria, Iraq and Persia. In 1936, Erika Mann, in exile from Munich, relocated her political cabaret *Die Pfeffermühle* (The Peppermill) to Zürich. The cabaret was attacked by Swiss pro-fascists, among whom were members of Annemarie's family. This fracas strained relationships all round. Annemarie's marriage to a gay French diplomat in Tehran in 1935 provided friendship, a useful diplomatic passport and some measure of distance from her family. Like Jane Bowles and Bryher – lesbians in 'lavender marriages' – Annemarie's androgynous looks appealed to the half-open closet. Erika Mann, for her part, seeking British citizenship, asked Christopher Isherwood's hand in marriage in 1934. He refused, but suggested his friend W.H. Auden. 'DELIGHTED', Auden cabled back, arranged a wedding party in a pub near the school where he was teaching, and invited colleagues and pupils. 'What are buggers for?' Auden later asked.[4]

By the time she encountered Ella Maillart in 1939, the inconsolable angel was an accomplished and prolific writer addicted to morphine. She had just checked out of a drug rehabilitation clinic in Yverdon. Both women were aware of the harbingers of another European war. Maillart thought

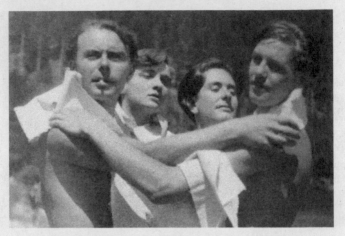

Klaus Mann, Annemarie Schwarzenbach, Erika Mann and
Ricki Hallgarten, shortly before the latter's suicide

she could save Annemarie from her demons, and their trip together was an
attempt by both of them to do exactly that. Maillart had succumbed to the
younger woman's charisma, but we have no evidence that their relationship had a physical component. Both writers later produced accounts of
their journey. Maillart's is suffused with knowledge of her travelling companion's death, but also of the devastation of war.

In her 2012 foreword to Maillart's *The Cruel Way* (1947), Jessa Crispin
contrasts the current American orientalism and Maillart's trailblazing:

> *We're so overstuffed with stories of blonde women finding spirituality in
> the East, as they blithely overlook poverty and patriarchy in these coun-
> tries and return to America to open up a vegan bakery/chakra cleansing
> studio. Our Western world went to the East, bought everything it could at
> the bazaar, and wonders why it doesn't feel any better. We're still picking
> international fights, we're still looking for enlightenment that can be pur-
> chased with a credit card, and we think because we know two dozen yoga
> poses that we understand Hinduism.*[5]

Maillart calls her travelling companion 'Christina', a pseudonym imposed
on the author by Renée Schwarzenbach following her daughter's death.
Both mother and Maillart must have tailored post-mortem description to
the mores of the time:

She was sitting on the bench – with hollowed chest, hugging her knees, her adolescent body leaning against the great stove built in the corner of the room ... her subtle body, her pensive face lighted by the pale brow, put forth a charm that acted powerfully on those who are attracted by the tragic greatness of androgyny.[6]

Ella and Annemarie set off from Geneva on 6 June 1939. Germany is mobilising for war. Switzerland, in contrast, is the picture of peace:

a streaming multitude was delighted with the clever 'Swiss Exhibition', which, on the eve of another world war, reminded the Confederates what Switzerland stood for ... I remembered a similar atmosphere during the Fête de Juin, the pageant that took place in Geneva in 1914. I saw the wide theatre whose vast stage opened onto the natural background of Lake Léman ... the huge barques sailed up to the stage full of Swiss soldiers of the past coming to liberate Geneva from Napoleon.[7]

The grand sweep of history here – Napoleon routed from Geneva, the First and Second World Wars – presents Switzerland as steadfast. Maillart is writing in 1946, the war over, Annemarie dead and the eastern world they explored together changed utterly.

Annemarie presents difficulties from the start. By the Balkans she is back on the drugs. Maillart finds a broken glass phial. Annemarie could be intense and withdrawn and for much of the trip she is taken as a boy. No doubt Maillart too could be strong-willed. Along the road people mistake them for Germans (there were still half a million Germans living in Yugoslavia) and give the Nazi salute to the passing car.

In Istanbul, after another relapse, Schwarzenbach puts herself in Maillart's hands:

I give you complete power over me, day and night. Don't leave me alone. If it happens again, I'll leave the car with you and go back. Let's go away quickly. I have to be far from towns. I can't help thinking: the temptation may come any moment, I shall yield, lured by the few minutes of forgetfulness it gives me.[8]

At Trebizond on the Black Sea, famous for its hazelnuts and dolphin oil, the two women encounter a Swiss buyer of nuts for chocolate factories back home. The trader has been told 'a lady and a boy of fifteen had just arrived from Switzerland'.[9]

Maillart at one point looks back on what it was that sent her out on the road in the first place: 'I am glad that I left home when I was young and followed the wake of the subtle Ulysses, glad to have lived the sea and the desert instead of helping father to air the silky softness of the deep sealskins, to value the bunches of ruffle-tailed silver foxes.'[10] Her driven character clashes with Annemarie's more fragile one. Annemarie is aware of her 'impetuous demands', that she exhausts those she is with. Maillart is more grounded, Annemarie 'a poet moving among ideas'.[11]

In Tehran they stay at the Nazi-infected German Legation. A chemist recognises Annemarie from her previous stay and presents an unpaid bill. Child labour and opium are prevalent:

> It was a fact that wherever crops were exploited and manufactured, boys and girls were good at their work until they were about eighteen. Then the boys took to opium and the girls to marriage and child-bearing.[12]

All three of our Swiss travellers present feudal Afghanistan as proudly independent. The irony is that the world has come calling throughout the nineteenth and twentieth centuries (Britain twice, Russia, the Americans). Afghanistan remains a powder keg to this day.

> You've come to the country where women are not seen, where men are capped with snowy muslin and walk with heavy shoes like gondolas. You've come to a country that has never been subjugated – neither by Alexander the Great nor by Timur the Lame, neither by Nadir nor by John Bull. It is the Switzerland of Asia, a buffer-state without colonies or access to the sea, a country whose great hills shelter five races speaking three totally different languages, a country of simple hillmen and well-bred citizens.[13]

Afghanistan's dilemma between mullahs and modernity is clear. The mullahs don't want education, certainly not for girls; education implies girls thinking for themselves. Modernity means information, science and independent thought; the mullahs are not keen on those either. They've got enlightenment: who needs thought? This is the nub of the problem across a swathe of countries coming into contact with western power. In the Hindu Kush, Annemarie notices 'the strangest mixture of races and tongues, the new proletariat of a state striving towards civilization'.[14] Afghanistan is where this clash of values has played itself out for over a century:

> Grouped around the mullahs, the ancients were against innovation. At a meeting where 1600 mullahs gathered, a programme of forty-eight points was drawn up; one demand was that the girls' school should be closed, for modern education only causes mischief in feminine heads. The government refused. Another point insisted on the closing of the cinema – where I saw men not used to chairs manage to squat on these uncomfortable pieces of furniture. This was also refused, government maintaining that films have an educative value: they bring a glimpse of the world to those not fortunate enough to travel.[15]

Annemarie notices the 'spoilt cheekiness of the little boys who soon scorn the women'. The government had just opened the first girls' school in Kabul:

> The little schoolgirls of Kabul were extremely gifted, lively, receptive creatures, a match for the boys, pretty and with such radiant eyes that it was impossible to imagine these slender little forms and delicate intent faces ever banished to the shadow of the harem walls, the sombre confinement of the chador.[16]

Both women travel without veils in an overwhelmingly patriarchal society, and we may wonder how they are viewed by Afghani men. Annemarie knows that Kabul has morphine aplenty. The two women part ways after months on the road. 'From the box containing our mountain boots, to my surprise, she produced a hypodermic needle which she gave me, saying: "This journey has freed me from the drug." I decided to believe her.'[17]

But Annemarie was lying.

Ella Maillart continued alone to South India, where she spent six years writing and meditating under a number of gurus. She had always been a spiritual seeker. The war over, she returned to Switzerland to spend half of every year in Chandolin, two thousand metres above Sierre and the Val d'Anniviers. When she first settled in this remote village you had to climb there from St Luc by mule, but these days the yellow Swiss Postbus hairpins its way right to the end of the road.

In an essay written from the United States in July 1940, Annemarie addresses early on the contentious question of Switzerland's neutrality.

Defences are already in place – trenches dug in the gardens of the Baur au Lac and Dolder hotels, barricades constructed all along the road between Basel and Zürich – some of which can still be seen to this day. She knows that Germany won't invade because of 'certain interests' and that Switzerland's vaunted freedom and independence are a comforting illusion:

> What could little Switzerland pretend to do if the Germans tomorrow insisted on passage of troops, or use of Swiss airbases, or the delivery of gold and goods, or merely the extradition of one lone German refugee enjoying Swiss political asylum?[18]

She acknowledges that neutrality has been a fiction right from the start of the war. Her assessment of potential German pressure on Switzerland – to return asylum seekers, to ban newspapers and books, to sack antifascist officials, to discriminate against the Jews – is chillingly accusatory. Her first-hand experience of the Swiss National Front comes from close to home:

> And for a long time the National Front has enjoyed the support of industrialists, the right-wing officer class and the rich, who see in this ersatz civil defence a bulwark against 'the socialist threat'.[19]

This extreme rightist party in Switzerland was a spent force by the time Annemarie was writing from the safety of Nantucket in 1941.

In his foreword to *L'Usage du monde* (1963), Nicolas Bouvier writes of having two years ahead of him in June 1953, and of quitting his native Geneva in a Fiat Topolino for Turkey, Iran, India, 'maybe further'. Twenty-three years old when he hit the road, he traces his wanderlust back to staring at atlases between the ages of ten and thirteen, dreaming of exotic music, strange glances and ideas. 'Something rises up in you and you lift anchor.'

Translated into English by Robin Marsack as *The Way of the World* (2009), Bouvier's magnum opus was completed ten years after the road trip of a lifetime. The Taoist echo is well placed. Patrick Leigh Fermor, another intrepid young traveller and Bouvier's English equivalent, introduced *The Way of the World* as 'nothing short of a masterpiece'. Bouvier,

Nicolas Bouvier, Thierry Vernet and the Fiat Topolino in Turkey, 1953

like Maillart and Schwarzenbach, records a spiritual journey. The stresses and strains of the imminent world war come through the women's 1939 accounts; Bouvier's journey is undertaken between the Beat era and the Beatles' first LP.

Bouvier emerged from Geneva's mandarin class. His grandfather was professor of German literature at Geneva University and his father director of the university library. Hermann Hesse, Robert Musil and Marguerite Yourcenar were guests at dinner.[20] Books in the house, lakeshore retreats and ancestral busts in the public buildings. *Grande bourgeoisie*. On his mother's side the inheritance was small lake nobility with a musical bent. Bouvier's maternal grandfather, Baron Maurice de Saint Germain, studied composition under Gabriel Fauré. Our young traveller benefited from the best Geneva had to offer. He couldn't wait to escape.

Nicolas met Thierry Vernet, seated beside him in 'Pion-Pion's' class, in the Collège Calvin. Decades later Thierry would come out as bisexual, so there was a bit of *amitié particulière* to the initial attraction. Neutral wartime Switzerland was a gilded cage. Bouvier completed a double degree at his grandfather's university, dreaming of east of Eden. Like the American writer Paul Bowles a decade earlier, the boys had an interest in folk music, in recording ethnographic sounds – what has come to be called world music. They read voraciously in several languages in a savvy way that the Beats, the young Americans of the post-war generation, did not.

The Way of the World opens in an artists' colony in a dusty Belgrade suburb in 1953. The sculptors are doing well, their monumental work in demand in a country throwing up revolutionary heroes every decade. Serbia is behind the Iron Curtain. Tito and the Party rule. The censors can't make up their minds whether irony is reactionary or progressive.

In Belgrade, a magazine asks Bouvier to write something about women in Switzerland: 'In your home country they don't have the vote. Write us a page on that. Your feelings.' This throws the reader somewhat, as it does Bouvier. We are accustomed to think of Switzerland as in the vanguard of democracy rather than keeping half its population without franchise. Bouvier's response is to soft pedal. Women should militate less and please more is his rather limp view. (In 1958 the Swiss community of Riehen was the first to grant women's suffrage; it was where I worked fifteen years later in 1973.) The editor finds his article frivolous, as might we with the benefit of hindsight. The rejection slip in 1953 pits feminist socialist Belgrade against a capitalist post-war Switzerland where women are without the vote.[21]

The two travellers shuttle between the popular districts of Belgrade and the diplomatic enclave, washing socks and handkerchiefs in the hot-water bathrooms of the rich, dining on plate, capturing the West-meets-East atmosphere of the Cold War. 'The warm glow of diplomatic cognac, the damascene napkins, the perfume of the lady of the house.'[22] Like Maillart and Schwarzenbach, Bouvier casts his mind back to comfy Switzerland as the epitome of prosperity. In Belgrade 'finery has disappeared along with a bourgeois clientele. Shop windows display barely finished goods: shoes piled higgledy-piggledy like logs, cakes of black soap, nails by the kilo or baby powder packaged like lard.'[23] In the same year, Patricia Highsmith was marvelling at the abundance of Switzerland in contrast to the privations of post-war rationing.

Bouvier bought a Remington typewriter in Ankara and started taking notes. Much more than a travelogue, *L'Usage du monde* is the story of a style, the awakening of the eye to the world. It is much better written, more closely observed, than the outpourings of *On the Road*. The Beat generation always seem to have their legs in the lotus position and their heads full of hallucinogens. Bouvier's mentors at the time were Robert Louis Stevenson, Julien Green, Jean Giono and Céline, all high stylists. He belongs to that line of French traveller poets – Blaise Cendrars and Valery Larbaud – tinted but not tainted by colonialism and classical training.

> *And then we return to the sunny street and the scent of watermelon, the central market where horses have children's names, and the disorderly houses spread out between two rivers, this old encampment nowadays called Belgrade ... There were formidable Muslim farm women snoring on benches between their baskets of onions, carters with pock-marked faces, officers sitting bolt upright in front of drinks, wielding toothpicks,*

jumping to offer you a light or engage in conversation. And nightly at the table flanking the entrance, four young whores chewing watermelon seeds and listening to the accordion player tickle delirious arpeggios from his ivory keys.[24]

With their ethnographic bent and use of the word bourgeois, Bouvier and Vernet remind me of earnest French *coopérants* I taught with in socialist Algeria in the late 1970s.

Bouvier spends time with the Kurds of northern Iran, appreciating their hospitality amid mutually suspicious cultures that have in our day spilled over into factional wars; 'In small war on the heels of small war,' as Robert Lowell put it in his poem 'Waking Early, Sunday Morning'. Sixty years on, Kurdish allegiance is still with us and Bouvier's description harks forward to the fragmented states of the second decade of the twenty-first century:

neither the Arabs nor the Mongols were able to dislodge the Kurdish shepherds from the high lyrical pastures which separate Iraq from Iran. There they feel at home, carving out a life as they see fit, and when they are called to defend their customs and settle a quarrel among themselves, Tehran authorities are hard put to be heard above the gunfire. Sometimes – in tough winters – they carry out a bit of extortion on the roads ... It must be said that numerous underhand influences are brought to bear: British, Russian, American, Kurdish separatists, not to speak of police and army at cross-purposes. Everyone belongs to a faction and the task is to determine which one.[25]

In Kurdish northwestern Iran, the Swiss travellers are lodged in the town prison for their own safety and to keep a close eye on their activities. The prison director thinks they are spies:

Around nine the prison began to come awake. We heard yawning and singing in the cells. The tea boy of the neighbouring eating establishment brought in the guards' tea perched on his head; then the barber turned up, leather strop on his shoulder, and did the rounds of the cells. Petitioners step over us to get to the prison director's office: prisoners' parents pitiably cowed, professional smugglers, rural mullahs leaving their donkeys at the door and, doubled up with bowing and scraping, heading in to intercede for one of their flock. Eyes half shut, at ground level, we watched this parade.[26]

At Tabriz the local mullah's attitude to schooling clashes with the idealism of an American Peace Corps worker trying to build a school. The stalemate underlines an enduring conflict of values, noted earlier by Maillart and Schwarzenbach. Months pass. Construction material disappears. Donors grow impatient. The villagers look to western benevolence askance. The mullah wants to hold on to power resting on ignorance; the clash of civilizations echoes down the decades to our own time's sorry mess. It reminds us of the 2014 Nobel Peace Prize awarded to Malala Yousafzai, shot in the face by the Taliban for daring to campaign for girls' schooling:

> the mullah is against the school. Knowing how to read and write is his privilege, his area of expertise. He draws up contracts, writes out petitions dictated to him, and deciphers prescriptions for the pharmacy. He carries out these services for six eggs, a fistful of dried fruits, and has no wish to lose this small revenue. Careful not to criticise the project openly, he makes sure his opinion is heard across the town's thresholds at night. And is listened to.[27]

Bouvier captures the American attempt to win the Cold War, but it is his grasp of physical detail and local colour that stays. His analysis applies to the many wars in the region since the 'tranquillised fifties'. The Great Game hasn't changed.

> We know that the American taxpayer is the most generous in the world. We know too that he is often ill informed, wants things done his way, and appreciates results flattering to his sentimentality. He is easily persuaded that building schools keeps communism in check – the cherished schoolhouse of memory. He has more difficulty admitting that what is good at home may not be elsewhere; that Iran, that old dowager of civilization who has seen it all – and forgotten much – is allergic to quick remedies and needs to be handled carefully.[28]

The French too had their *mission civilisatrice*: Gallic diplomatic puffery, frustrated missionaries and sundry expats taken to drink, opium or loose women. These are the outposts of French empire. I remember the Alliance Française – the 'Dalliance', we used to call it – in Bangkok, where film séances got cancelled without notice, reels never turned up, the *salle* was awash with floodwater as young cadres ponced around looking like a cross between Mormon missionaries and Maurice Chevalier.

After crossing Turkey, Iran, Afghanistan and India, Bouvier drew breath in a guesthouse at 22 Hospital Street, in Galle Fort, Ceylon. He began to see the direction the writing would take him. He took ship for Japan and returned to live there with his wife and children in 1964, the country appealing to his spiritual cast of mind.

When the Swiss go abroad, as they do in their millions, they can't help but notice how dirty it is, how bad the roads and inefficient the recycling. They are Brahmin travellers looking for leg room. (Americans must increasingly see 'abroad' through military night-vision glasses: are they for me or against me?) Long-term residents of Switzerland get habituated to the managed life, to things just pukka. One has to check the urge to Swiss thoroughness and organisation. When you step out of line you get slapped on the wrist once and then you do it the way it should be done. Step out of line twice and punishment ensues with Calvinist certainty.

Returning to Geneva after that first three-year trip, Bouvier had the opposite reaction. He noted the wealth, the cornucopia. He settled back into his parents' house at Cologny, into the red room he had painted himself as an adolescent. He remained there on and off all his life. Married, with three children, he became a paragon of the nomadic and the sedentary; the two are complementary. He wrote about Japan, about Scotland, about the Aran Islands off the west coast of Ireland.

In A Journal of Aran (1990) he traces the Irish monastic expansion of the fifth century CE as it moves into Gaul, Switzerland and beyond, comparing it to the wanderings of Tibetan lamas or Mongol shamans. Saints Columba and Gall set out from the west of Ireland to Christianise the heathen Swiss:

> In Burgundy, where they lectured the local baronets on their concubines, their bastards and gluttony – no less – they are asked to skedaddle. They move north to Lake Constance, into which they proceed to throw the most sacred idols of the Swabian tribe. There too, a bit fanatic. The monks flee and part ways. Saint Columba heads for Italy across the Alpine passes and founds the abbey of Bobbino. Saint Gall takes refuge in a wild valley to the west of the lake, overrun by bears. He gets rid of them with a swipe of his asperger – an asperger much revered by the Celts – always ready to cut a deal with capricious nature and its emissaries.[29]

In this apocryphal way the Irish saint founded the monastery of St Gallen in eastern Switzerland, and the noble bear was reduced to a mere emblem on the cantonal escutcheon. Irish monks brought a new system of musical

notation and lifted the level of Gregorian chant, like a whizz-kid music
teacher in a provincial school. They brought the art of manuscript illumination; to this day the library of St Gallen in eastern Switzerland has the
largest collection of mediaeval Celtic manuscripts outside of Ireland.

Bouvier's *Journal of Aran* is a return full circle on the wheel of hours:
the Swiss nomad revisits those wandering monks of a millennium and a
half ago. The Aran Islands present inhospitable weather, heating breaking
down, tinned salmon and sardines in the one shop, returned emigrants
from New York, a dilatory sense of time. 'The feeling of indigence, of emptiness, of nothingness born of this severing is not a surprise but a healthy
exercise.'[30] Bouvier, like Maillart, is always up for a bit of eastern mysticism,
wherever he finds it; Calvin under the bodhi tree. He notices too the parish
priest in those pre-scandal days, his hail-fellow well-met bonhomie:

> A *curly-haired burly curate, frenetically digging in the ribs, clasping
> hands, giving accolades and slaps on the back. Overplaying the forced
> familiarity, perhaps because of the weather. Not really the look of a holy
> man or a saint, more like a rugby coach after a converted try.*[31]

Literary recognition came late. In *The Scorpion Fish* (1981), one of Bouvier's
best books, we find him in Ceylon in 1955 at the tail end of his first big
journey. The narrative of fewer than a hundred pages, set in a guesthouse
in Galle Fort, achieves the grace of poetry. After a quarter century, the traveller's traumatic encounter with Ceylon accents the dark side of paradise.
Vignette after vignette illustrates how initiative fritters away in the east.
The oppression of the tropics weighs on the spirit: torpor, the end of the
road. It was his first book published by Gallimard in Paris, and earned him
the accolades of his peers. Always a traveller's writer, he became a writer's
writer.

Maintaining a comfortable relationship with Switzerland, he identified
a strain of what he called Swiss nomadic literature, writers emerging from a
country with little physical and psychological room; Ireland is another case
in point. One in six Swiss make their lives elsewhere:

> *Geneva is an artificial appendix with a mere six kilometers bordering
> the nearest canton as against a hundred kilometer border with France.
> The town looks towards France more than it does to Berne. It repudiates
> its illustrious men, Rousseau and Dunant (founder of the Red Cross):
> Geneva only recognises its sons when they're lauded elsewhere or dead.*

Bouvier knew that notoriety gets sorted out with death – thinking of Ella Maillart, of himself. This view also holds true in Switzerland as a whole. The country is small, Geneva tiny, a society very much kept under thumb; those who stick out, who are embarrassments, do well to leave.[32]

Bouvier was a child of the lake, born under the sign of Pisces. His errant life had a tidal rhythm – not the great surge of the ocean, perhaps, but the circumscribed loveliness of Lac Léman, fog wrapped, prey to sudden storms. How could you not be sedentary in such a landscape? In a late interview he recalled his watery childhood in the environs of Allaman:

We caught pike and char. This tin-coloured lake at dawn, from which we extracted superb fish, had a sort of adventurous, fairy-like atmosphere. I'm a Pisces, and so more at home in water than on land. Sometimes I set off from the shore at Allaman and arrived at Rolle or Morges after four or five hours swimming. People would let me telephone home or lend me a bike or a shirt, which I would send back by post. I loved that, being the drop-in swimmer.[33]

Maillart, Schwarzenbach and Bouvier trace the familiar arc of a journey. For much of the twentieth century the youth of the advanced technocratic economies searched for nirvana in the east. This might take the form of altered states and guitar riffs in Portland or Hari Krishnas on the Tottenham Court Road in London. These days it's a gap year filled with a spot of orphanage work, clubbing to hallucinogens on Ko Phangan. Bouvier's 1950s road trip seems the last authentic flourish of this romance, sparked by those first Romantics on Lake Geneva.

When you drive up to Chandolin on the switchback road above the Valais, you wonder why one might leave such a landscape. It's a vertical world, the valley disappearing and reappearing at every turn, growing more distant. Ella Maillart made her home here from the last snow to the first, in a chalet she named 'Atchala' after her beloved sacred mountain in India. A tiny converted chapel in Chandolin today houses a museum to her life and work. It was a Sunday when I made my way up, and a neighbour had left the door open for me. There were her Olympic medals, her old rucksack, her walking boots. I was the only visitor.

What made her set out on a spiritual quest? 'The last war sent me down to the clean life of the seas, for ever rid of illusions about our civilization. This war compels me to search for "the meaning of all this"'.[34]

Intrepid traveler and Olympic medalist Ella Maillart in Chandolin, 1982

In a caption to a photograph taken on the Simplon Pass, before leaving Switzerland for Afghanistan in June 1939, Annemarie Schwarzenbach asked herself the same question: 'Why do we leave this loveliest country in the world? What urges us to go east on desert roads?'[35]

Annemarie fell off her bicycle in the Engadin and suffered injuries from which she died at age thirty-four in 1942. The tiger mom burned her papers. In the 1980s her writing was rediscovered by a new generation of travellers, feminists and lesbian activists. She answered her own question about why she set out on the road: 'The real motivation of every true traveller is the yearning for the absolute.'

In a hotel clinging to the side of the mountain just below Chandolin, I watched the news feed from Ireland where the first ever referendum in support of gay marriage had just passed with a resounding majority. The country was jubilant. There was an impromptu party in Dublin Castle yard. I remembered the Special Branch parked outside the Rotunda Hospital in Dublin in the early 1970s, taking photographs of disco queens leaving the one Irish gay club. I thought of Patricia Highsmith on gay bars: 'a dark door somewhere in Manhattan, where people wanting to go to a certain bar got off the subway a station before or after the convenient one, lest they were suspected of being homosexual'.[36] And lovely Annemarie, my thin white duke, one foot up on the running board of the Ford. The mountain village was quiet. Outside my window was an old cheese hut up on posts, a relic, an original chalet. The woodwork precarious but still standing. It was Whit Saturday and church bells tinkled, echoed by others further down the valley. A thousand marriages got underway.

Our next group of writers belongs in the Swiss post-war world of the late twentieth century. The silver spoon is back in the mouth. Max Frisch, like Dürrenmatt, conducts a love–hate relationship with his home country, undermining its William Tell myth. Fritz Zorn's one novel set on Zürich's gold coast seems to point an accusing finger at terminal wealth. Daniel de Roulet takes stock of a politicised youth. Peter Stamm is Switzerland's best-known twenty-first-century writer, whose quiet, understated style might suggest a new direction. All of them present different facets of their home country to the world.

WILLIAM TELL FOR SCHOOLS

Frisch, Zorn, de Roulet and Stamm on the Swiss identikit

Swiss propaganda poster, 1916: Send the freeloaders flying

I am young and rich and educated, and I'm unhappy,
neurotic, and alone.
Fritz Zorn

On a May holiday weekend I'm taking the motorway from Basel to Zürich, passing through the Habsburg tunnel. It's a kilometre and a half long. Above me, looking out over the Aar river, sits the castle from which the dynasty traces its eleventh-century origins. The *Schloss* is in good shape, flying the family standard high above the valley.

Guntram the Rich was the daddy of them all: Rudolfs, Leopolds, Adolfs and Maximiliens land-grabbing down through the Dark Ages and the Middle Ages, the Reformation and the Restoration, the ages of enlightenment and industry, steam, electric power and on into the upheavals of the twentieth century. They became ever more powerful. They had the run of much of Europe and sundry possessions in the Americas for the best part of a thousand years. Now *that's* leadership. The First World War cut the dynasty down to size, as it did so many others, and the Second World War relegated them to shiny, happy people in *Hello!*, *Royalty* and *Majesty*. There they are leaning over their own baptismal fonts with new Maximiliens and Rudolfs in arms, in the paparazzi light.

Emerging from the tunnel, I drive into the Aargau hills. Habsburg is at the northernmost tip of the Jura, where the mountains come down to the Aar, the Reuss and the Limmat, threading their way through islands in the stream before losing themselves in the Rhine. It's an unassuming place from which to start a dynasty. There isn't much razzmatazz about the Habsburgs in Argovia, the Anglicised name for Aargau. No interpretive centre or theme park. The most you'll get on a Sunday is a bouncy castle. But a history of royal Europe is a history of forgotten corners and local bigwigs made good. I drive past the large, boxy aluminium factory with its shunting yards, through villages selling bio fruit and vegetables on the honour system, the produce laid out on folding roadside stands. Tractors putter in the neat vineyards. There's a smell of silage from the fields and wild garlic from the undergrowth.

From a distance it could be a manor farmhouse raised that bit higher with the village of Habsburg at its base. I park and climb. The forecourt has a large star-shaped *omphalos* (Greek for belly button) embedded in the cobbles, telling the distances to the far-flung corners of empire, most of them to the southeast. And a legend in three languages: *The empire on which the sun never sets*. It's hard to resist an Ozymandian moment: *nothing beside remains round the decay of that colossal wreck*. Well, perhaps the bank accounts remain, and an attractive property portfolio, and a sense of achievement.

Quite soon after building this family pile in 1020, the Habsburgs outgrew it. They moved into more spacious digs, commensurate with their holdings. In Muri, half an hour away, the hearts of the last Emperor, Charles I (1887–1922), and his wife, Zita of Parma-Bourbon (1892–1989), are buried in a family crypt in the monastery. Their son, Otto von Habsburg (1912–2011), was the last crown prince of the Austro-Hungarian Empire and pretender to the throne. We might think of him as an elegant old duffer who wanted to restore his illustrious line, but in fact he was an anti-Nazi of note (not all Austrians were) and a member of the European Parliament. He famously came to fisticuffs with his fellow MEP Ian Paisley in 1988 when Pope John Paul II visited the parliament. The Catholic Archduke landed a punch on the Free Presbyterian Doctor when Paisley publicly called Pope John Paul II 'the antichrist'. Here's Paisley in full flow before history swallows him up:

> *That vast Assembly erupted, and the books started to fly and the punches started to be thrown, and the kicking started, but I held my ground and maintained my testimony. There is no difference between Europe today and Europe in Reformation times. This afternoon I read again the story of Luther, at the Diet of Worms. Who presided over the Diet of Worms? The Emperor Charles, Head of the Holy Roman Empire. Who was he? He was a Habsburg. It is interesting to note that one of the men who attacked me is the last of the Habsburgs – Otto Habsburg, the Pretender to the Crown of Austria and Hungary. I said to myself, 'The Habsburgs are still lusting for Protestant blood. They are still the same as they were in the days of Luther.'*[1]

Switzerland's founding myth of William Tell is a revolt against the Habsburgs. The legend's plucky folk hero refuses to accept the dictates of Gessler, the Habsburg representative. The crossbow-wielding Tell is the good guy and Gessler the axis of evil, to use our contemporary parlance. The emergence of a confederation – one for all and all for one – is the story of the central cantons of Uri, Schwyz and Unterwalden carving out a destiny for themselves. 'We grew by resisting the Habsburgs' is the official story.[2] Max Frisch's essay 'Wilhelm Tell: A School Text' (1970) confronts this myth at a time when deconstruction was in the air and young radicals were in the streets.

Guillaume Tell absinthe label

Dürrenmatt and Frisch were witnesses to Switzerland's vexed neutrality during the Second World War. They viewed with scepticism the story that Switzerland told itself and bridled under too close an identification with the notion of the plucky little Homeland. Both make a plea for *écrivains sans frontières*:

> Friedrich Dürrenmatt, when asked by a Swiss critic how he deals with
> Switzerland as a problem, answered quite simply: 'You are mistaken, Herr
> Doktor. Switzerland is no problem for me. Sorry. It's just a pleasant place
> to work, that's all.'[3]

The Swiss reading public were used to its two *bêtes noires* castigating their history and cherished myths. Dürrenmatt alluded to wartime compromises:

> We all but held to our ideals, without definitely putting them into prac-
> tice. Tell stretched his crossbow to be sure, but he tipped a finger to the hat
> a little – almost but not quite – and we were spared heroism.[4]

Gessler, the Habsburg man, wears the imperial hat that William Tell slights or refuses to acknowledge. The hat was supposed to have been set on a pole as a sign of the Habsburg presence.

Max Frisch (left) and Friedrich Dürrenmatt (right) at the
Kronenhalle Restaurant in Zürich, 1963

he was a free man, he said, and didn't salute any Habsburg hat! The
plump knight was still stroking his horse, even smiled, for what hung on
the pole was no Habsburg hat but the imperial hat to which reverence was
due even in a valley like Uri with its imperial freedom.[5]

Frisch insinuates that the Tell story is a set of wartime and post-war blink-
ers: it allowed the Swiss to see what they wanted to see and turn a blind
eye to uncomfortable truths. When Schiller's *Wilhelm Tell* was performed
at the Schauspielhaus in Zürich during the Second World War, audiences
spontaneously burst out singing the Swiss national anthem.

Footnote number sixty-two in Frisch's essay about William Tell concerns Palestinian marksmen who shot at El-Al flight 432 as it was taking
off from Zürich airport on 18 February 1969, en route to Tel Aviv. The
four affiliates of the PLO opened fire with AK-47s, injuring crew members, one of whom later died. An Israeli security agent on the plane retal-
iated, killing one of the attackers. The terrorists had leaflets comparing
their actions to those of William Tell, drawing parallels between Hapsburg
heavy-handedness and Israeli appropriation. At their trial in Winterthur,
the terrorists were sentenced to twelve years of hard labour and the Israeli
security agent was acquitted.

In a speech on being awarded the George Büchner Prize in 1958, Frisch considered his own Swissness: 'Do I believe in a new Switzerland? I am Swiss and desire to be nothing else, but my commitment as a writer is not to Switzerland, nor to any other country.'[6]

Later Swiss writers share this view to varying degrees. Indeed, we could make the larger point that nationalism in art ended some time ago, if it ever existed. Writers on the right – where the money is – have a vested interest in a squeaky-clean national image, a pristine Heimat with its folksy sense of nationhood in part derived from 1930s Nazi gleanings. Writers of a liberal or left tendency confront a euphemistic history. Foreign views often shine a different light. A number of scandals in the last decades of the twentieth century contributed to public debate about Swiss identity. In 1970, members of the Swiss Writers' Association resigned in protest at toadying to government defence hysteria, forming the Gruppe Olten as an alternative. In 1989, the Swiss public discovered that federal police had kept secret files on many of them. Outcry followed the revelation that the Bührle arms company had profited from the illegal export of arms during the 1968 Nigerian Civil War (Biafran War). The Swiss government formed the Bergier Commission in 1996 to throw light on the country's Second World War activities. Looted assets, gold, 'Aryanisation policy', arms production and refugees all came under its remit. It presented a final report in 2002. In 1998, the German writer W.G. Sebald alluded to Switzerland's wartime profiteering: 'the gold, purchased at the expense of the immeasurable suffering of the Jews, which was to serve as a christening present for the generation of Swiss children born after the Second World War'.[7]

Fritz Zorn (1944–76) was one such writer born with a silver spoon in his mouth. His posthumously published *Mars* (1976) reckons with a privileged upbringing on Zürich's 'golden coast', inviting the reader to consider Zorn's malaise as rottenness in the state. He equates cancer with the inability to confront uncomfortable truths about material wellbeing. This illness as metaphor turned real: he died of cancer at age thirty-two.

Zorn, meaning 'anger', was a pseudonym chosen days before his death when the author knew his book would be published. His real name was Fritz or Federico Angst – *Angst* meaning 'anxiety'. Zürich's gold coast is a bejewelled world unto itself, a string of wealthy communities along the eastern shore of the lake, catching the setting sun. Zorn's was a typical gold coast upbringing:

Fritz Zorn (Federico Angst): Born with a silver spoon in his mouth

*I am young and rich and educated, and I'm unhappy, neurotic, and
alone. I come from one of the very best families on the east shore of Lake
Zürich, the shore that people call the Gold Coast. My upbringing has
been middle-class, and I have been a model of good behaviour all my life.
My family is somewhat degenerate, and I assume that I am suffering not
only from the influences of my environment but also from some genetic
damage. And of course I have cancer.*[8]

The writer Adolf Muschg – another gold coast boy – championed the book
and wrote the preface. It became a surprising international bestseller.

Zorn's Zürich is a world unto itself, one that Daniel de Roulet sees
as atypical of the time. Zorn was a dandy, poncing around town in a red
cloak, while de Roulet is a Lefty. Like Dürrenmatt, he is the son of a pastor,
from the Jura region. In *Un dimanche à la montagne* (2006) he revisits his
firebrand youth. In 1975, de Roulet burned the Gstaad chalet of publishing
magnate Axel César Springer to the ground. He wrongly thought that the
press baron was a Nazi sympathiser. The *récit* dramatises the polarised politics of post-war materialist Switzerland: 'There are two types of foreigners
here. Those who die digging our tunnels and building our Alpine dams,

and those who buy up our mountains."[9] In *Double* (1998), a novel about the author's own identity as much as Switzerland's, de Roulet follows the paper trail of Swiss police files on his own life at a time when East German Stasi files were being opened up. Fritz Zorn makes a fictionalised appearance, as a foil to de Roulet's more *engagée* Switzerland.

The identity question is especially acute in a country proud of independence from its bellicose neighbours. Swiss writers also have dialect to contend with: the language of the valley is not high German or literary French. Anglosphere publishing likes homogenised language and ideas. What sells in the airports is globlish. So a certain amount of hybridity – between languages, cultures, dialects – is characteristic of Swiss literature, as it is of contemporary English literature.

> *The younger among Max Frisch's contemporaries, especially if they write literary German, are not certain any longer whether they want to belong to a Swiss literature; and although they certainly feel at home in their villages and in their local dialects, they rightly suspect that too many demands would be made on them by the Establishment, who liked to see Swiss writers ossify in provincial sets of attitudes as predictable as the qualities of Emmental cheese or Sprüngli milk chocolate.*[10]

It is a false assumption that Zürich is a narrower world than New York or that Seattle has better coffee than a valley in Winterthur. The cosmopolitan shifts. Multilingual, multicultural Swiss cities are at the heart of Europe in a way that renders the Anglo world provincial, with its Costa coffee and easyJet swagger.

Perhaps the Swiss writer who has made the biggest splash internationally in recent years is Peter Stamm. *Seven Years* (2012) and *All Days Are Night* (2014) have garnered accolades both at home and abroad. Lauded as a quiet writer, a writer's writer, Stamm's cool style owes something to Ernest Hemingway and Raymond Carver, as well as to fellow Swiss Robert Walser.

Seven Years follows the fortunes of a group of Munich architecture students. The Wall falls, unification beckons, careers and marriages get underway. First house, first child, first affair, first root canal: a flat-pack world meticulously assembled from instructions. Alex's relationships with two different women – Sonia, beautiful and sophisticated, and Ivona, a religious frump from Poland – express the inadequacy of modernity. Alex marries Sonia and keeps the frump on the side. Sonia likes le Corbusier,

Peter Stamm: Cool, chiseled, lean writing

while Alex is more drawn to the wild: 'Ivona wasn't domesticated, under the quiet, long-suffering manner there was still something wild, a resolve I'd rarely come across in a human being.'[11]

Sonia, in contrast to Ivona, is disembodied and driven. More so than Alex, she hails from a class that recalls Fritz Zorn's golden coast:

> This was her social sphere, people who were demonstratively hiding their wealth and treated the staff in such a jolly, friendly way that it almost had the effect of condescension. They all seemed to be playing a game, and observing themselves and one another. They were playing at high society, the cultivated art lovers, hurrying out of the dining room to the events hall to catch the chamber music concert, as if there were no other possible way of getting through an evening.[12]

This triangular dilemma between Alex and his two women highlights a spiritual malaise. 'Perhaps I'm more interested in inner rather than external conflicts,' Stamm admits. Nebulous Swissness and national literature are secondary concerns to him:

I have, of course, a close relationship with some Swiss writers, not primarily because they were Swiss but rather because I treasure their books. Gottfried Keller, Robert Walser, Friedrich Glauser, Dürrenmatt and Frisch I particularly treasure, and also certain contemporaries. Perhaps it makes little difference that we stem from the same cultural origins. I particularly like Robert Walser's regional sense of place, the feeling he brings to the locality and people he describes, a place and people familiar to me.[13]

In Stamm's most recent novel, *All Days Are Night* (2014), Gillian is a television arts presenter in a world of 'openings and premieres'. Her face has been damaged in a car accident in which her husband Matthias died. Gillian undergoes reconstructive surgery, a reshaping of her physical but also psychological identity. Stamm fractures her and puts her back together as a different person. He abjures a grander statement about national identity for a precise rendering in a cool, efficient, chiselled style.

In both his recent novels Stamm has fun with the fluff belief systems that have supplanted organised religion. In *Seven Years*, a manager on the make starts a company called 'EGO plc':

He talked about spontaneous networks and people who had a sort of entrepreneurial approach to their lives, and kept asking themselves, okay, what are my strengths, my preferences, my assumptions? What am I making of them all? Where am I going, and how will I get there? That's where the future is, EGO plc.[14]

In *All Days Are Night*, the heliotherapy and dancing of a century ago, Hesse's oriental mumbo-jumbo, have been updated to 'power points' in the mountains, the caring and sharing rhetoric of self-help. Art too, of the conceptual kind, has become a sort of 'flummery': 'You could do something with teddy bears. Or with bear poop. Like that African guy who works with elephant dung.'[15]

The writer Tim Parks, like myself a fan of Stamm, sees him as 'not necessarily very "Swiss"':

Stamm's native language is a Swiss dialect but he writes in German, which is a literary construct for him. This helps him to be lean. One of the things clearly happening in this period of globalization is that we are getting a lot more writers writing in very lean styles.[16]

Switzerland emerged as a federation in protest at Habsburg power; whether Alsace burghers or Aargau castle Catholics is neither here nor there. Swiss identity for Max Frisch had an existential cast, ponderous with soul-searching. A new politicised talking-back to the state emerged in the later decades of the twentieth century, as hard historical facts came up against Swiss myth-making. Fritz Zorn bit the hand that fed him, but he is a maverick one-off. We might wonder what sort of writer he would have become had he lived, had illness not tragically presented him with a literal dead end and with his subject matter. Daniel de Roulet confronts his Leftist past with the wisdom of hindsight. Identity is central to Peter Stamm's work, not as a nationality or even a regional allegiance, but as a kind of spiritual quest. In literary terms there is no one Swiss identity, but a fairly fractured assembly of voices in several languages, all clamouring to be heard.

THE EMPEROR MOTHS

All quiet on the golden coast

Charlie Chaplin statue, Vevey, Switzerland

By the waters of Léman I sat down and wept.
T.S. Eliot

Many of the foreign writers in this book saw Switzerland as a haven – from two world wars in the twentieth century, from tax and celebrity towards its end. And not just writers: glitterati, rock aristocracy, royal and imperial has-beens, oily billionaires, anybody seeking the quiet slopes after life's fitful fever. Wealth helped, as it always does, with residence permits. Switzerland isn't exactly bohemian central, with poets in garrets living on the royalties of a slim volume. Celebrity comes into the mix too. Byron was the first of the bestseller bad-boy poets and Freddie Mercury was – well – mercurial and on his last legs.

Our haven-seekers span the twentieth century. The poet Rainer Maria Rilke, reluctant to return to Germany after the First World War, settled down and died in the Valais. Erich Maria Remarque wrote the century's most famous German novel, *All Quiet on the Western Front* (1929), about his traumatic war experience. Persona non grata in Germany once the Nazis came to power, he took American citizenship and spent much of his life in political exile in Switzerland. Jorge Luis Borges was no stranger to Geneva. Educated there as a teenager, he returned to the city as a blind old man, a Tiresias escaping the paparazzi. Graham Greene, after a life wandering the world's trouble spots and a bit of bother in Antibes, came to Switzerland to die. Anthony Burgess spent the last decades of his life in Monaco – Suisse-sur-Mer – but kept a flat in Locarno, shuttling between the two. They all slept easy and woke in rooms with a view.

These very different writers are our emperor moths. In his 1950 travelogue about Switzerland, John Russell describes the wealthy retirees wintering on the shores of Lake Geneva as the 'emperor-moths of western civilization'. On my way back and forth from the south of France, I often stop by Lake Geneva. I park the car in any of the small littoral towns, their grassy foreshores impeccably maintained, and take a power nap. Half an hour later the light has declined, the mountains turn flamingo pink, a mist creeps over the face of the water. It's like waking up in paradise. I drink from a thermos flask of coffee and imagine what it must be like to wake to this view every day. Women clad in burkas take the evening air in twos and threes, their toenails polished, diamonds or perhaps mere rhinestones in their toe rings. Well-heeled boys from Le Rosey lark around a pinball machine before they have to be back in their rooms – very Brideshead in cashmere and Nantucket red shorts.

Rising behind the north shore are a thousand years of vineyards, care-fully husbanded. The vines are up on trellises, trained high for more light. Before the emperor moths came winging in, this entire south-facing slope was grapes and fishing villages. The Romans took one look at it and thought: *vino*. Part of the shore's attraction for retirees is that it has many of the benefits of the French Riviera and few of the inconveniences. It's a UNESCO World Heritage site. Moths have always been attracted to rich pickings, to folds in the fabric. It's not just the vines looking for more light.

This corner of the world has been home to exiles and retirees of the better sort probably since the Romans. In the 1760s, an anonymous author remarked on the lake's attractions: 'It has even sometimes had the advan-tage of possessing some celebrated foreigners who have been drawn to retire there by its agreeable situation and the liberty which is enjoyed.'[1] Andrew Beattie catches this vesperal atmosphere:

> There is a strangely melancholic air about the lake, too. It is hard to
> pin down its exact nature: perhaps the huge, gloomy hotels that line the
> shore, clinging with quiet pride to a previous age of refinement and def-
> erence that has now virtually disappeared; or perhaps it is the sense of
> transience which cloaks the place: people come here, after all, to die, or to
> convalesce in a place bathed in cool air and soft light.[2]

Prague-born poet Rilke was attuned to transience and forever staying in other people's country houses. The First World War traumatised him. Even though he didn't see action on the front, his few months of service in the Austrian army, working in the War Records Office, were enough to send him scurrying to Switzerland in 1919. He wanted to get on with his poems, the *Duino Elegies*, the flow of which the war had had the temerity to interrupt.

Rilke's romantic involvement with Baladine Klossowska determined his stay in Switzerland. He first met her in 1907 when she was already preg-nant with the future painter Balthus. They crossed paths again in Geneva in 1919, at the Hotel Richemonde, by which time Baladine had separated from her husband and was the mother of two young sons. The poet had a penchant for the older woman – there had been a few – and if she came with apron strings he would be left to get on with his poems.

> On the night before Baladine went on a previously planned vacation
> to the resort of Beatenberg on Lake Thun near Berne, they spent a

Rainer Maria Rilke, Baladine and Balthus in Batenberg, 1922

memorable evening talking until all hours on the balcony of her apart-
ment. She left with some reluctance, only to be overwhelmed on her first
stopover in Berne by an abundance of flowers from Rilke. 'At five in the
morning, I was awakened by roses,' she wrote on August 13.[3]

Rilke came running to meet her at the Bellevue Palace in Bern at the con-
clusion of her holiday. He became a surrogate father to the boys, encourag-
ing the artistic talents of the young Balthus by writing a preface in French
to *Mitsou* (1921), the boy's pen-and-ink drawings of a cat.

In 1921, a friend offered Rilke an extended stay in yet another castle,
the Château de Muzot in Veyras, in the Valais. He'd seen a photo of it in
a shop window in Sierre: it was rent free, the views were splendid and he
could get on with his rhyming. Baladine furnished the rather forbidding
building, which had no electricity and no gas. 'I am saved,' the poet wrote
about their affair.[4] Later, Baladine described their domestic arrangements
with nostalgic affection: 'My sons were my school and my pleasure and I
was their playmate. When Rilke came, we were like four happy children.'[5]
The affair continued until Rilke's death in 1926.

He might have passed on his love of castles to Balthus, who in adult-
hood indulged a number of delusions of grandeur – that he was descended
from Lord Byron, the Romanoffs or the Polish Counts de Rola. As a young

The Grand Chalet at Rossinière, largest in Switzerland, home to the
painter Balthus

painter, Balthus had a studio at the Villa Diodati for a time, where Byron
stayed that rainy summer of 1816. Balthus also lived for many years in
the Villa Medici in Rome. Indulging this taste for gilt-edged dwellings,
he bought the Grand Chalet in Rossinière in 1977, one of the oldest in
Switzerland, built in 1754, and certainly the largest. It sits in the rolling
countryside behind Gstaad. Its roster of guests has included at one time
or another Victor Hugo, David Bowie and the Dalai Lama. Balthus, the
'king of cats', became one of the great painters of the twentieth century.
The Aga Khan and Henri Cartier-Bresson attended his funeral, while U2
frontman Bono sang at it. The painter is buried below the old whitewashed
village church. Rilke's grave is not far away as the crow flies, in Raron in
his beloved Valais, surrounded by roses and the towering mountains he
immortalised.

War and exile from Germany determined the long retreat in Switzerland
of the writer Erich Maria Remarque. Wounded by shrapnel in the First
World War, Remarque wrote from harrowing experience in *All Quiet on
the Western Front*, completed in just six weeks. By the time the National
Socialists came to power in Germany, he had bought a villa in Porto Ronco,
right on the Swiss border with Italy, facing the Brissago Islands and Lago
Maggiore. The Nazis banned and burned his books while trying to misrep-
resent him as Jewish. They beheaded his sister for speaking out against the

regime, a clear warning to him not to return. Finally, they stripped him of German nationality. Remarque began his long exile as a German writer of conscience, whose theme became political and psychological statelessness.

Handsome and fond of actresses, he went for the A-list: Heddy Lamarr, Marlene Dietrich, Greta Garbo and Paulette Goddard. He met Dietrich at the Venice Film Festival in 1937 and was bowled over. She was on the rebound from Douglas Fairbanks, Jr, and he had just broken up with Austrian actress Heddy Lamarr. Dietrich's opening line is a classic of its kind, designed to soften the heart of any writer: 'You look far too young to have penned one of the greatest novels of our time.'[6] To celebrate their relationship, he threw a bottle of his most valuable vintage into Lago Maggiore (for the record, a 1911 Hessische Staatsweingüter Kloster Eberbach Steinberger Riesling Kabinett). Remarque imagined a future diver coming across this love token. In 2012, a group of Remarque fans dived in search of the bottle off the lakeshore, and found it – intact after a century under water and authenticated by the label.[7]

Dietrich was notoriously chameleonesque, bisexual and a bit frosty, with a string of leading men as lovers. Like Remarque, she refused to return to Hitler's Germany and was a regular guest at the Hotel du Cap in Antibes, where she conducted her various assignations with the connivance of her husband. Here she also began an affair with Ambassador Joseph Kennedy, holidaying with his large family. Joe had always been fond of a showgirl, a penchant passed on to his son Jack. Dietrich managed to get her hand down Jack's trousers as well. Meanwhile, Remarque kept to his room, writing his bestseller *Arch of Triumph* (1945). Their correspondence, published as *Tell Me That You Love Me* (2002), is one of the great epistolary love stories, and has recently been adapted for the stage.

Remarque had been living in the Villa Monte Tabor in Ronco since 1931. It sits majestically on a cliff above Lake Maggiore, and had originally been owned by the artist Arnold Böcklin. In 1958 he married the actress Paulette Goddard, the former Mrs Chaplin. It was her fourth marriage and his second. Remarque liked mixing cocktails, collecting cars and artworks. There are moves afoot to turn the splendid residence above the lake into a museum.

What did Switzerland represent to this writer whose lasting value critics have sometimes thrown into doubt? *All Quiet on the Western Front* remains the best-known and most widely read German novel of the twentieth century. Remarque wrote about displacement and flight from the Nazi state, but rarely about the haven of Switzerland itself. In *Heaven Has No*

Favourites (1961), a couple of short stories and the screenplay for *The Other Love* (1947), he makes use of a Davos sanatorium as a backdrop to a love story between a racing car driver and a tubercular *femme fatale*, modelled somewhat on Dietrich. Like Nabokov, Highsmith and le Carré, success in the film world gave him an added material independence. Switzerland provided a haven from Germany's poisonous politics, as it did for Thomas Mann and Hermann Hesse. Remarque died in 1970 an American citizen and a German writer living in Italian-speaking Switzerland. The Great War and the great dictator, fast cars, actresses and a villa by the lake had turned him into a grand old man of gilded letters.

Argentine writer Jorge Luis Borges is an unlikely transatlantic moth. The Borges family moved to Geneva in 1914, when Jorge was fifteen. His father, a lawyer and psychology teacher with hereditary failing eyesight he passed on to his son, sought treatment from a Swiss ophthalmologist. Borges senior took early retirement and packed his family off to Europe: the strength of the Argentinian peso meant it was cheaper to live there than in Buenos Aires. The advent of war kept them in Geneva. The Irish writer James Joyce and his family were stuck in Zürich for the same reason. The young Borges had left behind a sheltered bilingual English–Spanish childhood in the colourful suburb of Palermo in Buenos Aires – 'a place of slaughter-houses, late-night bars, muleteers and smugglers', as his biographer James Woodall describes it.[8] Geneva must have been a sobering shock. Bookish, near-sighted, with sultry good looks, Borges affected English dress and manners, much like the young Nabokov at the same time in St Petersburg.

The Borges family lived at 17 rue de Malagnou (now 7 rue Ferdinand-Hodler), with a view of the Russian Orthodox Church and the cathedral. Decades later he acknowledged Geneva's multicultural influence, a city filled with war refugees like himself. But at the time the family encountered 'a certain disdain for the foreigner' among the Swiss.[9] Borges' two best friends during his years there were Jewish. He bought his books from the Librairie Jullien, still in business on Place du Bourg-de-Four. His maternal grandmother died in Geneva in 1917, in the Spanish flu epidemic. In *Atlas* (1986), his last book, he catalogues this psycho-geography:

> Of all the cities on this planet, of all the diverse and intimate places which a man seeks out and merits in the course of his voyages, Geneva strikes me as the most propitious for happiness. Beginning in 1914, I owe it the revelation of French, of Latin, of German, of Expressionism, of Schopenhauer, of the doctrine of Buddha, of Taoism, of Conrad, of

Lafcadio Hearn and of the nostalgia of Buenos Aires. Also: the revelation
of love, of friendship, of humiliation and of the temptation to suicide.[10]

No mention of Geneva or the Genevans themselves here, but rather an old man's bookish dream of his youth. At the time, the young Borges 'conceived a hearty loathing of Switzerland: it was terribly bourgeois, a place of hotels and chocolate factories'.[11] Time had clearly softened this view.

The 'humiliation' refers to Borges' first known sexual experience at age nineteen. Borges senior arranged for his son to be deflowered in a studio flat on Place du Bourg-de-Four, in time-honoured Latin tradition. The woman may have been one of his father's own mistresses, and the experience turned out to be traumatic:

Dr. Borges gave Georgie the address of a flat on the Place du Bourg-de-Four, which was in the red-light district not too far from where they lived, and told him that a woman would be waiting there. Most young men approach their first experience of sexual intercourse with considerable apprehension, and when Borges finally reached the woman's flat, he was in a state of high anxiety. As it turned out, it appears that he was too precipitate in his approach and did not fully go through with his initiation.[12]

Like Joyce, Borges spent many a stolen hour 'fluttering about the lamps of harlotry'.[13] Both writers suffered from progressive blindness and returned to Switzerland to die. In Borges' case it was after a long life as Latin America's premier writer. Against the wishes of his family, he married his secretary and companion, María Kodama, in Paraguay in 1986, a marriage not recognised under Argentine law. In May of that year Borges clarified in a press release his reasons for settling once again in the city of his adolescence:

I am a free man. I have decided to stay in Geneva, because Geneva corresponds to the happiest years of my life. My Buenos Aires is still one of guitars, of milongas, of water-wells and of courtyards. None of that exists now. It's a big city just like many others. I feel strangely happy in Geneva. This has nothing to do with the culture of my ancestors and the basic love of country. It seems strange that someone doesn't understand and respect this decision by a man who, like one of Wells's characters, has determined to be an invisible man.[14]

Already aware of approaching death, in 1985 Borges expressed a wish to become a dual Argentinian-Swiss citizen. In his poem 'The Confederates', he balances the fate of a torn-apart Argentina, following the Falklands War, and the solidarity inherent in the founding of the Swiss Confederation, where men 'resolved to forget their differences and accentuate their affinities'. Two weeks before he died in Geneva, he published a poem in *The New Yorker* titled 'The Web', questioning the notion of home, of a mother tongue, wondering where he might die. Geneva represented deracination but, paradoxically, the earth that nurtured him:

> *Which of my cities*
> *am I doomed to die in?*
> *Geneva,*
> *where revelation reached me*
> *through Virgil and Tacitus, certainly not from Calvin?*[15]

In the Cimetière des Rois, blustery rain was coming off the lake, primroses and daffodils pushed up from distinguished graves – Calvin's and Piaget's among them. Borges' has an inscription from the Old English poem 'The Battle of Maldon' – 'be not afraid'. His last acrimonious weeks in Geneva were in flight from family and the press, stumbling blind a stone's throw from the house where he had spent his teens and from the lake he hadn't seen in over sixty years.

Graham Greene was also a peripatetic moth, one of a number of English writer-spies flitting through Switzerland. He spent years away from his native Berkhamsted in the world's hot spots, but since 1966 had been living modestly in Antibes on the French Riviera. In novel after novel he anatomised shifting post-war power and the dilemmas of lonely men in colonial outposts. This was Greeneland: an idiosyncratic body of work as recognisable as Nabokov's hall of mirrors or Highsmith's murder machines. In 1982 Greene cried foul against organised crime and corruption in a short tract echoing Zola: *J'accuse – The Dark Side of Nice*. He goes for the jugular in his opening salvo:

> *Let me issue a warning to anyone who is tempted to settle for a peaceful life on what is called the Côte d'Azur. Avoid the region of Nice, which is the preserve of some of the most criminal organisations in the south of France.*[16]

His target was the Riviera mafia and the alleged corruption of Jacques Médecin, the then mayor of Nice. Médecin, whose father had also been mayor, initially responded with high dudgeon, but fled to Uruguay in 1993. Extradited back to France, he served time in prison for corruption. Greene had the last laugh in heaven, but in the meantime France banned his jeremiad and obliged the author to pay damages. He licked his wounds, sorted his tax affairs and retired to a flat outside Corseaux above Vevey in 1990, a year before he died from leukaemia. 'His last home, the final sanctuary, was in Switzerland, his anteroom to death. He shut the door on the world.'[17]

Charlie Chaplin was living in more opulent splendour outside the same village, in the fourteen-bedroom Manoir de Ban, with servants and garden. Chaplin too was a refugee from politics, having escaped the inanity of Senator McCarthy's Communist baiting in the United States. Chaplin read Greene parts of his autobiography in manuscript. Actor James Mason had the cottage next door to Greene's. Mason had played Humbert Humbert in Stanley Kubrick's *Lolita* and would take the role of Dr Fischer in the 1985 television adaptation of Greene's Swiss-based tale. The writer, the comic genius and the matinée idol were in and out of each other's houses.

Greene's reasons for visiting Switzerland since 1969 were mostly familial: his daughter and grandsons were living above Vevey. It was here, pulling Christmas crackers, that he conceived *Dr Fischer of Geneva* (1980), one of his last tales:

> At lunch on Christmas Day 1978, in Switzerland with my daughter and my grandchildren nine months after the publication of The Human Factor, *a new book*, Dr Fischer of Geneva, *came without any warning to my mind. At the age of seventy-five, I found my future still as unpredictable as when I sat down at my mother's desk in Berkhamsted and began to write my first novel.*[18]

The action of *Dr Fischer of Geneva* shuttles between Vevey where the narrator works and Geneva where his rich father-in-law holds court. Green spins a moral tale, cool as an after-dinner mint, from a group of wealthy elderly hangers-on. It's hard not to see their moneyed old-world swagger as a morality play, a comment on terminal wealth. The characters represent vices – vanity, hollowness and obsequiousness, but above all greed. Notoriously tight-fisted, Greene skewers the rich. Jones, his narrator, is a translator and one-handed letter writer in 'the immense chocolate factory of glass in Vevey'. (The headquarters of Swiss multinational Nestlé, the largest food company in the world, is in Vevey.) He lost his left hand in the Blitz. Dr Fischer is the inventor of a toothpaste called Dentophil Bouquet, 'which was supposed to hold at bay the infections caused by eating too many of our chocolates'.[19] The entanglement of one with the other – the sickly sweet and the squeaky clean – is Greene's sorry tale. The toothpaste mogul and the one-handed chocolate underwriter seem an allegory for Switzerland itself.

Greene's grotesques are all wealthy Toads – from toadies, a group of sycophants – gathered around Dr Fischer's table in Geneva in expectation of gifts. He humiliates them. Mrs Montgomery married well and enjoys a good widowhood; her matronly type makes an appearance in Anita Brookner's Hotel du Lac. She is a predatory bird of late plumage, 'an American with blue hair'.[20] The others include an alcoholic film actor past his best, an international lawyer, a tax adviser and a Swiss General called Krueger. They've all got some connection with money – Krugerrands are gold coins from South Africa. 'They were very well lined themselves. They had all settled around Geneva for the same reason, either to escape taxes in their own countries or take advantage of favourable cantonal conditions.'[21] Greene's group of sycophants satirises Switzerland as a tax haven for retirees.

Dr Fischer humiliates his guests by playing on their greed. Jones has married the doctor's daughter. '"Don't ever mention Dentophil to him," she said. "He doesn't like to be reminded of how his fortune was made."'[22] Is there a veiled reference to Swiss loot here? In a nod to how post-war victory quickly became commercial, the war-wounded Jones whiles away an hour in a Geneva pub, the aptly named Winston Churchill. Greene himself was a fire-fighter during the Blitz:

> There was what the Swiss call a Pub Anglais not far from the rank, named, as you would expect, the Winston Churchill, with an unrecognisable sign and wooden panelling and stained-glass windows (for some reason the white and red roses of York and Lancaster) and an English bar with china beer handles, perhaps the only authentic antiques, for that adjective could hardly be applied to the carved wooden settees and the bogus barrels which served as tables and the pressurised Whitbread. The hours of opening were not authentically English and I planned to drink up a little courage before I took a taxi.[23]

The other authentic antique in this faux interior, of course, is the war-wounded narrator himself, for whom Churchill represented sacrifice and not just an ersatz commercial killing.

Mr Kips, one of the Toads, is involved in shady arms deals. Greene's novel appeared at the time of the US-imposed Iranian arms embargo in 1979. He enlists Jones' help in translating a letter:

> There were references to Prague and Skoda, and Skoda to all the world
> means armaments. Switzerland is a land of strangely knotted business
> affiliations: a great deal of political as well as financial laundering goes
> on in that little harmless neutral state.[24]

We have come across arms and the launderette before: Glauser, Dürrenmatt, Frisch and le Carré have all pointed the finger at Swiss shady deals. In true Greeneland fashion, characters hear midnight Mass at the Abbey of Saint Maurice. They 'listened to that still more ancient story of the Emperor Augustus's personal decree and how all the world came to be taxed'.[25] The irony about Swiss taxation here is fleeting and subtle.

Greene shows an intimate knowledge of wealth, retirement and the emperor moths. His one-handed bandit gets caught up in the spiritual shallowness of rich people, much as Dürrenmatt's detectives do and Fitzgerald's Dick Diver in Tender Is the Night. The greed of the rich knows no bounds and masks the emptiness of their appetites. They need baubles, and they toy with people to get them. Dr Fischer remains Greene's only anatomy of mammon along the golden coast.

Anthony Burgess, like Graham Greene (the two famously didn't get on), was a globetrotting Englishman haunting the colonial service and the fallout of empire after the war. Burgess was a northerner, like D.H. Lawrence, who fell in love with the southern sun. His affair with exotica began in Malaya, from which emerged The Malayan Trilogy (1959). The novels A Clockwork Orange (1962) and Earthly Powers (1980) established his ebullient reputation. Film rights for the former and numerous screenplays made his fortune. He lived in Brunei (where he taught the Sultan's son), then in Malta and Italy, before settling in 1975 in Monaco. As a tax exile from Britain, a modestly born Mancunian Conservative, Burgess could rest easy in the little principality. He and his family spent the hot months at their chalet in Savosa outside Lugano, in Italian-speaking Switzerland:

Anthony Burgess, tax exile and man about Europe

Ticino looks like an udder drooping from the vaccine body of Switzerland, and Lugano is the teat of the udder. It looks as though it is dripping milch or lait or latte into the mouth of northern Italy.

In Lugano you will not find pasta-paunched deliverymen singing Puccini to the morning sun. Everybody is rather prim in the true Swiss manner, trim too, and there is not a single candy wrapper or cigarette packet thrown to disfigure the trim, prim streets.[26]

In 1975, Albert R. Broccoli and Guy Hamilton commissioned Burgess to write a screenplay for Ian Fleming's *The Spy Who Loved Me*. The script resurrects that old gothic-horror location of Swiss fiction, the private clinic. Burgess envisioned small nuclear devices inserted into the bodies of wealthy patients while they are under anaesthetic. This surgical procedure turns them into human bombs. The plan is for CHAOS (Consortium for Hastening the Annihilation of Organised Society) to blow up these walking explosives at a Royal Command Performance at Sydney Opera House. Bond's role is to perform acupuncture to extract the bombs. Burgess' script was rejected, but his wacky, not entirely serious imagination does anticipate the suicide bombers of our own CHAOS-filled century.[27]

By the time Burgess came to publish the second volume of his autobiography, *You've Had Your Time* (1990), the Swiss clinic, interestingly, has
become a German one, but the explosive plot remains the same. Burgess
describes his Lugano surroundings with characteristic bravado, including
that standard feature of all Swiss dwellings, a nuclear shelter: its 'massive
metal door ... a grim cell rather than use which one would prefer to be
nuclear-blasted'. He owned property all over the continent – in Rome,
Bracciano, Monaco – and his view of Switzerland is geographically aware,
not unkind, born of history and experience:

> *I am very much in Europe here in Lugano. This is the remotest point of*
> *the triangle formed with Monaco and Milan. It is a triangle within whose*
> *body shady deals are done, governments cheated, money stacked, high*
> *denomination plaques thrown onto green baize. Switzerland itself is not*
> *quite Europe: it remained aloof from Europe's last agony, as did Ireland,*
> *though it bought Nazi coal and was cautious about letting in refugees. It*
> *touches true Europe at four points, and it knows that its three linguistic*
> *cultures are mere tributaries of the main rivers.*[28]

Like Greene, and many of the writers in this book, Burgess has a jaundiced
view of Swiss hospitality and neutrality. He was always ready to play the
chip-on-the-shoulder northerner when it suited him, from the safety of his
various tax shelters. Like Borges, his take on Switzerland was bookish –
Lenin and Joyce rubbing shoulders in Zürich, the city as a cradle for modernism, a language backwater.

The novel that best captures the melancholy air of the emperor moths
is Anita Brookner's *Hotel du Lac* (1984). Her Vevey hotel is less swanky than
the Trois Couronnes of Henry James fame, downgraded from exclusivity to
faded grandeur, a daisy gone to seed. The guests are retiring types, among
them Edith Hope, a so-so writer of *romans de rose*, the ancestor of chic lit.
A little entertaining intrigue is the most Edith can hope for, rather than
the full game, set and match of Byronic romance. She glimpses Byron's
Château de Chillon in the distance, 'the outline of the gaunt remains', as
though all that's left her is toothlessness and sunken fires. The hotel offers
'a mild form of sanctuary, an assurance of privacy'.[29] Brookner has always
been good at plucking the faded English rose in the noonday sun. Edith
quickly ferrets out the unseemly behind privacy and discretion, but the
lake keeps intruding into view, 'spreading like an anaesthetic towards the
invisible further shore'.

Classic 1952 Samuel Henchosz poster for the Lac Léman Navigation
Company that criss-crosses the lake

An autumn sun, soft as honey, gilded the lake; tiny waves whispered onto
the shore; a white steamer passed noiselessly off in the direction of Ouchy;
and at her feet, on the sandy path, she saw the green hedgehog shape of a
chestnut, split open to reveal the brown gleam of its fruit.[30]

Unlike our emperor moths, Edith returns home to the world outside
Switzerland – Knightsbridge, in effect – leaving the gleaming chestnut
behind. She is the latest in a long line of arrivals to Switzerland, stretching
back to Byron and the Shelleys: refugees from the wars, from the scandal
sheets of romance, from history's noises off.

We could question the depth of attachment these emperor moths had
to the Federation. Switzerland itself is used to creative types flapping in
and sometimes settling; they are part of its self-image. Polanski in Gstaad.
Nabokov in Montreux. Chaplin in Vevey. They bring the glamour of
deposed royalty, these panjandrums of civilization, these *monstres sacrés*
of the writing and cinema worlds. Royalty comes winging in too. Such

celebrity confirms Switzerland's image as a first-class retirement home for foreigners, a happening place. Davos is a global talking shop; Art Basel trades in high-end canvas or perhaps merely high-end concepts; Montreux showcases established jazz. Switzerland's way of pulling in the punters may not be cutting edge or avant-garde, but it's well heeled, well connected, curated for the money. The problem with writers is that by and large they don't make money, although most of the above-mentioned moths didn't do too badly. You can't collect writers, but you can brand them when they're dead. The emperor moths settle by the lake or in the valleys, harming nobody, paying favourable taxes, sorting their affairs before night falls.

My power nap is over. Which way will I drive home? The back roads meander through vineyards, the lake appearing and disappearing below as I climb. Byron's university chum Hobhouse thought that the finest view of Lake Geneva was from Cossonay. Winding up their hike through the Bernese Oberland in 1816, they stopped there for a bite to eat. Hobhouse went behind the château to lie down in a field and take in the view:

> From this field I looked down upon the deep woody dell in which runs
> the Orbe, on the swelling plains of mead- and wine-land set with villages,
> on the Lake of Geneva and its Savoy hills, with the Clarens mountains
> – in short, on one of the most lovely prospects in Switzerland. The spot
> appeared to have been well selected for a view, as I found an overgrown
> bower. I lay down in the sun, enjoyed myself most entirely, and dared to
> write down in my pocket-book that I was happy.[31]

At Aubonne, further south, Hobhouse dined with their Swiss guide Berger, the two of them discussing taxes and pig killing, Napoleon and cantonal politics. Aubonne's oldest inn is the Hotel du Lion d'Or. The sign hanging in front has a prancing lion above the date: 1790. It's a small hotel built around a garden, where I take a room in what must once have been the stables. A trilingual Gideon's bible is by the bedside. When I ask the proprietor about Byron, he adds the title in deference, but seems unsure whether he wants his hotel associated with such a personage. Still mad, bad and dangerous to know.

The full realisation of Byron's exile from England, from wife and children, from his love for his half-sister Augusta, has been brought home to him in the mountains. In the final entry of his journal, written in the Golden Lion, he knows that the summer in Switzerland has come to its close. He has seen 'some of the noblest views in the world', but has not found solace:

> And neither the music of the Shepherd, the crashing of the Avalanche, not the torrent, the mountain, the Glacier, the Forest, nor the Cloud, have for one moment lightened the weight upon my heart, nor enabled me to lose my own wretched identity in the majesty and the power and the Glory around, above and beneath me. I am past reproaches, and there is a time for all things, I am past the wish of vengeance, and I know of none like for what I have suffered. But the hour will come, when what I feel must be felt, and the – but enough.[32]

Aubonne is one of those viewing points where you realise that Switzerland has had a long, fairly peaceful history, a place where not too much has changed. Nobody bombed the Lion d'Or. The castle above the town, built by gem merchant and orientalist Jean-Baptiste Tavernier, is intact and houses the village school. The view hasn't been tampered with.

Descending again to the lake, the car swings through roundabout after roundabout: Yverdon, Moudon, Nyon – the old Celtic stronghold names survive behind the Roman and Savoyard arrivals. A landscape rich in association. The Romans, Rousseau, the Romantics, refugee writers, the spies and detectives, bright young things of the Twenties and of the low, dishonest decade, the double agents and murderers, his master's butterflies and the emperor moths... they've all written about this immortal landscape and its effect on the viewer.

Early on it was Rousseau, a son of the soil, who drew the writers here. He was inspired by kicking the traces of Calvinism, spurning bourgeois habits and overhauling convention. The yearning and rebellion of his fictional young couple by the lake – Julie and Saint-Preux – imbued the landscape with feeling that got passed on to later tearaways. The Romantics imagined the Alps as authentic, impulsive, pure nature, unlike the civilisation they'd fled. For the most part the Romantics died young and thereby avoided the slippers and the comeback album. It's hard to imagine Byron as a big fat slob with a plummy voice, hauled up for a spot of jiggery-pokery with an underage Greek.

And it wasn't just a pretty landscape. The Romantics saw Switzerland as a functioning democracy and William Tell as a folk hero who sent the overlords packing. In the political sense too, Switzerland was the great good place. Topography helped foster the federation as a redoubt holding out against God's anointed kings who seemed always to be plotting for a piece of it. This conception of Switzerland lived on into the twentieth century when Russians were getting uppity against their tsars and conspired from the bars and tea-rooms of Zürich, Lausanne and Geneva.

Poets and travellers nurtured Switzerland as a psycho-geography: lacustrine, rocky, wild, Mother Nature on steroids. Victorian England followed in the poets' footsteps, clutching Baedekers and well-thumbed Tauchnitz editions. The prattle of guides and grasping innkeepers, milkmaids and slaphappy yodellers in *Lederhosen* added some local colour, a Swiss floorshow for the tourists. As the nineteenth century waned and tuberculosis ravaged industrial lungs, Switzerland morphed into an advertisement for health. Writers began to see the mountain sanatorium, the spa town, the grand hotel and the ski resort as havens and retreats. Foreign writers didn't get much beyond these confined spaces, into a more hardscrabble or authentic Switzerland. On the Grand Tour the locals are servants. Daisy Miller, besides being a little flirt, is a no-nothing heiress doing Europe on a gap year. Thomas Mann's talking heads are well fed but hardly ever leave the hotel. Switzerland becomes a terrace, a promontory above the world, an exclusive resort varnishing its woodwork for the visitors.

In the twentieth century, both Swiss and foreign writers imagined how Switzerland managed its neutrality during two world wars and the long Cold War that followed. From Sherlock Holmes at the Reichenbach Falls to le Carré's *The Constant Gardener*, the detective thriller, the spy novel, the Bond brand and a *noir* sensibility have had a century-long literary engagement with Switzerland and its secrets. Wheeling and dealing, cross-border practices, the wages of sin, arms and the high-level launderette have all cast a long shadow on the pure-as-the-driven-snow image of Switzerland.

Occasionally, my dormant Trotskyite reawakens here and I think: ah, so that's how the rich do it! It could be at a parent–teacher meeting. Or watching the world go by in St Moritz. Or crossing Bankverein in Basel, knowing gold is underfoot in the vaults, five floors beneath the pavement. We have been conditioned to think market capitalism benign, and sometimes forget that the rich become so on the backs of the rest of us. Does anybody any longer believe it's all a matter of innate intelligence plus elbow grease? The 99% and 1% model is back in business with a vengeance. 'Behind every fortune is a dead dog', as the saying goes in South America. Writers about Switzerland get a whiff of it. England's prosperity at one point rested on sugar and slavery in the Caribbean, America's on the bring-and-buy of a new continent. Switzerland's apple on the head of Tell Junior is tame as a founding myth in comparison to genocide, say. Between a spot of child labour and executive bonuses, many a company lies.

Switzerland took writers in, sometimes grudgingly, often with good grace. It gave them a room with a view and a place at the table – maybe not the *Stammtisch*, but you can't have everything. Service was brisk and efficient, the wine not too bad, the food rough and ready but nourishing. *Demi-pension*.

You're a writer, are you? We've had a few of those.

And the writers responded by doing what they do best: reportage, poems, horror fiction, travelogue, novel, detective and *Krimi*, great modern masterpiece. They bit the hand that fed them. They pointed out the dry rot. Suggested there's a smell under the floorboards. Often enough writers just got on with it – up some secluded valley or in a flat in Münchenstein. From time to time fruitful exchange between local scribblers and arrivistes led to new forms, mutual recognition. But this being Switzerland, they kept a wary eye on each other, knowing they might merely be passing through, taking shelter from the storm of history. Writers flitted into the gilded chalet, attracted by the light. What would the world be if there were no chalet, no refuge, no little lifeboat?

And are you paying cash or credit card?

It's impossible to move mountains: a certain resilience, inwardness and frugality are required of those who live in them. Caesar knew this. Latin, Germanic and Gallic cultures converge here, those three great linguistic streams. Peter Stamm makes a case for Switzerland being the watershed of Europe: 'water symbolises distance, a way to the sea that we sorely lack'.[33] And Swiss writers have often gone that distance and floated downstream. Just as the three great rivers of Europe have their source in its mountains, so the example of Swiss federal harmony has slaked the thirst of writers for centuries.

I hope this book has shown that Switzerland inspired a wealth of writing, and that writers from all over make it a rich literary landscape. *They came, they saw, they did a little shopping*. Switzerland is replete with small museums, writers' boltholes, hidden archives and literary landmarks: a truly inscribed and inspiring terrain A three hundred-year-old chalet still standing in Montbovon hosted Byron and Hobhouse for a fish supper. The archives are full of surprises.

And are you staying long, sir?

My journey is nearly over and I head up the motorway in the direction of Lake Biel and the Île St-Pierre. You remember that Rousseau was happiest there. You might recall that the green fairy sidetracked me the last time I attempted a visit. These days a causeway joins the island to the shore. Rousseau spent only five weeks on the island, but it was a period he never forgot.

> Emerging from a long and happy reverie, seeing myself surrounded by greenery, flowers and birds, and letting my eyes wander over the clear and crystalline water, I fused my imaginings with these charming sights and finding myself in the end gradually brought back to myself and my surroundings, I could not draw a line between fiction and reality.[34]

And so it is with me: no longer able to draw the line between fiction and reality; not even wanting to. I first read Rousseau studying French in Maynooth after that 1973 summer in Switzerland. I can't pretend I fully understood him. Who knows what understanding is? It might be a wine laid down long ago in the mind's eye until it is ready for drinking.

Solvitur ambulando, as Saint Augustine wrote, it is solved by walking. I left the books and the laptop in the car – 'all these gloomy old papers and books', Rousseau calls them[35] – and walked out on the causeway. Books were beginning to take over the chalet, to perch on every surface. You could do worse than to leave them behind, find a quiet island on a lake, and breed rabbits.

NOTES

Introduction

1. 'By Verona, Mantua and Milan, Across the Pass of the Simplon into Switzerland', extracted from Dickens, *Pictures from Italy*.
2. Twain, *A Tramp Abroad*, pp. 213–14.
3. Extract from 'Letter to Mick Flick' by Daniel de Roulet. English translation Daniel de Roulet, from a performance piece in Gstaad, 2014.
4. Conrad, *Under Western Eyes*, p. 180.
5. 'Geneva' in Rousseau, *Letter to d'Alembert, and Writings for the Theatre*, p. 241.
6. Caesar, *Gallic War*, trans. W.A. McDevitte and W.S. Bohn, Book 1, Chapter 2.
7. *Aus dem Tagebuch 1933*. Hoffmann and Piatti, *Europa Erlesen: Basel*, p. 167.
8. Ó Muraíle, *Turas na dTaoiseach nUltach as Éirinn*, p. 147. This sterling work of editing, translation and annotation, together with the earlier translation by Rev. Paul Walsh, represents a labour of love for these Maynooth men. Ó Muraíle's translation incorporates Walsh's earlier work published in Dublin in 1916. I have standardised the spelling of Basel.
9. Ibid., p. 157.
10. Ibid., p. 157.
11. Judt, *The Memory Chalet*, p. 220. The Swiss referred to here is Federal Police Chief Heinrich Rothmund, who recommended stamping a 'J' on the passports of German Jews as early as 1938.

1: Run Out of Town

1. Rousseau, *The Confessions*, p. 37.
2. Ibid., p. 59.
3. Ibid., p. 39.
4. Shelley, *Frankenstein*, p. 69.
5. *The Confessions*, p. 51.
6. Ibid., p. 102.
7. Ibid., p. 105.
8. Edmund Burke in 'Letter to a Member of the National Assembly', 1791. Burke was only the latest in a line of moralists who blamed reading as the cause of depravity. French physician Bienville's treatise *On Nymphomania* (1771) attributes sexual laxity in young girls to the loose reading habits and degeneracy of domestic servants.
9. *The Confessions*, pp. 146–7.
10. Rousseau, *Julie, or the New Heloise*, I, XIV.
11. *Oeuvres complètes de J.J. Rousseau: Corréspondance*, letters to the Maréchal de Luxembourg, 28 January and 20 February 1763, my translation.
12. Ibid.

13. *The Confessions*, p. 586.
14. Ibid., pp. 598, 603.
15. Maurice Cranston, *The Solitary Self: Jean-Jacques Rousseau in Exile and Adversity*, p. 57.
16. Rousseau, *Meditations of a Solitary Walker*, p. 28.
17. Byron, *Childe Harold's Pilgrimage*, Canto 3, LXXVII.
18. Hawthorne, *Passages from the French and Italian Notebooks*, pp. 532–3.
19. James, *Collected Travel Writings: The Continent*, pp. 625–7.
20. *Meditations of a Solitary Walker*, Fifth Walk.
21. Conrad, *Under Western Eyes*, pp. 239–40.

2: Here Come the Monsters

1. Percy Bysshe Shelley wrote the anonymous introduction to the first edition (1817) of *Frankenstein, or the Modern Prometheus*.
2. Shelley in a 3 October 1814 letter to Hogg, quoted at length in Spark, *Mary Shelley*, pp. 16–18.
3. *Mary Shelley*, p. 19.
4. Cited in Holmes, *Shelley: The Pursuit*, p. 238.
5. Published anonymously by T. Hookham & J. Ollier, London, in 1817 and including Percy Shelley's poem 'Mont Blanc', p. 40.
6. Ibid., pp. 49–50.
7. Ibid., p. 59.
8. *Shelley: The Pursuit*, p. 248.
9. Letter of Mary Shelley published with *History of a Six Weeks' Tour*.
10. *Shelley: The Pursuit*, p. 241.
11. Rossetti, *Diary of Dr. John William Polidori: 1816*, p. 96.
12. Byron's poem 'Childish Recollections' in his first book of verse, *Hours of Idleness*.
13. Hobhouse diary entry for July 19, 1811, following a meeting with Byron at Sittingbourne. See also Peter Cochran's comments on 'Leon' on www.newstead-abbeybyronsociety.org.
14. *History of a Six Weeks' Tour*, p. 110.
15. *Shelley: The Pursuit*, p. 335.
16. Ziegler, *The Swiss, the Gold and the Dead*, p. 210.
17. James, *Collected Travel Writings: The Continent*, p. 630.
18. Byron, *Letters and Journals*, Vol. V.
19. Galiffe to John Backhouse, quoted in John Clubbe, 'Byron in Switzerland', *Times Literary Supplement*, 6 February 1969. Jacques Augustin Galiffe (1773–1853) was a Genevan historian, exiled himself to Italy for his sins. He is buried in the Swiss-owned 'English' Cemetery in Florence.
20. Macfarlane, *Mountains of the Mind*, pp. 106–7.
21. *Frankenstein*, pp. 93, 95. The Bodleian Library holds Mary Shelley's manuscript of the novel, emended by Percy Shelley and with some passages in his hand. The bulk of the manuscript, however, is in her handwriting.

22. Ibid., pp. 31–2.
23. Ibid., p. 69.
24. Ibid., p. 198.
25. Ibid., p. 199.
26. Byron, *Fragment of a Novel*, 1816.
27. Byron, *Childe Harold's Pilgrimage*, Canto 3, LXXXVI.

3: The Blue Henrys

1. Ivo Haanstra examines this elegant item for inelegant purpose, with period illustrations, in *Blue Henry: The Almost Forgotten Story of the Blue Glass Sputum Flask*. Blue Henrys are now collectible items.

2. A Thomas-Mann-Way now links the Waldhotel Davos (former Waldsanatorium) and the Schatzalp, fixing in the landscape various scenes from Mann's novel. The spa town's connection with Nobel laureates has a pendant in the 1936 shooting of German Nazi Wilhelm Gustloff by a young Jewish man, David Frankfurter. Nobel laureate Günter Grass has fictionalised this incident in his novel *Crabwalk*.

3. Symonds corresponded with Venice resident Horatio F. Brown (1854–1926), and stayed with him on his summer visits to the city. Brown became Symonds' executor and published *John Addington Symonds, a Biography*. As such he was responsible for suppressing information and papers on Symonds' homosexuality. Symonds first befriended the schoolboy Brown at Clifton College, where the twenty-three-year-old Symonds was lecturing on the Greek poets. Later, Brown lived with his mother in a house on the Zattere, in company with a gondolier, Antonio Salin, and his family. Brown became a historian and leading light in the city, his public life recorded by another Venice man-about-town, Frederick Rolfe, the infamous Baron Corvo. Henry Scott Tuke painted Brown's portrait and he was connected to all the leading lights of his time, including Lord Roseberry and Robert Louis Stevenson, who wrote a poem for him.

4. Alan Bennett, *The Habit of Art*. Bennett wrote about the nexus of feelings and identities behind his play, in the *London Review of Books*, 5 November 2009.

5. Symonds, *The Memoirs*, p. 62.

6. Ibid., p. 78.

7. Nude photographs by the Arcadian photographers Baron von Gloeden (1856–1931) and Wilhelm von Plüschow (1852–1930), resident in Taormina, Sicily and Rome respectively. Von Gloeden's guest book was a who's who of turn-of-the-century pederasty, and included the signature of Oscar Wilde. Anne Thwaite's *Edmund Gosse: A Literary Landscape* cites Edmund Gosse in the choir stalls at Robert Browning's funeral in Westminster Abbey, peeping repeatedly at one such snap by von Gloeden, sent to him as a Christmas present by Symonds (p. 323).

8. Symonds, *The Memoirs*, pp. 94–95.

9. Symonds in a letter to Benjamin Jowett (1817–93), Master of Balliol College, Oxford.

10. *The Memoirs*, p. 117.

11. Ibid., p. 191.
12. Ibid., p. 138.
13. Ibid., p. 154.
14. Case XVII in Havelock Ellis, *Sexual Inversion*, which includes as part of Point 10: 'He was very curious to know why the Emperors kept boys as well as girls in their seraglios, and what the male gods did with the youths they loved.'
15. *The Memoirs*, p. 259.
16. Ibid., p. 261.
17. Ibid., pp. 265–6.
18. Symonds with his daughter Margaret, *Our Life in the Swiss Highlands*.
19. Tchaikovsky, in a letter to his brother, Modest, in *Letters to His Family*.
20. Ibid.
21. Stevenson, 'Health and Mountains', in *Essays on Travel*.
22. *The Letters of Robert Louis Stevenson*, Vol. II (1880–1887), p. 90.
23. Stevenson's 'Davos in Winter' first appeared in the *Pall Mall Gazette*, 17 February 1881, and was collected in *Essays on Travel*. The volume also included 'Health and Mountains', 'Alpine Diversion' and 'The Stimulation of the Alps', all originally appearing in the *Pall Mall Gazette* in February–March 1881.
24. Ibid.
25. Stevenson, 'Health and Mountains'.
26. Letter from Stevenson to his mother, 26 December 1881, in *The Letters of Robert Louis Stevenson*, p. 74.
27. Mann, *The Magic Mountain*, p. 104.
28. Conan Doyle, 'An Alpine Pass on Ski', *The Strand*, August 1894.
29. See Lellenberg et al., *Arthur Conan Doyle: A Life in Letters*.
30. Conan Doyle, 'The Final Problem', *The Strand*, December 1893.
31. Ibid.
32. Ibid.
33. See Kurzke, *Thomas Mann: Life as a Work of Art*.
34. Adair, *The Real Tadzio*, p. 93.
35. *The Magic Mountain*, p. 5.
36. Ibid., p. 7.
37. Behl and Gerberding, in the chapter dealing with the Schatzalp Hotel in Davos, in *Literarische Grandhotels der Schweiz*, p. 122. In 1950, Grand Duke Dimitri's remains were exhumed and reinterred on Mainau, an island on Lake Constance, in the Bernadotte family crypt. He was of the house of Holstein-Gottorps on the Romanov side. The tiny island belonged to Frederick II, Grand Duke of Baden (1857–1928), and is still administered as a 'flowering park island' by the Bernadotte family.
38. *The Magic Mountain*, p. 99.
39. Ibid., p. 54.
40. Ibid., p. 68.
41. Ibid., p. 73.
42. Ibid., p. 310.
43. Ibid., p. 316.

4: Going to Pot

1. James Guillaume's biographical sketch of Mikhail Bakunin, *Bakunin on Anarchy*. Guillaume was a founder of the First International in Geneva in 1866.

2. Mikhail Bode, 'Russian visions of Switzerland', in Pakhomova et al., *Russian Switzerland: Artistic and Historical Perspectives 1814–2014*.

3. From Sergei Nechayev's Revolutionary Catechism (1871), quoted in Annette Kobak's *Isabelle: The Life of Isabelle Eberhardt*, pp. 9–10. Nechayev was a twenty-three-year-old exile in Geneva when he wrote his catechism, which advocated a by-any-means-necessary approach to revolution. It was reissued by the Black Panthers in 1969.

4. 'Russian visions of Switzerland'.

5. This homemade weapon is on display in the Sisi Museum in Vienna.

6. Mark Twain, 'The Memorable Assassination', in *The Complete Essays of Mark Twain*.

7. Ibid.

8. Cited in Kobak, *Isabelle*, p. 17.

9. Ibid., p. 69.

10. Ibid., p. 75.

11. Ibid., p. 38.

12. From 'Choses du Sud-Oranais', published in *L'Akhbar* in 1903–04 and cited in Kobak, *Isabelle*, p. 216.

13. Eberhardt, *In the Shadow of Islam*, p. 27. Her journalist friend Victor Barrucand published this posthumous account of Eberhardt's 1904 journey to Ain Sefra and Kenadsa near the Moroccan–Algerian border in 1920. The original text was found in an urn in the house where she drowned in a flash flood. Barrucand's tampering (he claimed co-authorship) is evident from the overwrought style.

14. Kobak, *Isabelle*, p. 83.

15. Ibid., p. 56.

16. 'Deuil' in Eberhardt, *Amours nomades*, p. 137. My translation.

17. From the short story 'Zoh'r et Yasmina' in *Amours nomades*, p. 111. My translation.

18. *The Nomad: The Diaries of Isabelle Eberhardt*, p. 185.

19. Eberhardt's *Dans l'ombre chaude d'Islam*, controversially edited and arranged by Victor Barrucand, was re-issued in 1921. The appendix 'Choses du Sahara', in which 'Joies noires' appears, has not been included in the English translation by Sharon Bangert (2003). The original French of Barrucand's 1921 text has been published by l'Association Les Bourlapapey, bibliothèque numérique romande at http://www.ebooks-bnr.com/. This translation mine.

20. One of the first to recognise a kindred spirit in Eberhardt's singular life and prose was the Scottish-Austrian writer Norman Douglas. Reviewing *Dans l'ombre chaude d'Islam* and *Notes de route* (1906) as early as 1911 for the *North American Review*, Douglas wonders, in an essay entitled 'Intellectual Nomadism', about 'the effective affinity of some women for wild and destructive races of mankind: is it their development has been arrested at the emotional stage when as children, we were wont to delight in pirate adventures and redskin scalpings ...?' Douglas had been

expelled as a British diplomat from Russia for sexual impropriety; like Isabelle he was a linguist, nomad and stood at the sexual margins: 'like many of her sex, she always had a weakness for the soldiery'. Unlike her, he lived until the ripe old age of 84 and died on Capri with the words 'get those nuns off me' on his lips.

21. Clemenceau quoted by Revenin, *Homosexualité et prostitution masculines à Paris*, p. 225.
22. Kobak, *Isabelle*, p. 212.
23. Quoted in ibid., p. 213.
24. Quoted in ibid., p. 212.
25. *In the Shadow of Islam*, p. 42.
26. Ibid., pp. 39–40.
27. Ibid., p. 46.
28. Ibid., pp. 65–6.
29. Ibid., p. 83.
30. Ibid., pp. 91–2.
31. Ibid., p. 83.
32. Kobak, *Isabelle*, p. 225.
33. *In the Shadow of Islam*, p. 84.
34. *The Oblivion Seekers*, translated with a preface by Paul Bowles, pp. 54–5.
35. Ibid., p. 33.
36. Ibid., p. 8.
37. Ibid., pp. 71, 74.
38. Dessaix, *A Mother's Disgrace*, p. 9.
39. *The Nomad: The Diaries of Isabelle Eberhardt*, p. 146.
40. Conrad, *Under Western Eyes*, p. 145.
41. Ibid., p. 119.
42. In a letter to Apollon Maikov, cited in Frank, *Dostoyevsky: The Miraculous Years, 1865–1871*, p. 231.
43. *Under Western Eyes*, p. 182.
44. Ibid., p. 238.
45. Ibid., p. 240.
46. Ibid., p. 276.

5: The Infinity Pool

1. Quoted in Washington, *Madame Blavatsky's Baboon*, p. 118.
2. Ibid., p. 156.
3. Kafka, *The Diaries 1910–1923*, pp. 47–9.
4. *Madame Blavatsky's Baboon*, p. 233.
5. Ibid., pp. 233–4.
6. Details from Martin Green's excellent *Mountain of Truth: The Counterculture Begins, Ascona, 1900–1920*.
7. Wells, *A Modern Utopia*, Chapter 1.
8. Ibid., Chapter 2.
9. Ibid., Chapter 7.

10. Ibid.
11. Wells, *A World Set Free*, Chapter 1.
12. Lawrence, *Twilight in Italy*, p. 115. The 1990 Barrie & Jenkins edition is beautifully printed and bound in Spain, and published with photos by Paul Strand, Henri Cartier-Bresson and watercolours by John Ruskin, Walter Tyndale and others.
13. Ibid., p. 120.
14. Ibid., p. 121.
15. Ibid., p. 130.
16. Ibid., p. 135.
17. In a July 1912 letter to Edward Garnett, following Heinemann's rejection of *Sons and Lovers*.
18. *Twilight in Italy*, p. 137.
19. Ibid., p. 142.
20. Ibid., p. 144.
21. Ibid., p. 152.
22. Ibid., p. 153.
23. Ibid.
24. Hesse, *Klingsor's Last Summer*.
25. Hesse, *Basler Erinnerungen*.
26. Cited in 'As far away from Berlin as I can get!', a lecture given by Volker Michels on Hermann Hesse on Lake Constance. See www.hermann-hesse.de.
27. 'Journey to Nuremburg' (1926), collected in *Autobiographical Writings*, translated by Theodore Ziolkowski.
28. Hesse, *Steppenwolf*, p. 35.
29. Ibid., p. 47.
30. Greene, *Dr Fischer of Geneva or The Bomb Party*, p. 12.
31. 'Moving to a New House' in *Autobiographical Writings*.
32. *Autobiographical Writings*.
33. Byatt, *The Children's Book*.
34. Ibid.
35. FBI-Bericht von J.E. Hoover vom 7. Juli 1952, in: NARA RG 65 FBI File 029424.
36. Museum Rietberg press release April 2013.

6: Keeping the Wars at Arm's Length

1. Ellmann, *Selected Joyce Letters*, p. 40.
2. Crivelli, *James Joyce: Itinerari Triestini/Trieste Itineraries*, p. 150.
3. A verse composed by Joyce and cited in Ellmann, *James Joyce*, p. 420.
4. Lenin's speech to the Swiss Social Democrats cited by Bode, 'Russian visions of Switzerland', p. 35.
5. de Botton, *The Art of Travel*, p. 37.
6. Commentary by Ellmann in *Selected Joyce Letters*, p. 214.
7. Nora's letter to Joyce from Locarno, cited in Maddox, *Nora: The Real Life of Molly Bloom*, p. 148.
8. *Selected Joyce Letters*, p. 226.

9.   Ellmann, *James Joyce*, p. 455.
10. Cited in Brivic, *Joyce the Creator*, pp. 36–7.
11. O'Brien, *James Joyce*, p. 88.
12. August Suter's reminiscences of James Joyce in the *James Joyce Quarterly*, Vol. 7, No. 3 (Spring 1970), University of Tulsa.
13. Joyce's lyrics quoted by Edna O'Brien in *James Joyce*, p. 107.
14. Caws, *Maria Jolas, Woman of Action*.
15. PACS (Paris-American Committee to Stop War).
16. *Maria Jolas, Woman of Action*, p. 104.
17. 'que je ne suis pas juif de Judee mais aryen d'Erin', quoted in Ellmann, *James Joyce*, p. 736.
18. Ibid., p. 738.
19. Lester's fascinating account of the Joyce family's day in Geneva is included in *The Joyce We Knew: Memoirs of Joyce*, edited and with an introduction by Ulick O'Connor.
20. Ibid., p. 120.
21. *Selected Joyce Letters*, p. 408.

7: Loony Bins and Finishing Schools

1.   *The Stories of Vladimir Nabokov*, p. 488.
2.   *Financial Times*, 3–4 January 2015.
3.   Hemingway, *A Moveable Feast*, p. 52.
4.   Hemingway, *A Farewell to Arms*, p. 218.
5.   Ibid., p. 258.
6.   Ibid., p. 262.
7.   Ibid., p. 268.
8.   In the short story 'One Trip Abroad', published in the *Saturday Evening Post*, 11 October 1930.
9.   Fitzgerald, *Tender Is the Night*, p. 129.
10. Ibid., p. 133.
11. Ibid., pp. 134–5.
12. Meyers, *Scott Fitzgerald: A Biography*, p. 110.
13. *Tender Is the Night*, pp. 162–3.
14. Ibid., p. 171.
15. Ibid., p. 189.
16. Ibid., p. 195.
17. Ibid., p. 213.
18. *Scott Fitzgerald: A Biography*, p. 195.
19. Ibid., p. 65.
20. *Tender Is the Night*, p. 268.
21. Haig Simonian, 'Charm academy: Switzerland's last finishing school', *Financial Times*, 30 September 2010.
22. Brent-Dyer, *The Chalet School in Exile*, pp. 119–20.
23. Friends of the Chalet School website, www.chaletschool.org.uk.

24. Information from crime writer Val McDermid's BBC Radio 4 broadcast on the Chalet School series.
25. Spark, *The Finishing School*, pp. 4–5.
26. Ibid., p. 46.
27. Ibid., p. 197.

8: The Playground of Europe

1. Fleming, *Thrilling Cities*, pp. 207–8.
2. Ibid., p. 213.
3. Ibid., p. 216.
4. Ibid., p. 221.
5. Ibid., p. 226.
6. Maugham, *Ashenden*, p. 8.
7. Ibid., p. 9.
8. Ibid., p. 29.
9. West, *Historical Dictionary of British Intelligence*, p. 380.
10. *Ashenden*, pp. 109–10.
11. Ibid., pp. 148–9.
12. Ibid., p. 161.
13. Woods, *Neutral Ground: A Political History of Espionage Fiction*, p. 55.
14. *Ashenden*, pp. 170–71.
15. Boulton, *The Letters of D. H. Lawrence*, pp. 162, 166. Lawrence unfavourably reviewed Maugham's *Ashenden* for *Vogue*, July 1928, describing the stories as 'faked', 'instruments of the author's prejudice' and 'rancid'.
16. Glauser, *In Matto's Realm*, p. 6.
17. Ibid., p. 10.
18. Ibid., p. 206.
19. Ibid., p. 103.
20. Ibid., p. 119.
21. Ibid., p. 127.
22. Glauser, *The Spoke*, p. 105.
23. Ibid., pp. 127–8.
24. Ibid., p. 150.
25. Diogenes Verlag, author page.
26. Schneider, *Flattermann*, p. 20. My translation.
27. Ibid., p. 31.
28. Capus, *Almost like Spring*, p. 33.
29. Ibid., p. 42.
30. Ibid., p. 97.

9: His Master's Voice

1. Nabokov advised his students at Cornell to pronounce the second syllable to rhyme with 'gawk'. In *Strong Opinions* he suggests: 'A heavy open "o" as in

"Knickerbocker". My New England ear is not offended by the long elegant middle "o" of Nabokov as delivered in American academies. The awful "Na-bah-kov" is a despicable gutterism. Well, you can make your choice now.'

2. Andrei Bely (1880–1934) published *Petersburg* in 1916, which is among Nabokov's four 'greatest masterpieces of twentieth century prose', the others being Joyce's *Ulysses*, Kafka's *Metamorphosis* and the first half of Proust's *In Search of Lost Time*. Bely's horseman is Pushkin's, the Bronze Horseman, Peter the Great on Senate Square beside the Admiralty. A second rider, Nicholas I, sits on a prancing steed in Marie Square (St Isaac's Square) fronting the cathedral and also figures prominently in Bely's novel. Rudolf Steiner's anthroposophical movement, based in Dornach, influenced Bely, who spent from January 1914 to April 1916 in Dornach, across the valley from where I write, and where he re-wrote and tweaked much of *Petersburg*.

3. Boyd, *Vladimir Nabokov: The Russian Years*, p. 57.

4. Howells, *A Little Swiss Sojourn*, p. 103.

5. See Wyllie, 'Nabokov and Cinema'. Nabokov's deal with Harris and Kubrick was $150,000 plus 15 per cent of producers' profits. Nabokov also picked up $100,000 for writing the screenplay. The film earned $3,700,000 in the US box office alone.

6. Lev Grossman, 'The Gay Nabokov', *Salon*, 17 May 2000.

7. Russell, *The Unreal Life of Sergey Nabokov*, p. 20.

8. Nabokov, *Ada or Ardor: A Family Chronicle*, p. 510.

9. Boyd, *Vladimir Nabokov: The American Years*, p. 423. See also Tappe, *Nabokov*, p. 53.

10. Boyd, *Vladimir Nabokov: The American Years*, p. 416.

11. Nabokov, *Speak, Memory*, p. 35.

12. Nabokov, *Strong Opinions*, pp. 78, 194.

13. Nabokov, *The Stories of Vladimir Nabokov*, p. 27.

14. Svetlana Polsky wrote about 'Easter Rain' in *Nabokov Studies*, Vol. 4, 1997. Translated from Russian by Dmitri Nabokov and Peter Constantine, 'Easter Rain' appeared in *Conjunctions*, 38, Spring 2002.

15. Nabokov, *Lolita*, p. 9.

16. Ibid., p. 10.

17. Cited in *Vladimir Nabokov: The American Years*, p. 422.

18. Nabokov, *Pale Fire*, p. 232.

19. Nabokov in a 1965 television interview with Robert Hughes, quoted in *Strong Opinions*, pp. 76–7. The cedar is still there, growing tall.

20. *Ada or Ardor*, p. 553.

21. Ibid., p. 527.

22. Ibid., p. 554.

23. Ibid., p. 522.

24. Ibid., p. 557.

25. See Tappe, *Nabokov*.

26. Unveiled by Dimitri Nabokov in 1999 to mark the centenary of his father's birth, the statue is by Alexander Rukavishnikov. Rukavishnikov was Vladimir Nabokov's mother's maiden name.

27. Nabokov, *Transparent Things*, p. 15.
28. Ibid., p. 34.
29. In *Strong Opinions*, originally a 1971 interview for Bayerische Rundfunk.
30. Le Carré, *The Night Manager*, p. 184.
31. *Vladimir Nabokov: The Russian Years*, p. 263.
32. *Transparent Things*, pp. 50–51.

10: Ticino Noir

1. Highsmith, quoted in Wilson, *Beautiful Shadow: A Life of Patricia Highsmith*, p. 179.
2. Highsmith letter to Kate Kingsley Skattebol, 26 October 1952, Swiss Literary Archives.
3. Highsmith diary, 5 December 1952, Swiss Literary Archives.
4. Swiss Literary Archives, Highsmith archive, Cahier 22, A-05/22.
5. Ibid.
6. Ibid.
7. Highsmith, *Strangers on a Train*, p. 3.
8. Highsmith, *The Price of Salt*, p. 17.
9. Ibid., p. 191.
10. Swiss Literary Archives, Highsmith archive, Cahier 22, A-05/22.
11. Ibid.
12. Plath, *The Bell Jar*.
13. 'A Long Walk from Hell', published in French as 'La longue marche hors de l'enfer' in *Le Nouvel Observateur*, 1988.
14. Quoted in Meaker, *Highsmith: A Romance of the 1950s*, p. 178.
15. 'A Long Walk from Hell', Swiss Literary Archives.
16. Schenkar, *The Talented Miss Highsmith*, p. 490.
17. See Highsmith's article 'Winter in Ticino' in Dicks, *Ticking along with the Swiss*.
18. Ibid.
19. *Highsmith: A Romance of the 1950s*, pp. 3, 118.
20. *The Talented Miss Highsmith*, p. 314.
21. *Beautiful Shadow*, p. 219.
22. Swiss Literary Archives, Highsmith archive, Cahier 22, A-05/22.
23. *Highsmith: A Romance of the 1950s*, p. 190.
24. Dessaix, *Night Letters: A Journey through Switzerland and Italy*, pp. 25–6. Dessaix appends a fine comment to Highsmith's drawling indifference: 'Yet a civilized life is a matter of depth, surely, not surfaces. Otherwise it's just civility, expensive manners. We love all this in the late twentieth century.'
25. *Highsmith: A Romance of the 1950s*, p. 155.
26. *Beautiful Shadow*, pp. 170–71.
27. *The Talented Miss Highsmith*, p. 240.
28. Ibid., p. 485.
29. Swiss Literary Archives, Highsmith archive, B-01-02. Marijane Meaker confirms the virulence of Highsmith's racism: 'She said that black men got physically ill if they didn't have sexual intercourse many times a month' (Meaker, *Highsmith*, p. 196).

30. *The Talented Miss Highsmith*, p. 26.
31. Meaker, *Highsmith*, p. 198.
32. Terry Castle, 'The Ick Factor', *The New Republic*, 10 November 2003.
33. *Beautiful Shadow*, p. 255.
34. Typescript in the Highsmith archive, Swiss Literary Archives.
35. Highsmith, *Small g: A Summer Idyll*, p. 56.
36. Ibid., p. 25.
37. 'The Ick Factor'.
38. *Small g*, p. 83.
39. Crédit Suisse Bulletin.
40. Ibid.
41. *The Talented Miss Highsmith*, p. 480.
42. 'The Ick Factor'.

11: Truffles Missing from the Bonbon Box

1. Dürrenmatt, *Suspicion*, p. 205.
2. Ibid., p. 110.
3. Dürrenmatt, *The Judge and His Hangman*, p. 63.
4. Ibid., p. 35.
5. Ibid., p. 41.
6. *Suspicion*, pp. 110–11.
7. Ibid., p. 143.
8. Ibid., p. 104.
9. Stage directions for *The Physicists*, pp. 1–2.
10. *Suspicion*, p. 178.
11. Ibid., p. 183.
12. See Profit, *The Devil Next Door*, p. 37.
13. *Suspicion*, p. 184.
14. Ibid., p. 174.
15. *The Pledge*, p. 1.
16. Ibid., pp. 30–31.
17. Ibid., p. 111.
18. Ibid., p. 158.
19. Ibid., p. 161.
20. Ibid., p. 162.
21. Ibid., p. 167.
22. *The Physicists*, pp. 23–24.
23. *The Pledge*, p. 168.
24. Ibid., p. 107.
25. Ibid., p. 172.
26. 'Switzerland – A Prison' in Dürrenmatt, *Selected Writings Volume 3: Essays*, p. 67.
27. Ibid. p. 68.
28. Ibid., pp. 68–9.

29. Ibid., p. 69.
30. Ibid., p. 70.

12: Hard Boiled in Bern

1. *The Guardian*, 5 March 2005.
2. Conversation with Miriam Gross, 1980, in Bruccoli and Baughman, *Conversations with John le Carré*, p. 66.
3. Prize-giving speech for the Oxford German Olympiad 2013, Bodleian Library, 18 June 2013.
4. Le Carré, *A Perfect Spy*, p. 140.
5. Le Carré, *Smiley's People*, p. 184.
6. BBC television interview with Jon Snow, 2011.
7. *A Perfect Spy*, p. 159.
8. Macintyre, *A Spy among Friends: Kim Philby and the Great Betrayal*, pp. 91–2.
9. Ziegler, *The Swiss, the Gold and the Dead*, p. 19.
10. Ibid., p. 36.
11. Ibid., p. 71.
12. Ibid., p. 192.
13. Ibid., pp. 49–50.
14. Dulles, *The Craft of Intelligence*, pp. 202–3.
15. Le Carré's Afterword to Macintyre, *A Spy among Friends*.
16. *A Perfect Spy*, p. 194.
17. Ibid., p. 194.
18. Ibid., pp. 194–5.
19. Ibid., pp. 208–9.
20. Ibid., p. 219.
21. *Smiley's People*, p. 254.
22. Ibid., p. 255.
23. Ibid., p. 259.
24. Le Carré, 'The Unbearable Peace', *Granta*, 35, Spring 1991, p. 18.
25. Ibid., p. 52.
26. Ibid., p. 72.
27. Ibid., p. 56.
28. Ibid., p. 71.
29. Le Carré, *The Night Manager*, p. 19.
30. Interview with Jon Snow, 2011.
31. Ziegler, *The Swiss, the Gold, and the Dead*, p. 265.
32. *The Night Manager*, p. 29.
33. Cited in Beattie, *The Alps: A Cultural History*, p. 164.
34. *The Craft of Intelligence*, p. 54.
35. Le Carré, *Democracy Now* interview, broadcast 11 October 2010.
36. The documentary exposes the protective patent legislation that keeps the cost of retroviral drugs artificially high so that western pharmaceutical companies turn a profit and only rich people can afford them.

37. Article by Ben Goldacre in *The Guardian Weekly*, 25 April 2014.
38. *Democracy Now* interview.
39. Le Carré, *The Constant Gardener*, p. 362.
40. Ibid., pp. 363–4.
41. Ibid., p. 504.
42. Markus Haefliger, reviewing *The Constant Gardener* on swissinfo.ch, 15 January 2001.
43. *Democracy Now* interview.
44. *The Constant Gardener*, p. 364.
45. *The Craft of Intelligence*, p. 216.
46. Ibid., p. 210.
47. Le Carré, *Our Kind of Traitor*, p. 245ff.
48. *The Independent*, 26 October 2008.
49. *Our Kind of Traitor*, p. 157.
50. Ibid., p. 273.
51. Ibid., p. 300.

13: On the Road

1. Obituary of Ella Maillart, *The Independent*, 10 April 1997.
2. Roger Martin du Gard in dedicating one of his books to her.
3. In Carson McCullers' unfinished autobiography *Illumination and Night Glare*.
4. Edward Mendelson, 'The Secret Auden', *New York Review of Books*, 20 March 2014.
5. Foreword by Jessica Crispin to Maillart, *The Cruel Way: Switzerland to Afghanistan in a Ford*, 1939.
6. Maillart, *The Cruel Way*, pp. 3–4.
7. Ibid., p. 10.
8. Ibid., p. 33.
9. Ibid., p. 40.
10. Ibid., p. 45.
11. Ibid., p. 75.
12. Ibid., p. 89.
13. Ibid., p. 117.
14. Schwarzenbach, *All the Roads Are Open: The Afghan Journey*, p. 47.
15. Ibid., p. 195.
16. Ibid., p. 59.
17. *The Cruel Way*, p. 197.
18. 'La Suisse – le pays qui n'a pas tiré un coup de feu' in Schwarzenbach, *De monde en monde: Reportages 1934–1942*, p. 253. My translation.
19. Ibid., p. 266. My translation.
20. Laut, *Nicolas Bouvier: L'oeil qui écrit*, p. 27, my translation.
21. Bouvier, *L'usage du monde*, pp. 26–7, my translation.
22. Ibid., p. 36.
23. Ibid., p. 29.

24. Ibid., pp. 37–8.
25. Ibid., pp. 184–5, 194.
26. Ibid., p. 196.
27. Ibid., pp. 218–19.
28. Ibid., p. 220.
29. Bouvier, *Oeuvres*, p. 950. My translation.
30. Ibid., p. 970.
31. Ibid., p. 973.
32. Laut, *Nicolas Bouvier*, p. 287. My translation.
33. From 'Routes et Déroutes', interviews with Nicolas Bouvier collected in *Oeuvres*, pp. 1271–2. My translation.
34. *The Cruel Way*, p. 204.
35. Cited in Roger Perret's Afterword to *All the Roads Are Open*, p. 137. Photo by Schwarzenbach in the Swiss Literary Archives in Bern.
36. Highsmith's Afterword to the 1984 reissue of *The Price of Salt/Carol*, p. 291.

14: William Tell for Schools

1. Ian Paisley's 'None Dare Call Him Antichrist' sermon, Martyrs' Memorial Free Presbyterian Church, 16 October 1988.
2. Swiss Economics Minister Doris Leuthard speaking in 2008, designated Habsburg memorial year.
3. 'Emigrants', Frisch's speech on being awarded the George Büchner Prize, 1958, in Frisch, *Novels, Plays, Essays*, p. 332.
4. Dürrenmatt's 1972 essay 'Zur Dramaturgie der Schweiz'. My translation.
5. 'Wilhelm Tell: A School Text' in *Novels, Plays, Essays*, pp. 126–7.
6. 'Emigrants', p. 330.
7. Sebald, *A Place in the Country*, p. 105.
8. Zorn, *Mars*, p. 1.
9. De Roulet, *Un dimanche à la montagne*, p. 23. My translation.
10. Foreword to *Novels, Plays, Essays*.
11. Stamm, *Seven Years*, p. 62.
12. *Novels, Plays, Essays*, pp. 157–8.
13. Peter Stamm interview with the author. My translation.
14. *Seven Years*, p. 233.
15. Stamm, *All Days Are Night*, p. 103.
16. Interview with Tim Parks on www.prohelvetia.ch.

15: The Emperor Moths

1. 'Geneva' in Rousseau's *Letter to d'Alembert, and Writings for the Theatre*, pp. 245–6.
2. Beattie, *A Cultural History of the Alps*, p. 220.
3. Freedman, *Life of a Poet: Rainer Maria Rilke*, p. 455.

4. In a letter to Baladine, February 9, 1921, quoted in ibid., p. 492.
5. Ibid., p. 485.
6. Reported in Maria Riva's memoir *Dietrich by Her Daughter*, p. 501.
7. See 'Porto Ronco', https://www.youtube.com/watch?v=QNoyr_NFRow
8. Woodall, *Borges: A Life*, n.p.
9. Cited in Williamson, *Borges: A Life*, p. 58.
10. Borges, *Atlas*.
11. Williamson, *Borges: A Life*, p. 62.
12. Ibid., pp. 64–5.
13. Ibid., p. 88.
14. Borges' letter to Spain's Agencia Efe news agency, dated 6 May 1986.
15. *The New Yorker*, 26 May 1986. Translation by Alastair Reid.
16. Greene, *J'accuse – The Dark Side of Nice*, p. 7.
17. Sherry, *The Life of Graham Greene: Vol. 3, 1955–1991*, p. 790.
18. Greene, *Ways of Escape*, p. 300.
19. Greene, *Dr Fischer of Geneva or The Bomb Party*, p. 9.
20. Ibid., p. 10.
21. Ibid., p. 10.
22. Ibid., pp. 24–25.
23. Ibid., p. 25.
24. Ibid., p. 77.
25. Ibid., p. 80.
26. Anthony Burgess in *The New York Times*, 22 November 1987.
27. *New Statesman*, 9 April 2013.
28. Burgess, *You've Had Your Time*, p. 384.
29. Brookner, *Hotel du Lac*, pp. 7, 14.
30. Ibid., pp. 51–2.
31. The late Peter Cochran's site provided invaluable comparison and commentary on Byron's and Hobhouse's trek through the Bernese Oberland. https://peter-cochran.wordpress.com
32. Byron, *Letters and Journals*.
33. Stamm in an interview with the author.
34. Rousseau, *Meditations of a Solitary Walker*.
35. Ibid.

BIBLIOGRAPHY

Adair, Gilbert. *The Real Tadzio: Thomas Mann's Death in Venice and the Boy Who Inspired It*. London: Short Books, 2001.

Anderson, Chester G. *James Joyce*. London: Thames and Hudson, 1998.

Baghli, Sid Ahmed. *Nasreddine Dinet: Un maître de la peinture algerienne*. Alger: SNED, 1977.

Beattie, Andrew. *The Alps: A Cultural History*. Oxford: Signal Books, 2006.

Bedenig Stein, Katrin. 'Auf dem Zauberberg: Thomas Mann als Kurgast in der Schweiz', in Felix Graf & Eberhard Wolff (eds), *Zauber Berge: Die Schweiz als Kraftraum und Sanatorium*. Zürich: Swiss National Museum, 2010.

Behl, Silke & Gerberding, Eva. *Literarische Grandhotels der Schweiz*. Zürich-Hamburg: Arche Literatur Verlag, 2008.

Bennett, Alan. *The Habit of Art*. Faber & Faber, 2009.

Bewes, Diccon. *Slow Train to Switzerland*. London: Nicholas Brealey Publishing, 2013.

Bolton, Zoe. 'Collaborative Authorship and Shared Travel in History of a Six Weeks' Tour', in L. Adam Mekler and Lucy Morrison (eds), *Mary Shelley: Her Circle and Her Contemporaries*. Newcastle upon Tyne: Cambridge Scholars Publishing, 2010.

Borges, Jorge Luis. *Atlas*. New York: E.P. Dutton, 1985.

Boulton, James T. (ed.). *The Letters of D.H. Lawrence*. Cambridge: Cambridge University Press, 1984.

Bouvier, Nicolas. *L'usage du monde*. Paris: Éditions Payot & Rivages, 2001.

Bouvier, Nicolas. *Oeuvres*. Paris: Quarto Gallimard, 2004.

Bower, Tom. *Blood Money: The Swiss, the Nazis and the Looted Billions*. London: Macmillan, 1997.

Boyd, Brian. *Vladimir Nabokov: The Russian Years*. London: Chatto & Windus, 1990.

Boyd, Brian. *Vladimir Nabokov: The American Years*. Princeton, NJ: Princeton University Press, 1991.

Boyd, Brian. *Stalking Nabokov*. New York: Columbia University Press, 2011.

Brent-Dyer, Elinor. *The Chalet School in Exile*. W.R. Chambers, 1950.

Brivic, Sheldon. *Joyce the Creator*. Madison, WI: University of Wisconsin Press, 1985.

Brookner, Anita. *Hotel du Lac*. London: Guild Publishing, 1984.

Brown, Horatio F. *John Addington Symonds, a Biography*. New York: Scribner's, 1895.

Bruccoli, Matthew J. & Baughman, Judith S. (eds). *Conversations with John le Carré*. Jackson, MS: University Press of Mississippi, 2004.

Burgess, Anthony. *You've Had Your Time*. London: Penguin, 1991.

Byatt, A.S. *The Children's Book*. London: Chatto & Windus, 2009.

Byron, *Letters and Journals*, Vol. V, ed. Leslie A. Marchand. New York: Harvard University Press, 1976.

Caesar, *Gallic War*, trans. W.A. McDevitte & W.S. Bohn. New York: Harper & Brothers, 1869.

Capus, Alex. *Almost like Spring*. London: Haus Publishing, 2013.

Carpenter, Humphrey. *Geniuses Together: American Writers in Paris in the 1920s*. London: Unwin Hyman, 1987.

Castle, Terry. 'The Ick Factor', *The New Republic*, 10 November 2003.

Caws, Mary Ann (ed.). *Maria Jolas, Woman of Action: A Memoir and Other Writings*. Columbia, SC: University of South Carolina Press, 2004.

Codevilla, Angelo M. *Between the Alps and a Hard Place: Switzerland in World War II and the Rewriting of History*. Washington, DC: Regnery Publishing, 2000.

Coller, Ian. 'Rousseau's Turban: Entangled Encounters of Europe and Islam in the Age of Enlightenment', *Historical Reflections*, Vol. 40, Issue 2, Summer 2014.

Conrad, Joseph. *Under Western Eyes*. London: Penguin, 2007.

Cranston, Maurice. *The Solitary Self: Jean-Jacques Rousseau in Exile and Adversity*. Chicago, IL: University of Chicago Press, 1997.

Crivelli, Renzo S. *James Joyce: Itinerari Triestini/Trieste Itineraries*, trans. John McCourt. Trieste: MGS Press, 2001.

Dangerfield, Elma. *Byron and the Romantics in Switzerland*. London: Ascent Books, 1978.

De Bellaigue, Christopher. *Patriot of Persia: Muhammad Mossadegh and a Very British Coup*. London: Bodley Head, 2012.

De Botton, Alain. *The Art of Travel*. London: Hamish Hamilton, 2002.

Debrunner, Albert M. *Literarische Spaziergänge durch Basel*. Zürich: Huber, 2011.

De Roulet, Daniel. *Un dimanche à la montagne*. Paris: Buchet/Chastel, 2006.

De Roulet, Daniel. *Double*. Geneva: Metropolis, 2006.

Dessaix, Robert. *Night Letters: A Journey through Switzerland and Italy*. Sydney: Pan Macmillan, 1997.

Dessaix, Robert. *A Mother's Disgrace*. Angus & Robertson, 2002.

De Tonnac, Jean-Philippe. *Les Promenades de Hermann Hesse*. Paris: Éditions du Chêne, 1996.

Dickens, Charles. *Pictures from Italy*. Penguin Classics, 1998.

Dickens, Charles. *On Travel*, edited by Pete Orford. London: Hesperus Press, 2009.

Dicks, Dianne (ed.). *Ticking along with the Swiss*. Basel: Bergli Books, 1988.

Dulles, Allen W. *The Craft of Intelligence*. Guilford, CT: Lyons Press, 2006.

Dürrenmatt, Friedrich. *The Pledge*. London: Penguin, 2001.

Dürrenmatt, Friedrich. *The Inspector Barlach Mysteries: The Judge and His Hangman and Suspicion*. Chicago, IL: University of Chicago Press, 2006.

Dürrenmatt, Friedrich. *The Physicists*. New York: Grove Press, 2006.

Dürrenmatt, Friedrich. *Selected Writings Volume 3: Essays*. Chicago, IL: University of Chicago Press, 2006.

Eberhardt, Isabelle. *The Nomad: The Diaries of Isabelle Eberhardt*. Chichester: Summersdale Travel, 2002.

Eberhardt, Isabelle. *Amours nomades*. Paris: Éditions Joelle Losfeld, 2003.

Eberhardt, Isabelle. *In the Shadow of Islam*. London: Peter Owen, 2003.

Eberhardt, Isabelle. *The Oblivion Seekers*. London: Peter Owen, 2010.

Ellis, David. *Byron in Geneva: That Summer of 1816*. Liverpool: Liverpool University Press, 2011.

Ellis, Havelock. *Sexual Inversion*. London: Wilson and Macmillan, 1897.

Ellmann, Richard (ed.). *Selected Joyce Letters*. New York: Viking Press, 1975.

Ellmann, Richard. *James Joyce*. Oxford: Oxford University Press, revised edition 1982.

Fitzgerald, F. Scott. *Tender Is the Night*. London: Penguin Classics, 2000.

Fleming, Ian. *Thrilling Cities*. London: Vintage, 2013.

Frank, Joseph. *Dostoyevsky: The Miraculous Years, 1865–1871*. Princeton, NJ: Princeton University Press, 1995.

Freedman, Ralph. *Life of a Poet: Rainer Maria Rilke*. London: Farrer Straus & Giroux, 1996.

Frisch, Max. *Novels, Plays, Essays*. New York: Continuum, 1989.

Frisch, Max. *I'm Not Stiller*. New York: Harvest Books, 1994.

Frisch, Max. *Homo Faber*. London: Penguin, 2006.

Frisch, Max. *Drafts for a Third Sketchbook*. London: Seagull Books, 2013.

Glauser, Friedrich. *In Matto's Realm*, trans. Mike Mitchell. London: Bitter Lemon Press, 2005.

Glauser, Friedrich. *Fever*. London: Bitter Lemon Press, 2006.

Glauser, Friedrich. *The Spoke*, trans. Mike Mitchell. London: Bitter Lemon Press, 2008.

Green, Martin. *Mountain of Truth: The Counterculture Begins, Ascona, 1900–1920*. Lebanon, NH: University Press of New England, 1986.

Greene, Graham. *Dr Fischer of Geneva or The Bomb Party*. London: Penguin, 1980.

Greene, Graham. *Ways of Escape*. London: Bodley Head, 1980.

Greene, Graham. *J'accuse*. London: Bodley Head, 1992.

Greer, Germaine. *The Boy*. London: Thames & Hudson, 2003.

Grivat, Olivier. *Un roi en Suisse: La jeunesse helvétique du roi Bhumibol de Thaïlande*. Lausanne: Éditions Favre, 2011.

Guillaume, James. *Bakunin on Anarchy*. Paris: P.V. Stock, 1907.

Haanstra, Ivo. *Blue Henry: The Almost Forgotten Story of the Blue Glass Sputum Flask*. Toronto: Cortex Design, 2010.

Hasler, Hans. *The Goetheanum*. Dornach: Verlag am Goetheanum, 2005.

Hawthorne, Nathaniel. *Passages from the French and Italian Notebooks*. Boston, MA: Houghton Mifflin, 1896.

Heilbut, Anthony. *Thomas Mann: Eros and Literature*. New York: Alfred A. Knopf, 1996.

Hemingway, Ernest. *A Moveable Feast*. London: Jonathan Cape, 1964.

Hemingway, Ernest. *The Collected Stories*. London: Everyman's Library, 1995.

Hemingway, Ernest. *A Farewell to Arms*. London: Arrow, 2004.

Hesse, Hermann. *Klingsor's Last Summer*. Berlin: S. Fischer Verlag, 1919.

Hesse, Hermann. 'Basler Erinnerungen', *Merian*, 9, no. 7, 1956.

Hesse, Hermann. *Autobiographical Writings*, trans. Theodore Ziolkowski. London: Picador, 1975.

Hesse, Hermann. *Reflections*. London: Jonathan Cape, 1977.

Hesse, Hermann. *Steppenwolf*. London: Penguin, 2011.

Highsmith, Patricia. *The Talented Mister Ripley*. London: Vintage Crime, 1992.

Highsmith, Patricia. *Small g: A Summer Idyll*. London: Bloomsbury, 1995.

Highsmith, Patricia. *Strangers on a Train*. London: Vintage, 1999.

Highsmith, Patricia. *Ripley under Water*. London: Bloomsbury, 2003.

Highsmith, Patricia. 'Winter in the Ticino', in Dianne Dicks (ed.), *Ticking along with the Swiss*. Basel: Bergli Books, 2003.

Highsmith, Patricia. *The Price of Salt*. New York: W.W. Norton, 2004.

Hoffmann, David Marc & Piatti, Barbara. *Europa Erlesen: Basel*. Klagenfurt: Wieser Verlag, 2006.

Holmes, Richard. *Shelley: The Pursuit*. London: Weidenfeld and Nicolson, 1974.

Howells, W.D. *A Little Swiss Sojourn*. New York: Harper & Brothers, 1893.

James, Henry. *Collected Travel Writings: The Continent*. New York: Library of America, 1993.

James, Henry. *The Aspern Papers*. New York: Dover Thrift Editions, 2001.

Judt, Tony. *The Memory Chalet*. London: William Heinemann, 2010.

Kafka, Franz. *The Diaries 1910–1923*, ed. Max Brod. London: Penguin, 1975.

Kobak, Annette. *Isabelle: The Life of Isabelle Eberhardt*. New York: Knopf, 1989.

Kurzke, Hermann. *Thomas Mann: Life as a Work of Art*. Princeton, NJ: Princeton University Press, 2002.

Laut, François. *Nicolas Bouvier: L'oeil qui écrit*. Paris: Éditions Payot & Rivages, 2008.

Lawrence, D.H. *Twilight in Italy*. London: Barrie & Jenkins, 1990.

Le Carré, John. *Smiley's People*. London: Hodder & Stoughton, 1979.

Le Carré, John. *A Perfect Spy*. New York: Alfred A. Knopf, 1986.

Le Carré, John. 'The Unbearable Peace', *Granta*, 35, Spring 1991.

Le Carré, John. *The Night Manager*. New York: Alfred A. Knopf, 1993.

Le Carré, John. *The Constant Gardener*. London: Hodder & Stoughton, 2001.

Le Carré, John. *Our Kind of Traitor*. London: Penguin Viking, 2010.

Lellenberg, Jon, Stashower, Daniel and Foley, Charles (eds). *Arthur Conan Doyle: A Life in Letters*. New York: Harper Perennial, 2007.

Levy, Bertrand. 'Borges et Genève: Entre mythe et réalité', *Le Globe*, Vol. 150, 2010.

Lloyd, Roger. *A Week on the Lake*. Bloomington, IN: iUniverse, 2014.

Lüscher, Jonas. *Barbarian Spring*. London: Haus Publishing, 2014.

Macfarlane, Robert. *Mountains of the Mind: A History of a Fascination*. London: Granta Books, 2003.

Macintyre, Ben. *A Spy among Friends: Kim Philby and the Great Betrayal*. London: Bloomsbury, 2014.

Maddox, Brenda. *Nora: The Real Life of Molly Bloom*. Boston, MA: Houghton Mifflin, 1988.

Maillart, Ella K. *The Cruel Way: Switzerland to Afghanistan in a Ford, 1939*. Chicago, IL: University of Chicago Press, 2013.

Mann, Thomas. *The Magic Mountain*, trans. John E. Woods. New York: Vintage International, 1996.

Maugham, W. Somerset. *Ashenden*. London: Vintage, 2000.

McCullers, Carson. *Illumination and Night Glare*. Madison, WI: University of Wisconsin Press, 1999.

Meaker, Marijane. *Highsmith: A Romance of the 1950s*. San Francisco, CA: Cleis Press, 2003.

Meier, Daniela. *Helvetias guter Draht zum Pfauenthron: Die Beziehungen der Schweiz zu Iran (1946–1978)*. Zürich: Orell Füssli Verlag, 2002.

Meyers, Jeffrey. *Scott Fitzgerald: A Biography*. London: Macmillan, 1994.

Milani, Abbas. *The Shah*. New York: Palgrave Macmillan, 2012.

Monney, Jean-Jacques. *La vie de Jean-Jacques Rousseau en cartes postales*. Geneva: Éditions Slatkine, 2012.

Mottahedeh, Roy. *The Mantle of the Prophet: Religion and Politics in Iran*. New York: Pantheon Books, 1985.

Nabokov, Vladimir. *Speak, Memory: An Autobiography Revisited*. New York: G.P. Putnam's Sons, 1966.

Nabokov, Vladimir. *Ada or Ardor: A Family Chronicle*. London: Weidenfeld & Nicolson, 1969.

Nabokov, Vladimir. *Lolita*. London: Everyman Library Classics, 1992.

Nabokov, Vladimir. *The Stories of Vladimir Nabokov*. New York: Alfred A. Knopf, 1995.

Nabokov, *Pale Fire*. London: Penguin Modern Classics, 2000.

Nabokov, Vladimir. *Strong Opinions*. London: Penguin Classics, 2011.

Nabokov, Vladimir. *Transparent Things*. London: Penguin Classics, 2011.

O'Brien, Edna. *James Joyce*. London: Weidenfeld & Nicolson, 1999.

Ó Cianain, Tadhg. *The Flight of the Earls*, edited with translation and notes by Paul Walsh. Dublin: Gill & Son, 1916.

O'Connor, Ulick (ed.). *The Joyce We Knew: Memoirs of Joyce*. Dingle: Brandon Press, 2004.

Ó Muraíle, Nollaig. 'The Learned Family of Ó Cianáin', *The Clogher Record: Journal of the Clogher Historical Society*, 19, 387–436, 2005.

Ó Muraíle, Nollaig (ed.). *Turas na dTaoiseach nUltach tar Sáile: From Ráth Maoláin to Rome – Tadhg Ó Cianáin's Contemporary Narrative of the Journey into Exile of the Ulster Chieftains and Their Followers, 1607–8*. Rome: Pontifical Irish College, 2007.

Pakhomova, Anna et al. *Russian Switzerland: Artistic and Historical Perspectives, 1814–2014*. Prégny-Genève: Éditions de Penthes, 2014.

Perrottet, Tony. *The Sinner's Grand Tour: A Journey through the Historical Underbelly of Europe*. New York: Broadway Paperbacks, 2011.

Pifer, Ellen. 'Dark Paradise: Shades of Heaven and Hell in Ada', *Modern Fiction Studies*, Vol. 25, No. 3, 1979.

Pitzer, Andrea. *The Secret History of Vladimir Nabokov*. New York: Pegasus Press, 2013.

Plath, Sylvia. *The Bell Jar*. New York: HarperCollins, 1963.

Powers, Thomas. *Intelligence Wars: American Secret History from Hitler to Al-Qaeda*. New York: New York Review of Books, 2004.

Profit, Vera B. *The Devil Next Door: Toward a Literary and Psychological Definition of Human Evil*. Amsterdam: Rodopi, 2014.

Revenin, Régis. *Homosexualité et prostitution masculines à Paris*. Paris: L'Harmattan, 2005.

Rippl, Daniela. *Vladimir Nabokov: Sein Leben in Bildern und Texten*. Berlin: Alexander Fest Verlag, 1998.

Riva, Maria. *Dietrich by Her Daughter*. New York: Alfred A. Knopf, 1993.

Rossetti, William Michael (ed.). *Diary of Dr. John William Polidori: 1816*. London: Elkin Mathews, 1911.

Rousseau, Jean-Jacques. *Lettres écrites de la montagne*. Paris: La Renaissance du Livre, n.d.

Rousseau, Jean-Jacques. *Oeuvres complètes: Correspondance, Tome II*. Paris: Dupont, 1824.

Rousseau, Jean-Jacques. *Meditations of a Solitary Walker*. London: Penguin Books, 1979.

Rousseau, Jean-Jacques. *The Confessions*. Ware: Wordsworth Editions, 1996.

Rousseau, Jean-Jacques. *Julie or the New Heloise*, trans. and ed. Philip Stewart and Jean Vaché. Dartmouth College, NE: University Press of New England, 1997.

Rousseau, Jean-Jacques. *Letter to d'Alembert, and Writings for the Theatre*, trans. & ed. Allan Bloom et al. Dartmouth College, NE: University Press of New England, 2004.

Rousseau, Jean-Jacques. *The Social Contract*. London: Penguin, 2004.

Russell, Paul. *The Unreal Life of Sergei Nabokov*. Berkeley, CA: Cleis Press, 2011.

Schenkar, Joan. *The Talented Miss Highsmith*. New York: St. Martin's Press, 2009.

Schneider, Hansjörg. *Flattermann*. Zürich: Diogenes Verlag, 2013.

Schneider, Hansjörg. *Hunkeler und die goldene Hand*. Zürich: Diogenes Verlag, 2013.

Schwarzenbach, Annemarie. *All the Roads Are Open: The Afghan Journey*. London: Seagull Books, 2011.

Schwarzenbach, Annemarie. *De monde en monde: Reportages 1934–1942*. Carouges-Genève: Éditions Zoé, 2012.

Sebald, W.G. *A Place in the Country*. New York: Random House, 2013.

Semochkin, Alexander. *Nabokov's Paradise Lost: The Family Estates in Russia*. St. Petersburg: Liga Plus, 1999.

Shawcross, William. *The Shah's Last Ride*. London: Chatto & Windus, 1989.

Shelley, Mary. *Rambles in Germany and Italy, 1840, 1842 and 1843*. London: E. Moxton, 1844.

Shelley, Mary. *Frankenstein or the Modern Prometheus*. New York: Everyman's Library, 1992.

Shelley, Percy B. *Poems, Selected by Isabel Quigley*. London: Penguin Books, 1956.

Sherry, Norman. *The Life of Graham Greene: Vol. III*. New York: Viking Penguin, 2004.

Smolik, Pierre. *Graham Greene: The Swiss Chapter*. Geneva: Call Me Edouard Publishers, 2013.

Spark, Muriel. *The Finishing School*. London: Penguin Viking, 2004.

Spark, Muriel. *Mary Shelley*. Manchester: Carcanet Press, 2013.

Stamm, Peter. *Seven Years*. London: Granta, 2012.

Stamm, Peter. *All Days Are Nights*. London: Granta, 2014.

Stamm, Peter. *We're Flying*. London: Granta, 2015.

Stevenson, Robert Louis. *Essays on Travel*. London: Chatto & Windus, 1905.

Stevenson, Robert Louis. *The Letters of Robert Louis Stevenson, Vol. III*, edited by Bradford A. Booth & Ernest Mehew. New Haven, CT: Yale University Press, 1995.

Stevenson, Robert Louis. *Selected Letters*, edited by Ernest Mehew. New Haven, CT: Yale University Press, 1997.

Symonds, John Addington. *Italian Byways*. London: Smith, Elder, 1883.

Symonds, John Addington. *The Memoirs*, edited and introduced by Phyllis Grosskurth. New York: Random House, 1984.

Symonds, John Addington & Symonds, Margaret. *Our Life in the Swiss Highlands*. London: A. & C. Black, 1892.

Tappe, Horst. *Nabokov*. Basel: Christoph Merian Verlag, 2001.

Tchaikovsky, Piotr Ilyich. *Letters to His Family*. New York: Stein and Day, 1982.

Thwaite, Anne. *Edmund Gosse: A Literary Landscape, 1849–1928*. London: Secker & Warburg, 1984.

Twain, Mark. *A Tramp Abroad*. London: Penguin, 1997.

Twain, Mark. *The Complete Essays of Mark Twain*. Boston, MA: Da Capo Press, 2000.

Volcker, Paul et al. *Report on Dormant Accounts of Victims of Nazi Persecution in Swiss Banks*. Bern: Staempfli Publishers, 1999.

Washington, Peter. *Madame Blavatsky's Baboon: A History of the Mystics, Mediums, and Misfits Who Brought Spiritualism to America*. New York: Schocken Books, 1993.

Wells, H.G. *A Modern Utopia*. London: Penguin Classics, 2006.

Wells, H.G. *A World Set Free*. Project Gutenberg online edition.

West, Nigel. Historical Dictionary of British Intelligence. Lanham, MD: Scarecrow Press, 2005.

Williamson, Edwin. *Borges: A Life*. New York: Penguin Viking, 2004.

Wilson, Andrew. *Beautiful Shadow: A Life of Patricia Highsmith*. London: Bloomsbury, 2004.

Wood, Michael. *The Magician's Doubts: Nabokov and the Risks of Fiction*. London: Chatto & Windus, 1994.

Wood, Michael. 'Nabokov's late fiction', in Julian W. Connolly (ed.), *The Cambridge Companion to Nabokov*. Cambridge: Cambridge University Press, 2005.

Woodall, James. *Borges: A Life*. New York: Basic Books, 1996.

Woods, Brett F. *Neutral Ground: A Political History of Espionage Fiction*. New York: Algora Publishing, 2005.

Wraight, John. *The Swiss and the British*. Salisbury: Michael Russell, 1987.

Wyllie, Barbara. 'Nabokov and Cinema', in Julian W. Connolly (ed.), *The Cambridge Companion to Nabokov*. Cambridge: Cambridge University Press, 2005.

Ziegler, Jean. *The Swiss, the Gold, and the Dead: How Swiss Bankers Helped Finance the Nazi War Machine*. New York: Harcourt Brace, 1997.

Zorn, Fritz. *Mars*, trans. Robert Kimber & Rita Kimber. London: Pan, 1982.

INDEX

ACKNOWLEDGEMENTS

Many Swiss museums and their staff proved informative and useful in the writing of this book: the Dürrenmatt museum in Neuchâtel; the Hermann Hesse museums in Montagnola (Ticino) and Gaienhofen on Lake Constance; the James Joyce Foundation in Zürich; the Thomas Mann Archives in Zürich; the Rousseau museums in Geneva and Môtiers; the Absinthe House in Môtiers; the Museum of the Swiss Abroad in Pregny; the Sherlock Holmes museums in Meiringen and Lucens; the museum complex at Monte Verità (Ticino); the Éspace Ella Maillart in Chandolin (Valais); the Goetheanum at Dornach; Laténium outside Neuchâtel; and Schloss Habsburg in Aargau.

Stéphanie Cudré-Mauroux and her staff at the Swiss Literary Archives in Bern were particularly helpful with my research on Patricia Highsmith. The University Library in Basel and the library at International School Basel also gave me congenial surroundings in which to read. Librarians Susan Clarke and Robyn Stewart made suggestions and pointed me towards the stacks.

Thank you to Diogenes Verlag for permission to quote from the unpublished papers of Patricia Highsmith.

A number of sterling hotels and hostelries provided sustenance of various sorts, as they did to their literary guests: The Three Kings in Basel; The Bellevue Palace in Bern; the Richemonde in Geneva; the Palace and the Posthotel Rössli in Gstaad; the Kulm in St Moritz; the Palace Hotel in Montreux.

A special thank-you goes to Garni Barbatè in Tegna (Ticino) and to its garden table in memory of Hannah Arendt.

Patrick Cramer and Jean-Charles Giroud were helpful and generous with the cover illustration by Hans Eggimann.

I received patient guidance in shepherding this book to completion from my editor Nicholas Brealey and his team.

Thank you to Kirsten Jaehde for accompanying me on walks in the Bernese Oberland and the Val de Travers in the footsteps of Byron, Hobhouse and Rousseau, and for help with translations.

André Ehrhard, Christophe Müller, Brigitta Louisa Merki, Professor George Lüdi and Markus Fischer proved invaluable and forthcoming with information about and memories of Fritz Zorn.

Many thanks to Peter Stamm and to Daniel de Roulet for graciously answering my questions.

Thank you to the following for reading chapters and offering insightful comments: Paul Doolan, Denis McClean, Val Carey, Hilary and Ewart Cole, Elsa Fischer, Richard Begbie, Mattias Rüegger and David Burleigh.

CREDITS

Front cover: Hans Eggimann poster for the Grand Hotel Belvédère in Davos, 1905, in *A Century of Swiss Winter Sports Posters* by Jean-Charles Giroud, Patrick Cramer Publisher, Geneva.

Page 0: First World War cartoon by Charles Addy, in the Lausanne satirical magazine *l'Arbalète*, Swiss National Library.

Page 4: Davos sanatorium patients, ca. 1910, Dokumentationsbibliothek Davos.

Page 5: Monte Verità Foundation.

Page 7: Wikimedia Commons, public domain.

Page 8: 2007 stamp, courtesy of the Basel Paper Museum.

Pages 12, 14, 19: postcards in the collection of Jean-Jacques Monney, *La vie de Jean-Jacques Rousseau en cartes postales*.

Page 16: A facsimile from Beza's 1580 edition of icons, Hekman Digital Archive, jointly maintained at Calvin College by Hekman Library and Heritage Hall.

Page 22: Poster by Ernest Bièler for the 1905 Fête des Vignerons, Confrérie des Vignerons de Vevey.

Page 26: National Portrait Gallery of Scotland.

Page 29: Print ca. 1820 in the New York Public Library Print Collection.

Page 37: George Henry Harlow's 1815 drawing of Byron, private collection.

Page 40: Photographer unknown. Courtesy Logan Reed, Chicago.

Page 47: In the collection of the British Library.

Pages 52, 53, 57: Bristol University Library, John Addington Symonds papers.

Page 56: Swiss bobsleigh team, Davos 1910, Wikimedia Commons.

Page 61: *Strand Magazine*, 1893.

Page 68: Luggage label for the Grand Hôtel de Russie in Geneva, late nineteenth century.

Page 74: Photos taken by Louis David, Geneva, 1895, Isabelle Eberhardt archive in Le Centre des Archives d'Outre-Mer, Aix-en-Provence.

Page 81: Photo attributed to Swiss photographer Jean Geiser (1848–1923), Algiers.

Page 85: 1890 Postcard of Pont des Bergues and Rousseau's Island in Geneva.

Page 87: Three graces on Max Emden's Brissago Islands in the 1930s. Huber Verlag (Orell Füssli).

Page 90: Rudolf Steiner Archive, Dornach.

Page 92, 94, 95, 103, 104: Monte Verità Foundation Archive.

Page 105: 1928 brochure for Emil Fahrenkamp's Bauhaus hotel at Monte Verità.

Page 107: Sketch by Frank Budgen donated by his daughter Joan Budgen to the James Joyce Centre in Dublin.

Page 111: 1929 poster for the Café Odéon.

Page 116: Frank Budgen as the sailor on publicity material for Players Navy Cut cigarettes.

Page 117: Huber Verlag, Zürich.

Page 121: Courtesy of James Joyce Foundation, Zürich.

Page 123, 131: Vintage postcards from the Gstaad Valley collection, http://gstaadvalley.com.

Page 128: Drawings by Gordon Bryant: Zelda Fitzgerald published in *Metropolitan* magazine, 1922; Scott Fitzgerald published in *Shadowland* magazine, 1921.

Page 134: Cover art by Nina K. Brisley.

Page 136: Photo by R. Ricksel, courtesy of Widmer family, Gstaad.

Page 138: Still of Sean Connery as James Bond from the 1962 film *Dr. No*, Eon Productions.

Page 146: W. Somerset Maugham's *Ashenden*, 1966 Avon paperback edition.

Page 150: Glauser collection, Swiss Literary Archives, Bern.

Page 151: *Matto Regiert* by Friedrich Glauser, Jean Christophe-Verlag, 1936.

Page 154: David Herrliberger's 1761 copper engraving of the Rhine at Basel, from Hermann Spiess-Schaad: *David Herrliberger. Zürcher Kupferstecher und Verleger 1697–1777*. Verlag Hans Rohr: Zürich 1983.

Page 157: Statue of Vladimir Nabokov in Montreux by Alexandre & Philipp Rukavishnikov.

Page 160: Horst Tappe's 1965 photograph of Vladimir Nabokov with butterfly net, © Horst Tappe/Lebrecht Music & Arts.

Pages 172, 175: © Swiss Literary Archives, Bern.

Pages 174, 187: Swiss Literary Archives, Bern.

Page 180: Photo © F. J. Goodman. Swiss literary archives, Bern.

Page 184: Photo © Rolf Tietgens. Swiss literary archives, Bern.

Page 189: Still from *The Pledge* (1958): Praesens-Film, Central Cinema Company Film (CCC) et al.

Page 191: Pino Musi © Centre Dürrenmatt Neuchâtel.

Page 193: Still from the BBC 1961 production of *The Judge and His Hangman*, © BBC.

Page 202: Photo of Friedrich Dürrenmatt, 1979: Peter Friedli, Bern/ Archives littéraires suisses, courtesy of Centre Dürrenmatt Neuchâtel.

Page 205: Map by Matthäus the Elder in *Flugbild der Schweizer Stadt*, 1963, Kümmerly & Frey, Geographischer Verlag, Bern.

Page 207: Photo by Deborah Elliott.

Page 214: Schweizer Radio und Fernsehen (SRF).

Page 216: Photo by Peter Hebeisen, © Dolder Hotel AG.

Pages 224, 226: Photos © Fonds Ella Maillart/Musée de l'Elysée, Lausanne.

Page 227: Photo by Esther Gambaro, © Fonds Marie-Louise Bodmer-Preiswerk.

Page 228: Courtesy of Monacensia Literary Archive and Library, Munich.

Page 233: Photo © Fonds Nicolas Bouvier/Musée de l'Elysée, Lausanne.

Page 240: Photo © A. Hollmann, 1982.

Page 242: Artist unknown, courtesy of Swiss National Library.

Page 246: Courtesy of Max Frisch archive, Max Frisch Foundation, ETH-Bibliothek, Zürich.

Page 248: Schweizer Radio und Fernsehen (SRF).

Page 250: Photo courtesy of Gaby Gerster.

Page 253: Statue by British sculptor John Doubleday, photo © Bruce Whitehill.

Page 256: German History in Documents and Images (GHDI), German Historical Institute, Washington, DC.

Page 257: Postcard of le Grand Chalet at Rossinière ca. 1910, photographer unknown.

Page 265: Photo by Graham Wood/Daily Mail/Rex Features.

Page 267: 1952 poster for Lac Léman Compagnie Générale de Navigation, designed by Samuel Henchosz (1905-1976).

Back cover:

Top l. to r.: James Joyce photographed by Alex Ehrenzweig in Zürich in 1915 (Google Images); Jean-Jacques Rousseau as a youth, 1902 postcard in the private collection of Jean-Jacques Monney; 1815 sketch of Lord Byron by George Henry Harlow, private collection; Hermann Hesse photographed in 1935 by his son Martin; Ian Fleming in his study in 1958.

Middle l. to r.: Patricia Highsmith photograph © F. J. Goodman, courtesy of the Swiss Literary Archives, Bern; Hotel Byron at Villeneuve, nineteenth-century poster; Elinor M. Brent-Dyer's *Chalet School in the Oberland* (1952) with cover art by Nina K. Brisley; 1964 Reprint Society's edition of Ian Fleming's *Thrilling Cities.*

Bottom l. to r.: Luggage sticker for the Hotel de Russie in Geneva; Friedrich Dürrenmatt 1979, Peter Friedli, Bern/Archives littéraires suisses, courtesy of Centre Dürrenmatt Neuchâtel; Nicolas Bouvier on the road to Afghanistan, courtesy of Musée de l'Elysée, Lausanne; H.G. Wells photographed by George Charles Beresford in 1920, National Portrait Gallery; Wells's *The World Set Free* with cover art by Caspar David Friedrich; 1921 drawing of F. Scott Fitzgerald by Gordon Bryant.